AF314018

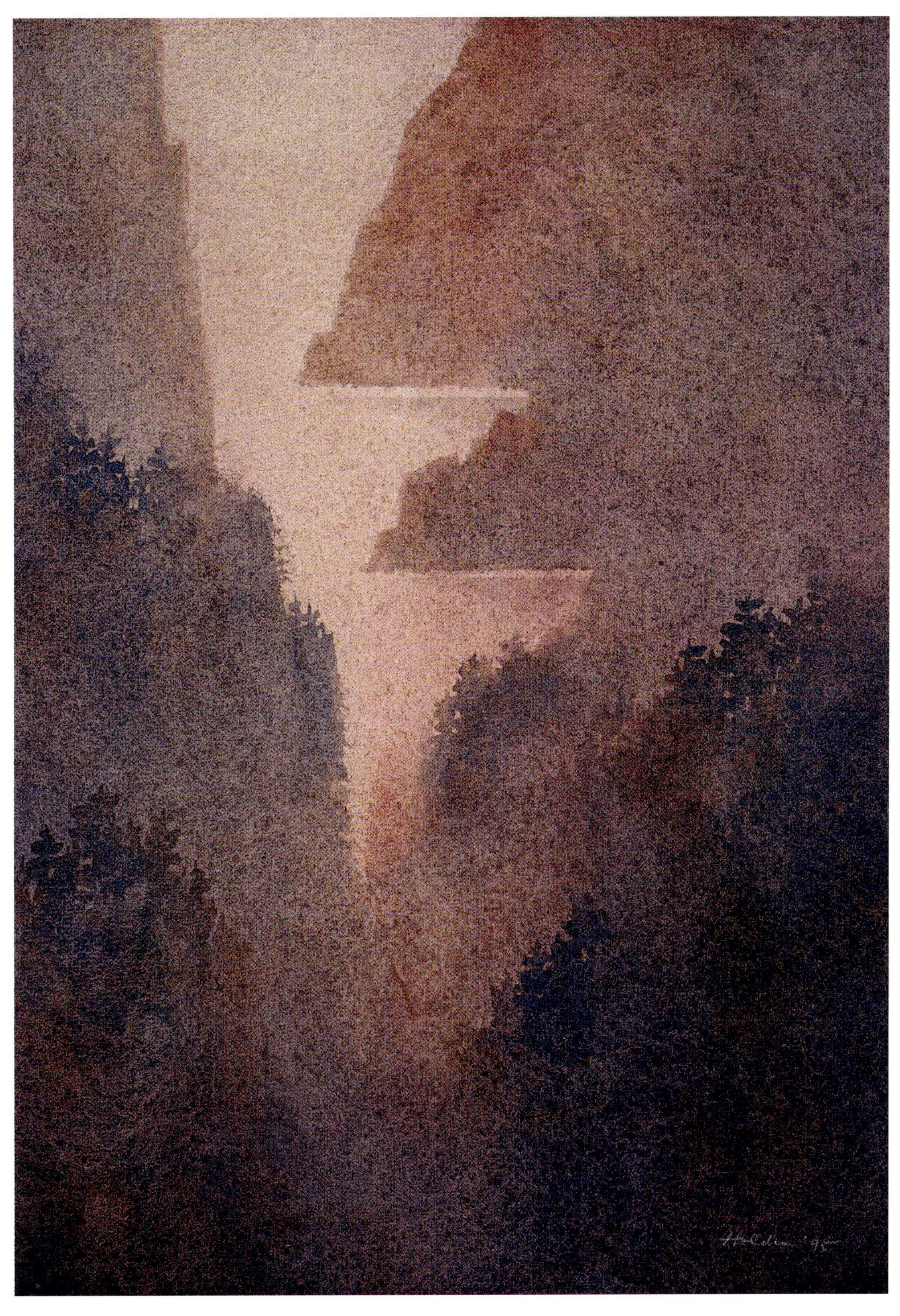

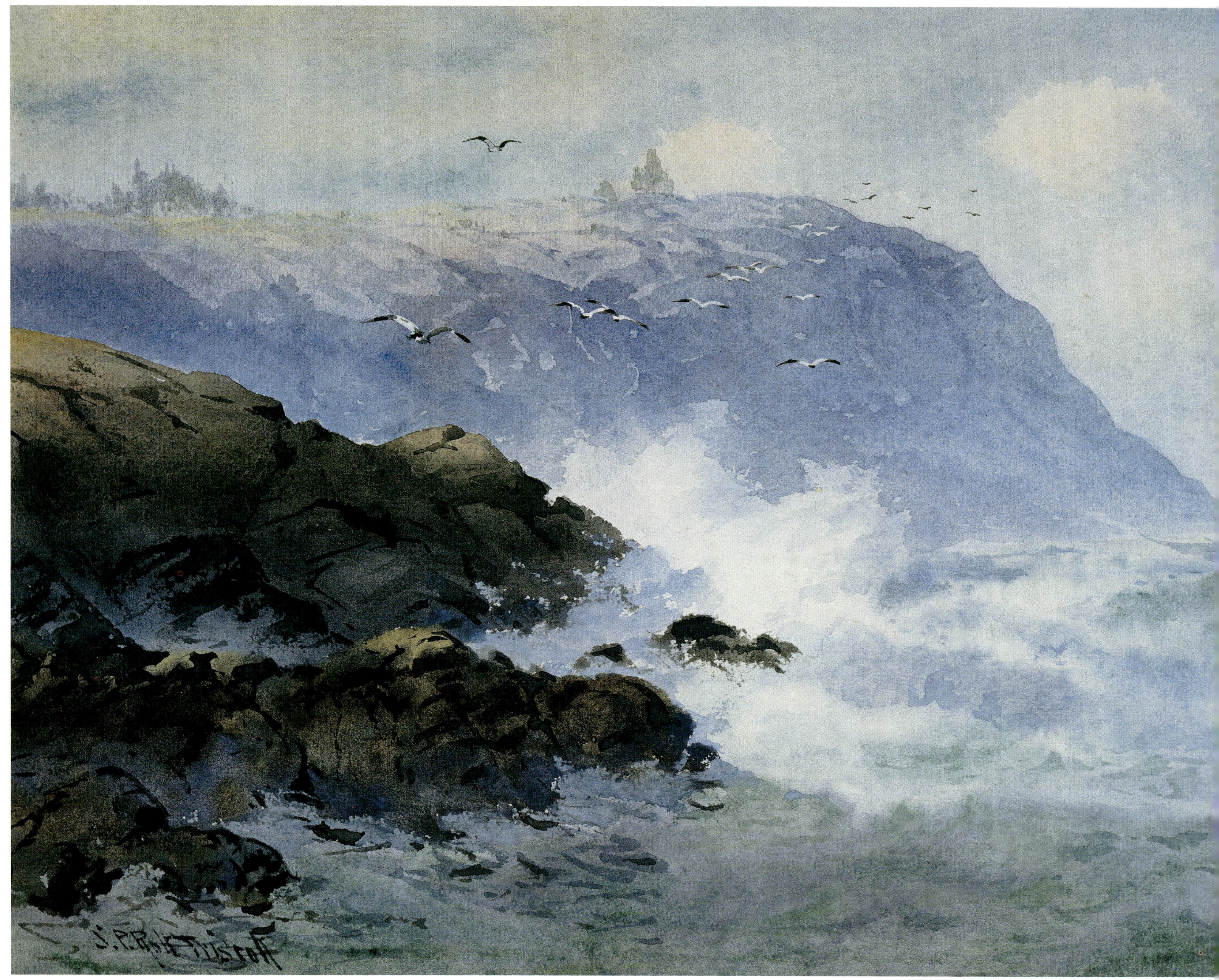

S.P.Rolf Liscoff

The Art of Monhegan Island

By Carl Little

Picture Editor, Arnold Skolnick

Foreword by Jamie Wyeth

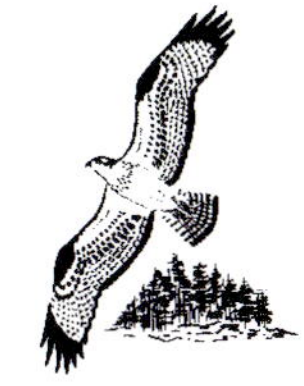

DOWN EAST BOOKS, CAMDEN, MAINE, 2004

A Chameleon Book

Copyright © 2004 by Chameleon Books, Inc.
Text © 2004 Carl Little

All rights reserved. No part of this book may be reproduced
or transmitted in any form or by any means, electronic or mechanical,
including photocopying, recording, or by any information storage and
retrieval system, without permission in writing from the publisher.

Published by
Down East Books
P.O. Box 679
Camden, ME 04843
Book Orders: 800-766-1670
(website) *www.downeastbooks.com*
(e-mail inquiries) *books@downeast.com*

Produced by
Chameleon Books, Inc.
Chesterfield, MA 01012
chambooks@earthlink.net

Designer/Picture Editor: Arnold Skolnick
Editorial Assistants: Jone Messmer & Martha Hoppin
Copy Editor: Jamie Nan Thaman
Design Assistant: K. C. Scott

Printed in China

ISBN: 0-89272-648-2

Library of Congress Control Number: 2004107409

(HALF-TITLE) DONALD HOLDEN, *MONHEGAN MORNING IV*, 1995
WATERCOLOR ON PAPER, 13 X 9 IN., PORTLAND MUSEUM OF ART, MAINE,
GIFT OF THE ARTIST IN MEMORY OF JOANNE WAXMAN

(FRONTISPIECE) S. P. ROLT TRISCOTT, *BLACKHEAD, MONHEGAN*, C. 1903
WATERCOLOR ON PAPER, 9 1/2 X 14 IN., COLLECTION OF WILLARD BOYNTON AND JACQUELINE BOEGEL

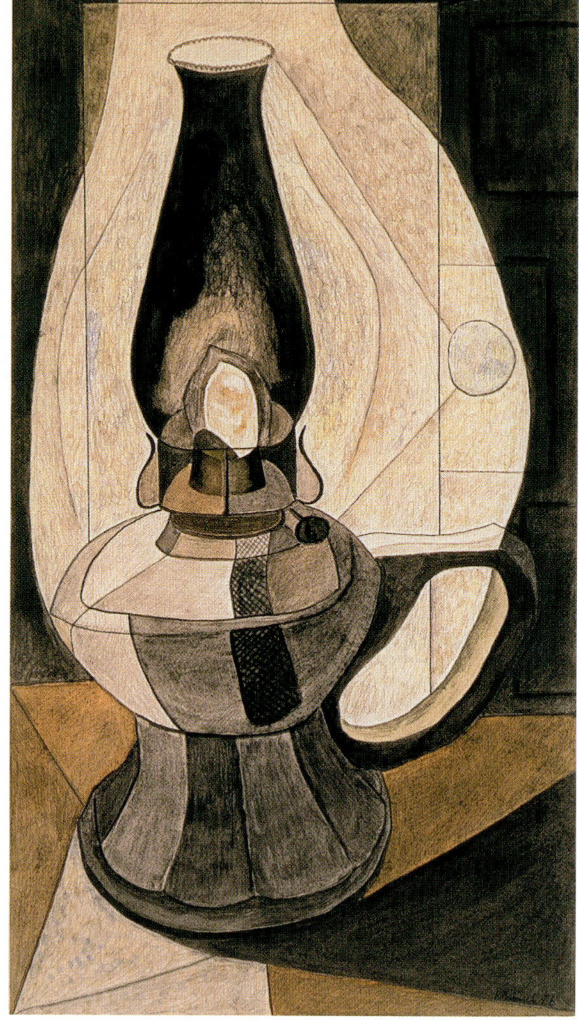

WILLIAM KIENBUSCH, *KEROSENE LAMP, MONHEGAN*, 1948
CASEIN ON PAPER, 22 1/2 BY 11 3/4 IN.
COLLECTION OF JULIANA LITTLE

Dedication:

To Peggy, Emily and James, who know and love Monhegan.

Acknowledgments

In assembling the images in this book, we came to rely on the extraordinary expertise of Edward Deci, director of the Monhegan Museum. It is doubtful that any one person has a greater knowledge of those who painted on the island than he. In his tenure, Deci has expanded the museum, organized remarkable summer exhibitions, stewarded a growing collection, and interviewed numerous artists.

Monhegan Island brings out the best in the passions of collectors. We thank the following for their contributions to this book: Edward Deci, Remak Ramsey, George Schwarz, John M. Day, Anne Vartabedian, C. L. Morehead and several anonymous individuals.

Additional thanks go to the following: Earle G. Shettleworth Jr.; Sally Rand; David Little; Juliana P. Little; Valerie Livingston; the staff of the Ellsworth Public Library; the Mt. Desert post-office crew for special deliveries; Tralice Bracy, Monhegan Museum; Sally MacVane, Gallery-by-the-Sea; Dennis and Marty Gleason, Gleason Fine Art; Susan Maasch, Clark House Gallery; Wiscasset Bay Gallery; River Gallery; Elizabeth Moss Gallery; Owen Gallery; Bayview Gallery; Spanierman Gallery; and Sherry French Gallery.

We are also grateful to the Farnsworth Art Museum, Portland Museum of Art, Florence Griswold Museum, Mint Museum of Art, Philadelphia Museum of Art, Plattsburgh State Art Museum and Whitney Museum of American Art.

Special thanks go to Jamie Wyeth for his foreword and for his contributions to Monhegan art.

As with so many of the books we have produced together (ten in all), Arnold Skolnick and I faced a bounty of great work to choose from. This book was perhaps our most daunting, by virtue of the sheer amount of material available. With the exception of four paintings reproduced herewith, we avoided using the images collected by our dedicated predecessors, Will and Jane Curtis and Frank Lieberman—the authors of *Monhegan: The Artists' Island*. We thank all the island-passionate artists who submitted work.

—Carl Little

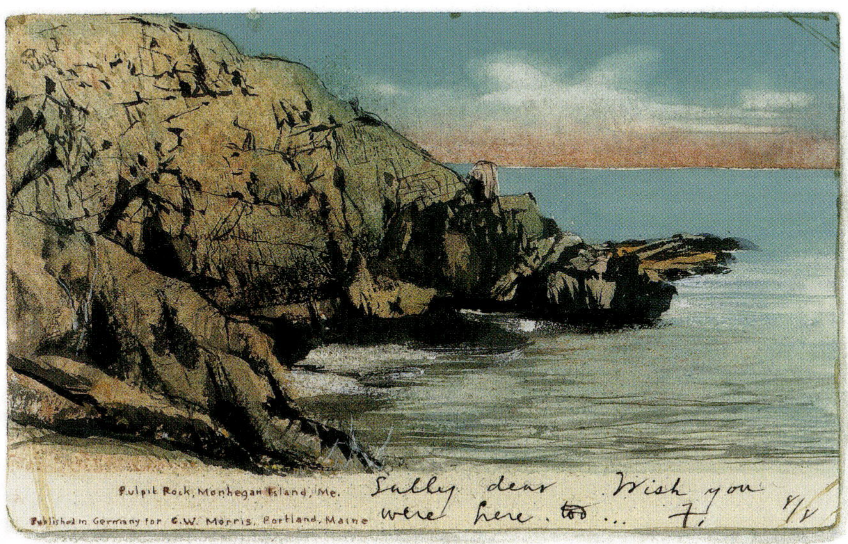

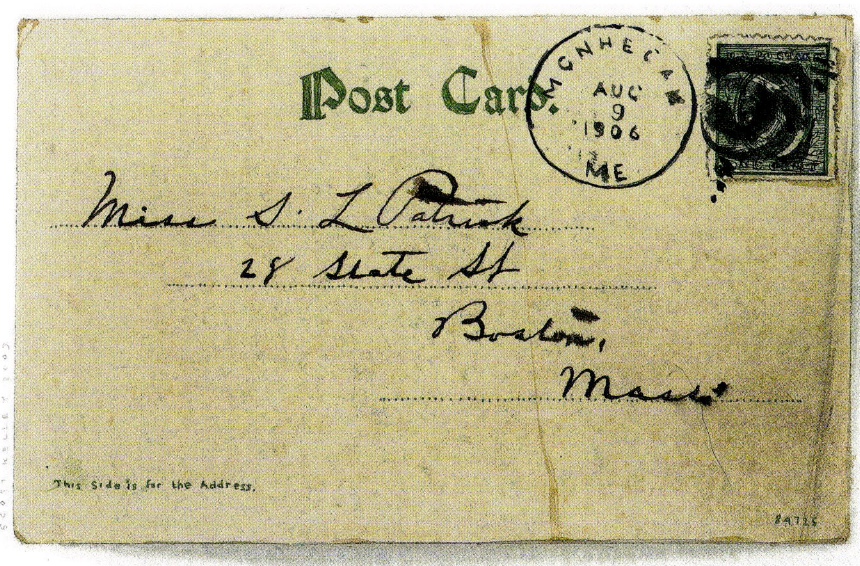

Scott Kelley, *Sally Dear Wish You Were Here*, 2003
watercolor on paper, 14 x 10 1/4 in.
courtesy of Gleason Fine Art, Boothbay Harbor, Maine

Monhegan, My Lover

I have a problem with Monhegan Island. Let me explain: Everybody remembers their first lover, don't they? Perhaps passionately, occasionally longingly, sometimes angrily, but always.

I am peculiar. And one of the ways I am peculiar is that my first lover was not a person—it was an island. As a child, growing up on the coast of Maine, I dreamed of living aboard a ship completely surrounded by the sea. I longed for the sounds: gull cries, bell-buoy chimes, foghorn moans, and the constant pulse of the waves. On my twenty-first birthday, this recurring dream came true. With the sales from my first one-man show in New York, I purchased Kent House on Monhegan Island. Not only could I now live on the next best thing to a ship—a remote island—but I could dwell in a house built by the painter who, in my estimation, best understood the sea: Rockwell Kent.

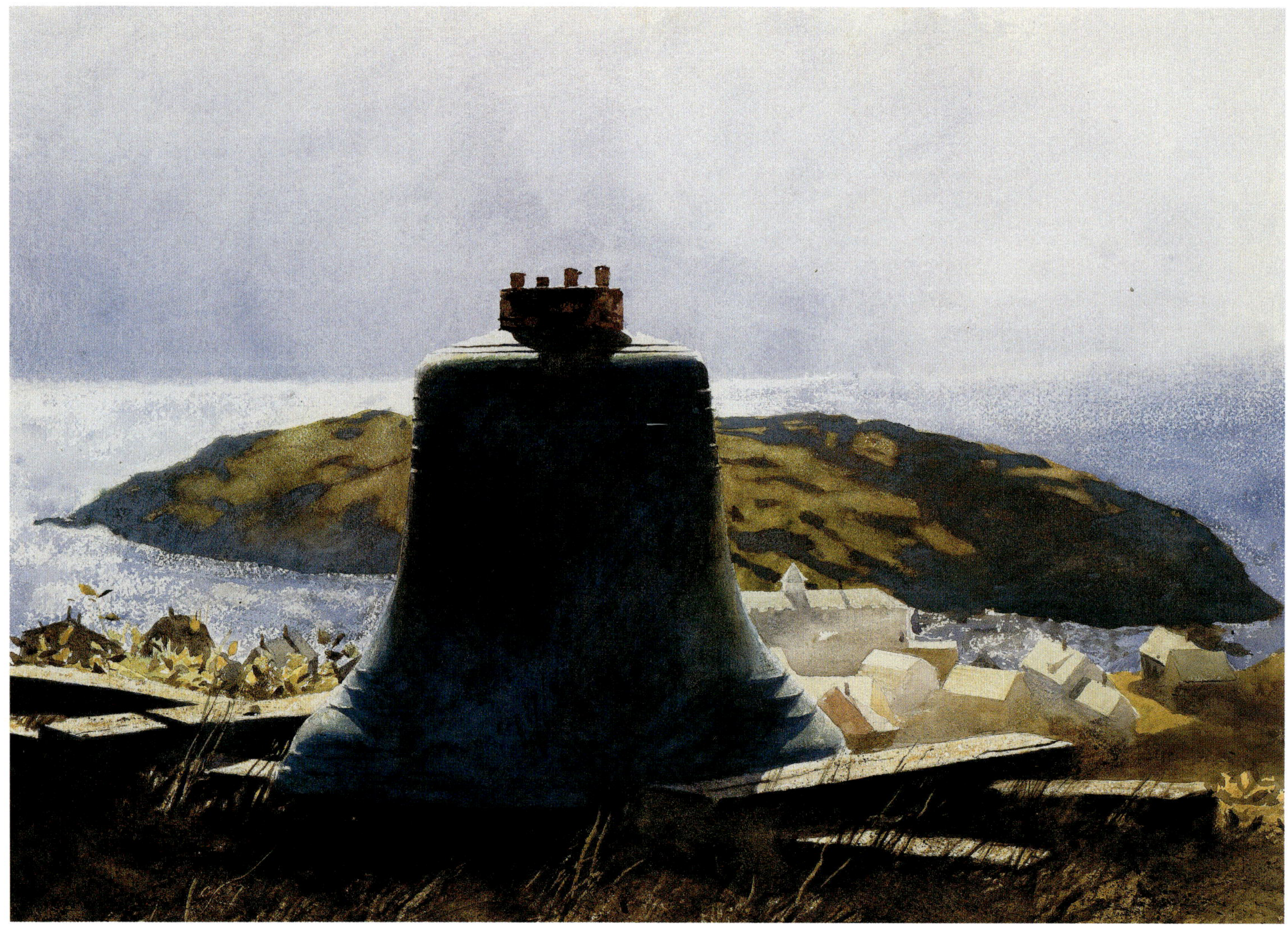

JAMIE WYETH, *Obelisk*, 1976, WATERCOLOR ON PAPER, 22 x 30 IN.
COLLECTION OF STAR FORD WHITNEY, BRIN FORD, REED FORD AND MILLS FORD

Kent's time on the island was relatively short—1905–1910, with occasional visits between 1947 and 1953. During those periods, he produced some of American art's most timeless and monumental images. His paintings, abstract in their simple forms, describe the stark winter headlands and ink-black spruce with a power unequaled to this day.

This power I found almost daunting. Living in his house, painting his island—How dare I! But I dared and lived and worked on the island for twenty-five years, finding "my own Monhegan." Present and future painters "will dare," and they too will find "their own Monhegan."

How this one-mile-long by half-mile-wide island, thirteen miles out to sea, could hold enough magic to beguile Mr. Kent, myself, and hundreds of other painters over the years truly amazed me. But therein lies my problem. I grew jealous of sharing my love with so many suitors, so many painters. I began to wish that Monhegan would become a retreat for dentists, not artists, and that I could have the island's visual riches all to myself. But, of course, that was not to be. I eventually moved to a nearby island down the coast, and I am alone on Southern Island.

I will keep Kent House and return to Monhegan to work and bask in her beauty and power. But we both have other lovers, and it will never be as it was. Or will it?

Almost every night before I go to sleep on my island, I scan the southwest horizon from my bedroom window until I catch the flash of the distant Monhegan lighthouse—the "wink" of my former lover.

Now, wouldn't you say there is a problem?

Jamie Wyeth
March 2004

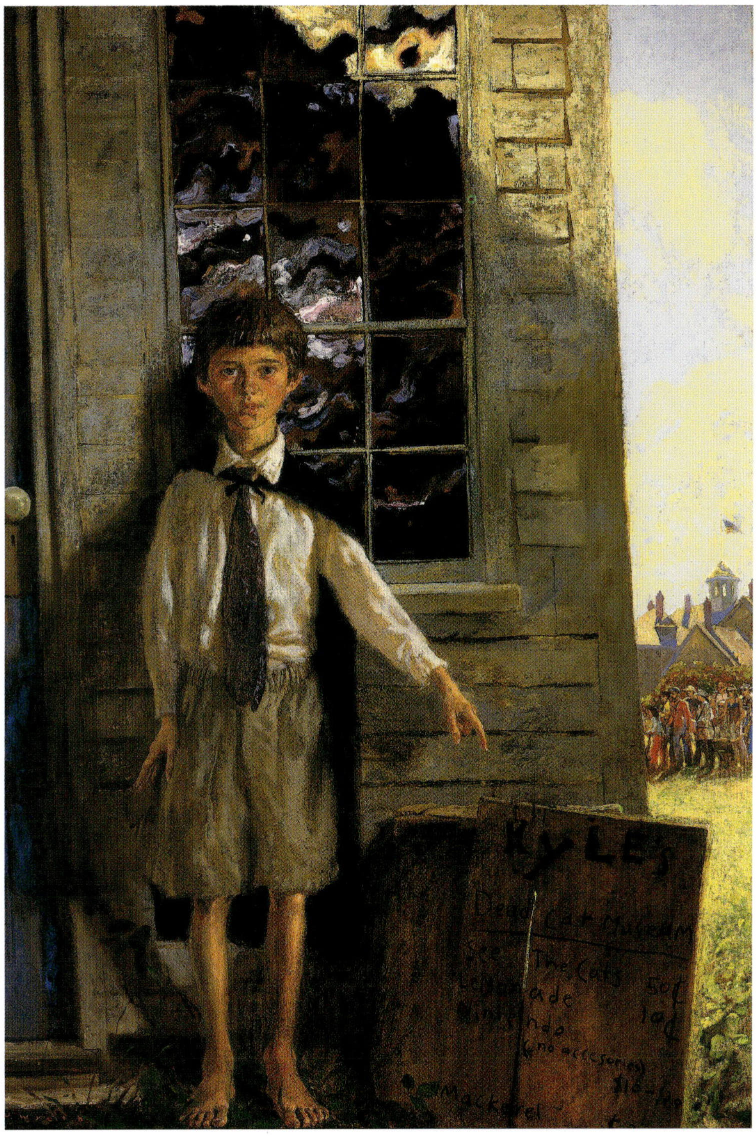

Jamie Wyeth, *Dead Cat Museum, Monhegan Island*, 1999
oil on canvas, 60 x 40 in., collection of the Cawley Family

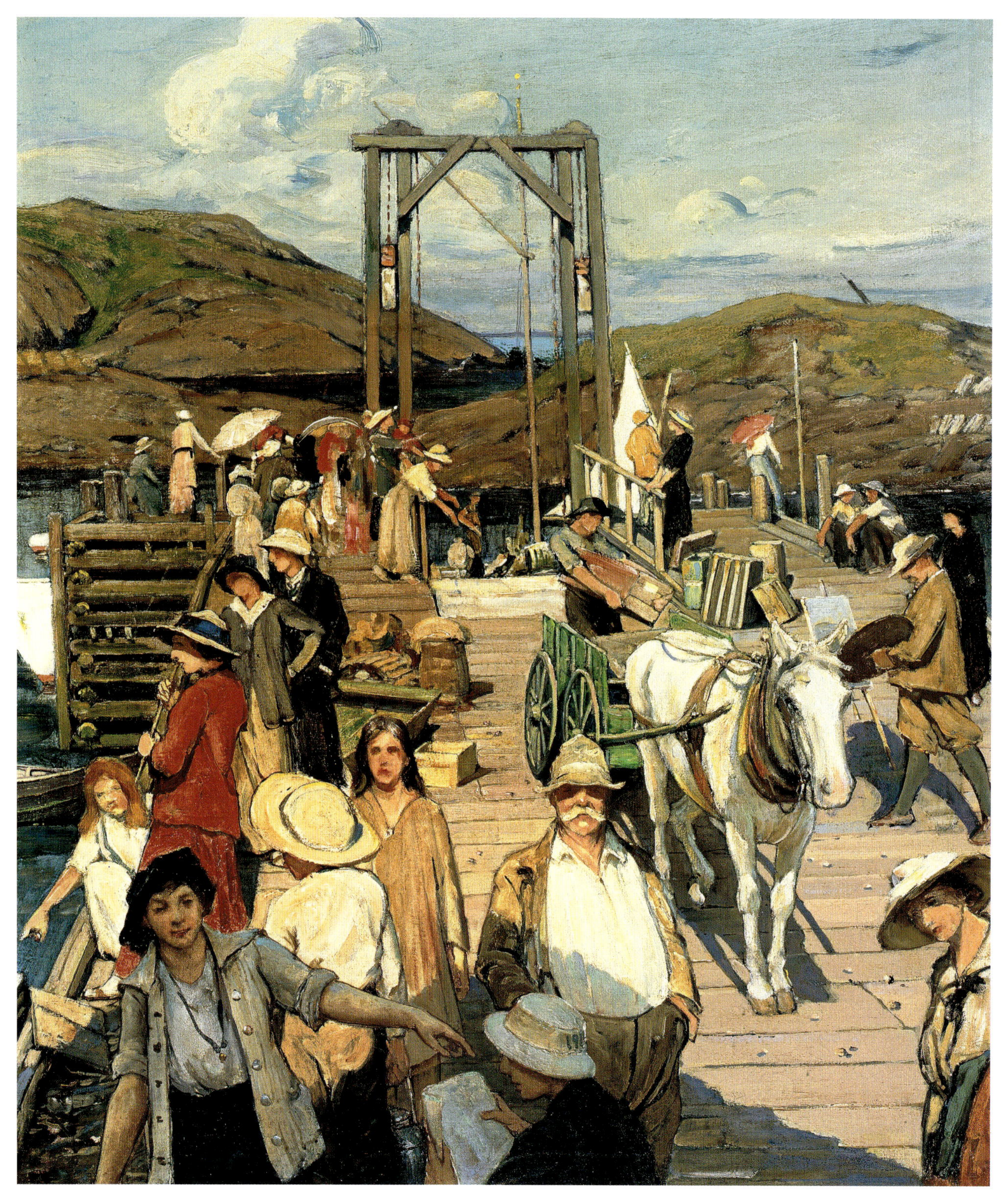

Robert Van Vorst Sewell, *At the Dock*, 1916, oil on linen, 36 x 30 in.
collection of Monhegan Museum, gift of Jacqueline Hudson

If you have the time and inclination to visit only one island of the Maine coast, Monhegan should be that island.

I'm not counting as islands places you can reach by car over bridges, although I suppose that technically they are. But it takes more than encirclement by water to make an island. There must also be inaccessibility except by boat. An island becomes a peninsula, to my mind, the minute it becomes available by bridge, no different from any other cape or promontory. Part of visiting an island is the change of means of transportation, with the accompanying change of pace and viewpoint. You haven't visited an island unless you have seen it rise from the sea, seen it change from cloud on the horizon to a solid bastion of earth and rock, with houses small and clear in the sunlight.

. . . Monhegan is the best island to visit because of its remoteness and because of its small size. Both factors contribute to an evocation of the true island spirit.

—LOUISE DICKINSON RICH, *THE COAST OF MAINE,* 1975

Introduction

*as we cast off   the feeling is
we're off to see the island now
the wonderful island that is.*
—RICHARD ALDRIDGE, "A BOATLOAD TO MONHEGAN BOUND"

The art of Monhegan Island entered my consciousness in a bold manner in 1990 when the Farnsworth Art Museum in Rockland, Maine, invited me to lecture on the subject. I knew that artists had been visiting Monhegan for nearly 150 years. I understood that the concentrated grandeur of this mighty island out in the Atlantic had swayed the hearts and aesthetics of painters from nearly every school of American art: Hudson River, Impressionist, Ashcan, Modernist, Realist, Abstract Expressionist.

What I didn't fully appreciate was the breadth of the passion this multitude of artists has brought to their island work nor the remarkable transforming power of the place and its people on their sensibilities. Painters known for their urban landscapes or society portraits have found themselves transfixed by the dramatic headlands and inspired by the stoic island families.

In preparation for my presentation at the Farnsworth, I listened to, and took notes on, a tape of Edward Deci, director of the Monhegan Museum, lecturing on the artists who had found inspiration on the island. I then selected eight painters out of literally hundreds to focus on: Robert Henri, Rockwell Kent, George Bellows and Edward Hopper from the early twentieth century, and Reuben Tam, Hans Moller, Alan Gussow and Jamie Wyeth from more recent times. Last but not least, I boarded the venerable mailboat, the *Laura B,* for Monhegan.

The latter activity seemed absolutely requisite. How could I, in all good conscience, give an account of artists on this island without having paid Monhegan a visit? Wouldn't time on the island serve to add authenticity to my remarks?

It was mid October, and fog greeted my family and me. The island lay in a kind of caul of moisture, with an occasional light shower adding a wet blessing to our baptismal island explorations. Visitors with binoculars gathered here and there to gaze at hawks, peregrines, song- and shorebirds and other migratory and nonmi-

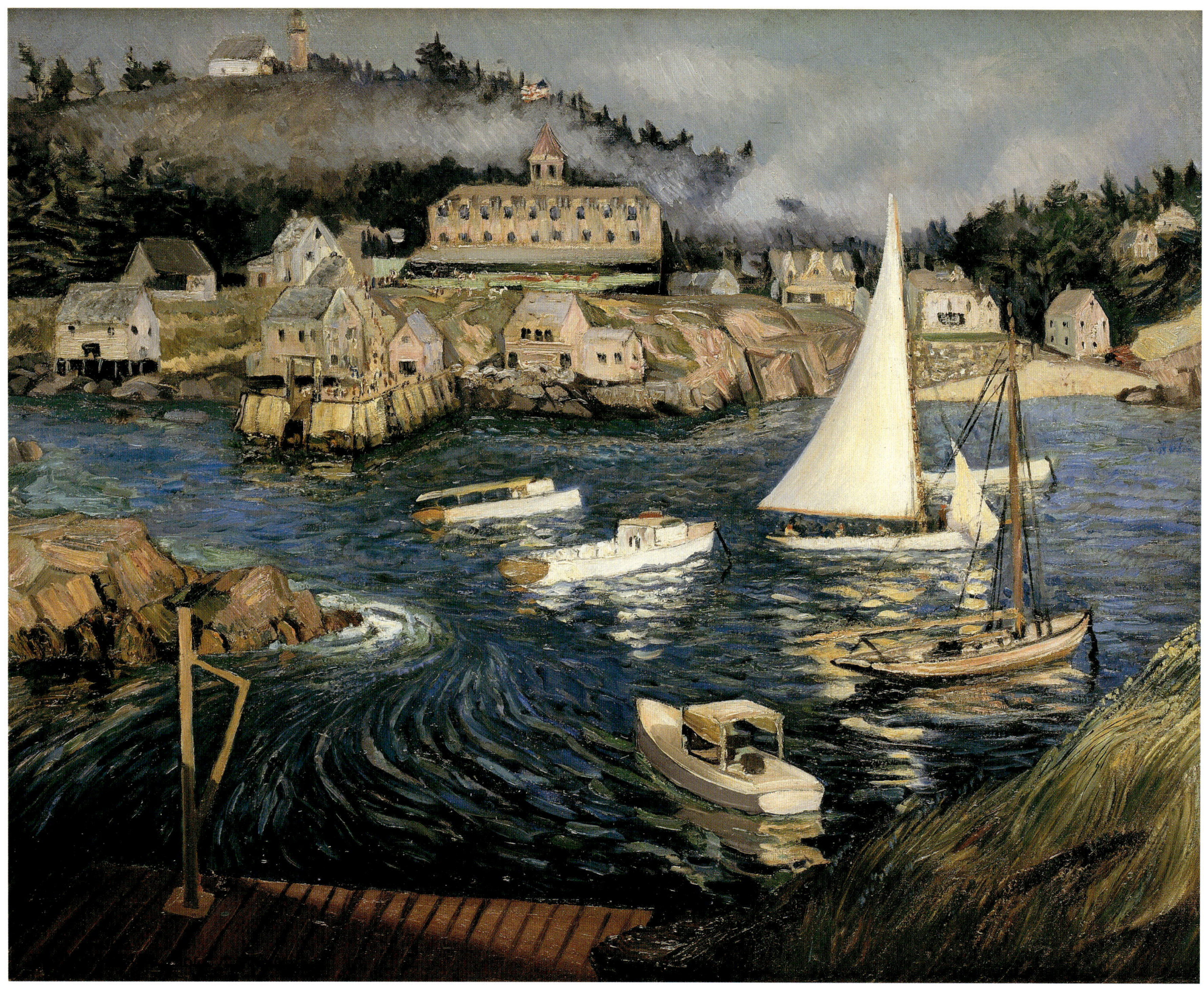

 HAYLEY LEVER, *MONHEGAN,* 1941, OIL ON BOARD, 25 X 30 IN., SCHWARTZ FAMILY COLLECTION. PHOTO COURTESY OF SPANIERMAN GALLERY, LLC. NEW YORK

gratory visitors (the island lies on the Atlantic flyway). Few artists were seen, for many depart in September. A greater hush comes over Monhegan after Columbus Day—a sigh of sorts, mixing sadness and relief, when the seventy five or so year-round residents begin to hunker down for winter.

We stayed at the Trailing Yew, a collegial hostelry with, if memory serves, watercolor views of the island by S. P. Rolt Triscott on the walls. We dined mess-hall style and carried flashlights to our sleeping quarters. The fog signal atop Manana, Monhegan harbor's protector island, blew at regular intervals through the night. We might have been on a ship far out to sea. (The explorer Samuel de Champlain named the island *La Nef*—the ship— "because it looked like one from a distance.")[1]

Even in its foggy embrace, the island worked its magic on all of us, so much so that when Deci invited me to speak at the opening of the new Monhegan Museum in 1998, my family clamored to return. They remembered the fairy houses in Cathedral Woods, hikes over the headlands and the vaporous embrace of the island. Our second trip offered an island in the sun and vistas that left us awestruck. Now I could fully understand the seemingly hyperbolic reactions of so many artists to the handsome harbor, magnificent cliffs and waves crashing against the rocky shore. Now it made sense to me that George Bellows, writing to his wife, Emma, from Monhegan, would compare the island to the Rocky Mountains. And how true rang Rockwell Kent's claim that this sea-girt continent offered a painter's plenitude—"enough for me, enough for all my fellow artists, for all of us who sought 'material' for art."[2]

✳   ✳   ✳

It appeared a meane high land, as we found it, being but an Island of some six miles in compasse, but I hope the most fortunate euer discovered.
—JAMES ROSIER, 1605

The distance from the mainland to Monhegan depends on where you're measuring it from, but the average seems to be twelve miles from Port Clyde and farther from other embarkation points, including Boothbay Harbor and New Harbor. The island lies about midway between the mouths of the Kennebec and Penobscot Rivers, in the mouth of Muscongus Bay. On a clear day

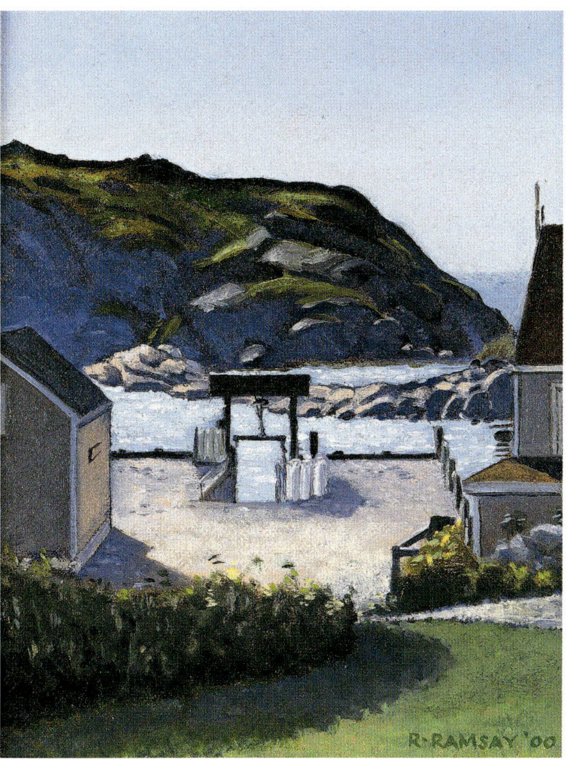

REMAK RAMSAY, *THE WHARF, MONHEGAN* 2000, OIL ON CANVAS BOARD, 9 x 7 IN. COLLECTION OF THE ARTIST

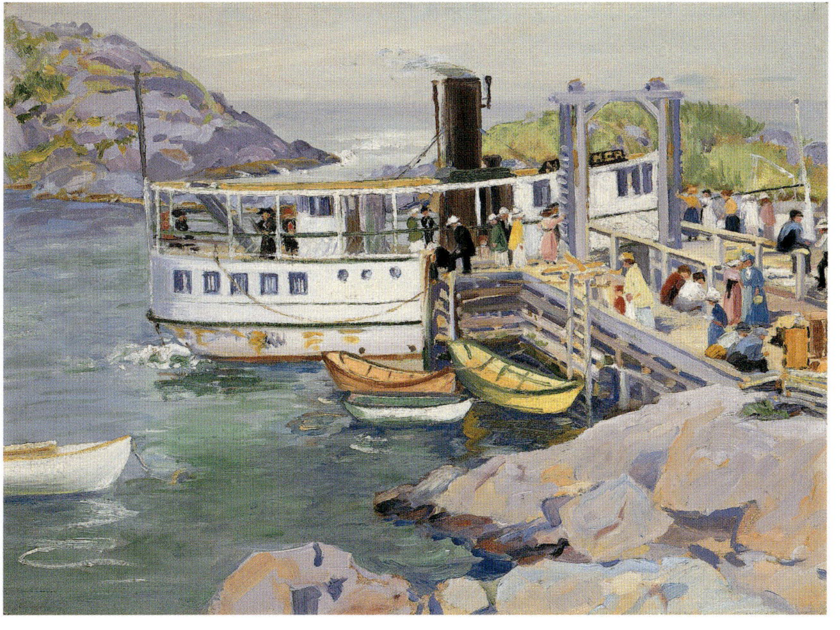

UNKNOWN, *THE MAY ARCHER*, C. 1920, OIL ON CANVAS, 18 x 24 IN. SCHWARTZ FAMILY COLLECTION

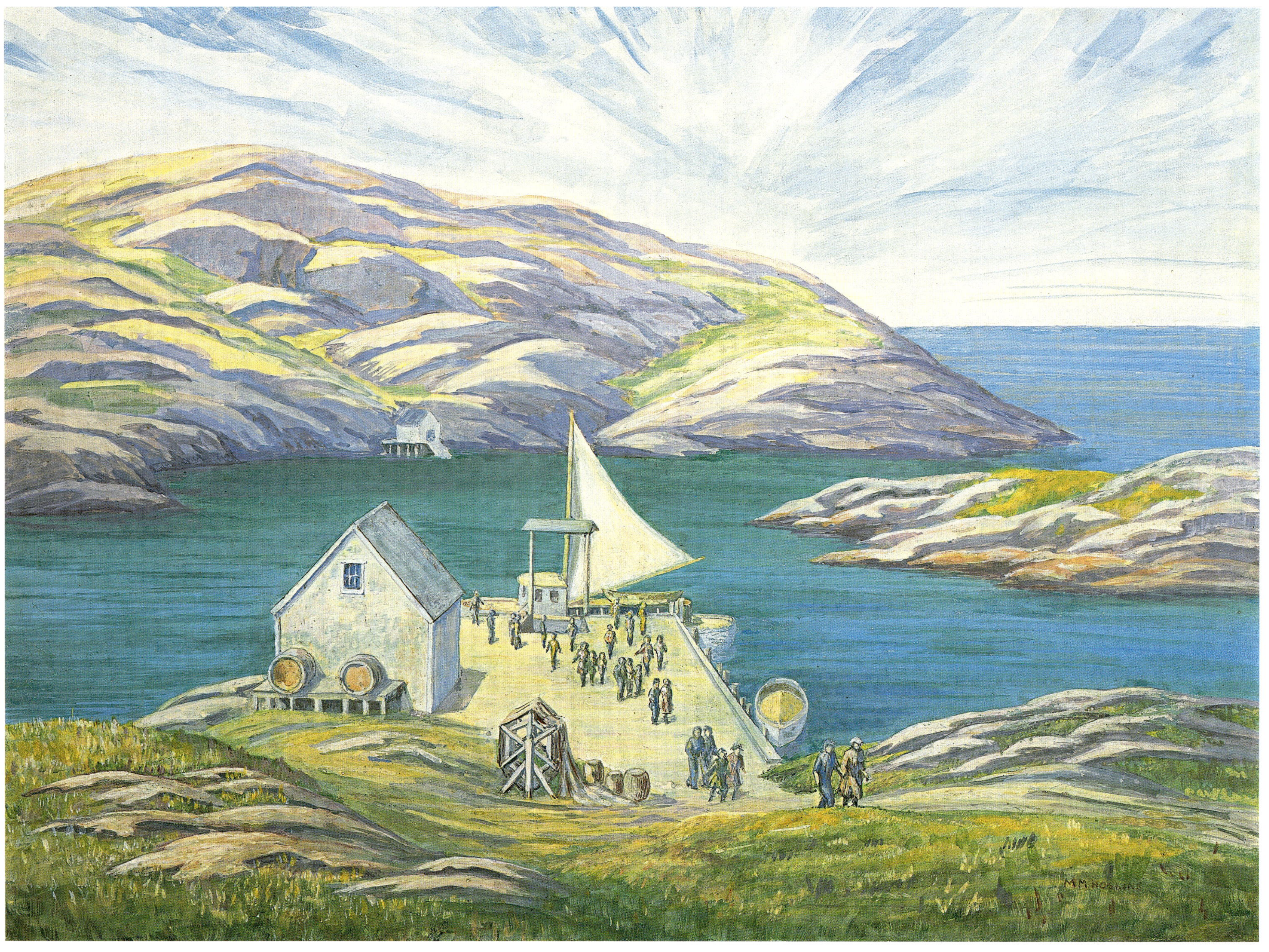

 Margaret Morris Hoskins, *The Ferry Dock*, n.d., oil on board, 18 x 24 in., River Gallery Collection, Damariscotta, Maine

you can make out the Camden Hills in the distance and glimpse an assortment of distinguished Maine islands, among them Isle au Haut, Matinicus, Criehaven and Matinicus Rock.

Part of one's orientation might include situating the island in a broader geographical scheme. Rockwell Kent provided coordinates in his autobiography *It's Me O Lord*: "a small island lying in latitude 43°46' North, longitude 69°19' West." From the top of Whitehead, one of the island's famed headlands, Kent looked "far out to sea toward Africa and England."[3] Other sight lines would take in Nova Scotia, France and Spain.

The island's size varies from one writer to the next. The trail map distributed by the Monhegan Associates, which serves as steward for much of the undeveloped part of the island, offers these measurements: "about .7 of a mile wide and 1.7 miles long." The island's six-mile "compasse" given by the British explorer James Rosier would no doubt change if modern technology, such as Geographic Information Systems, were used to measure its many indentations.

The actual spelling of the name, which is native American for *the* Island" or "Great Island," seems to change from map to map in the centuries of exploration: Monahigan, Monahegan, Menhegan, Manhegin. So does that of its "nursling," Manana Island, which provides partial protection to the harbor: Monanis ("Small Island"), Menana and other variants appear throughout island literature.

Monhegan features a series of landmarks with somewhat curious names, many of them inspired by their physical characteristics. Describing his first hike around the island, Kent led the readers of his autobiography from one spot to the next, naming the places as he went: Washerwoman rock, Norman's ledge, Burnt Head, Whitehead and Blackhead, Pulpit Rock, Green Point and Deadman's Cove. Other sites derive their names from nature: Gull Rock, Seal Ledges, Lobster Point, Boar's Head, the Crow's Nest and Inner Duck Rock. And then there's Squeaker Cove, a place of dramatic surf that rivals Acadia National Park's Thunder Hole.

Some of these remarkable sites ended up on postal cards produced for the use of island visitors. In one of a series of trompe l'oeil watercolors of turn-of-the-century postcards *(p. 5)* by Scott Kelley (b. 1968), the legend reads "Pulpit Rock Monhegan, Island, Me," and carries the message, "Sally dear Wish you were here, too . . ." When Kelley arrived on Monhegan in 2002, he was tempted to join

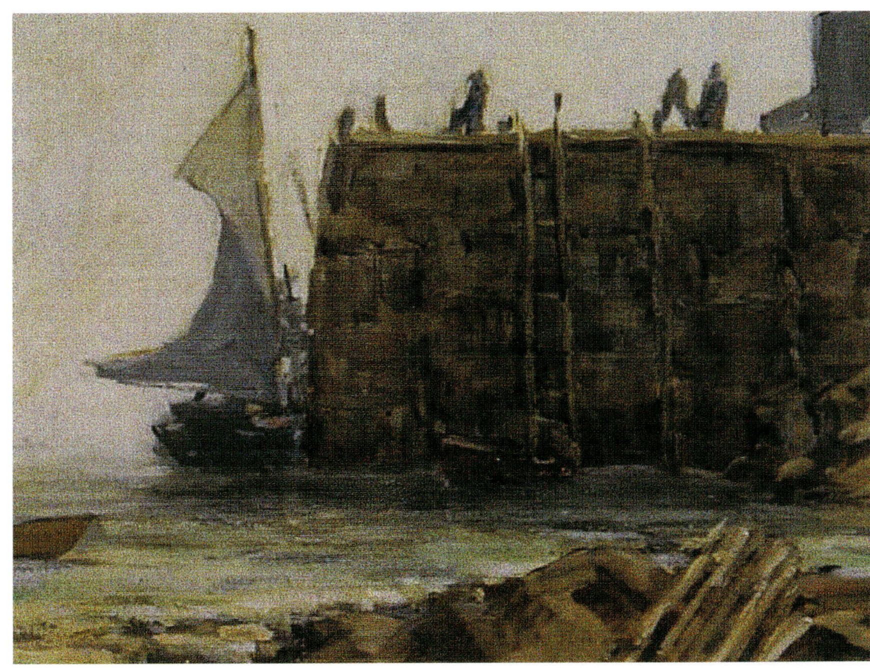

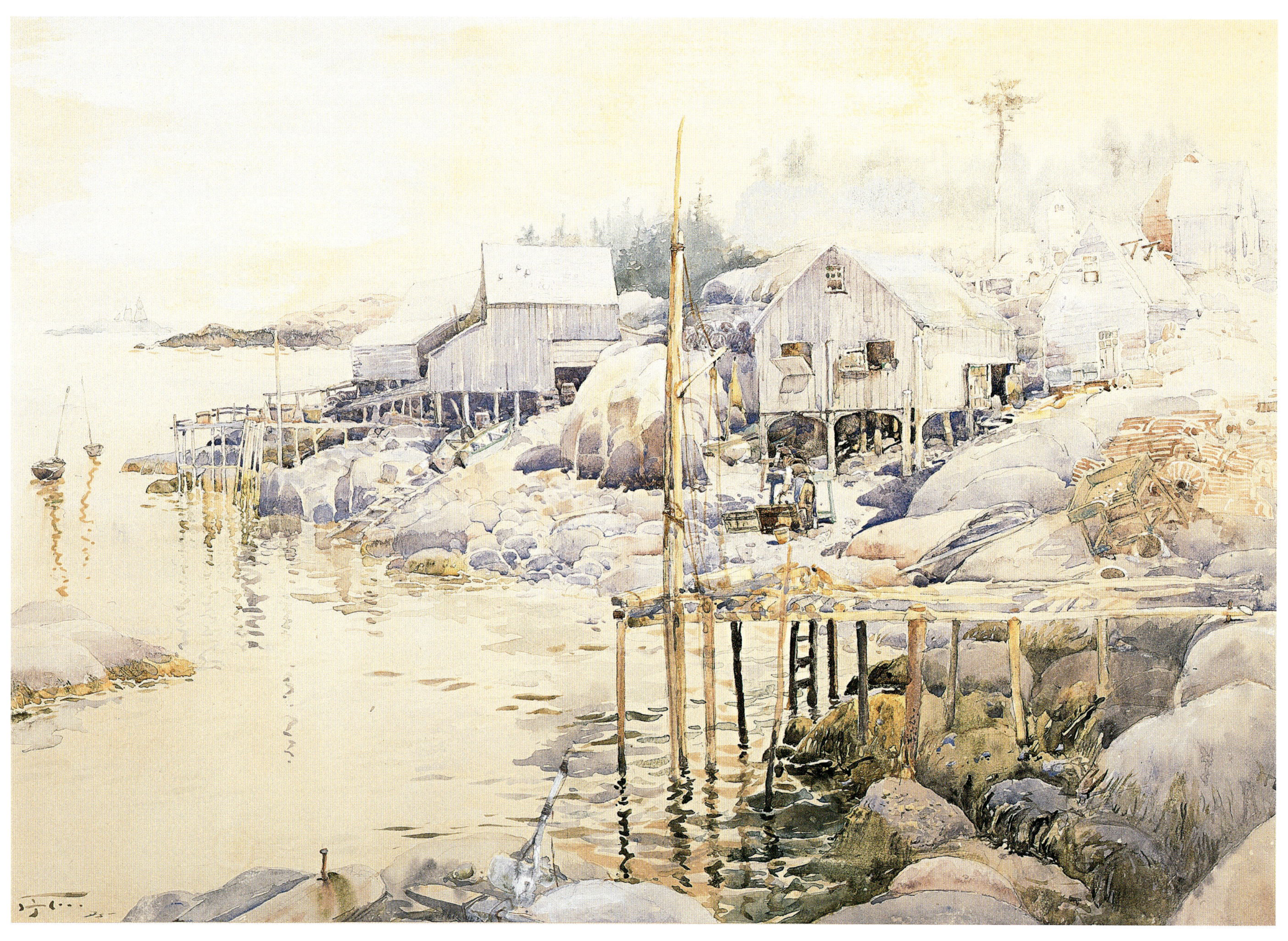

Harry Fenn, *A Silvery Morning on the Coast of Maine*, 1895, watercolor, graphite, gouache on paper, 17 ¹/₂ x 25 in.
River Gallery Collection, Damariscotta, Maine

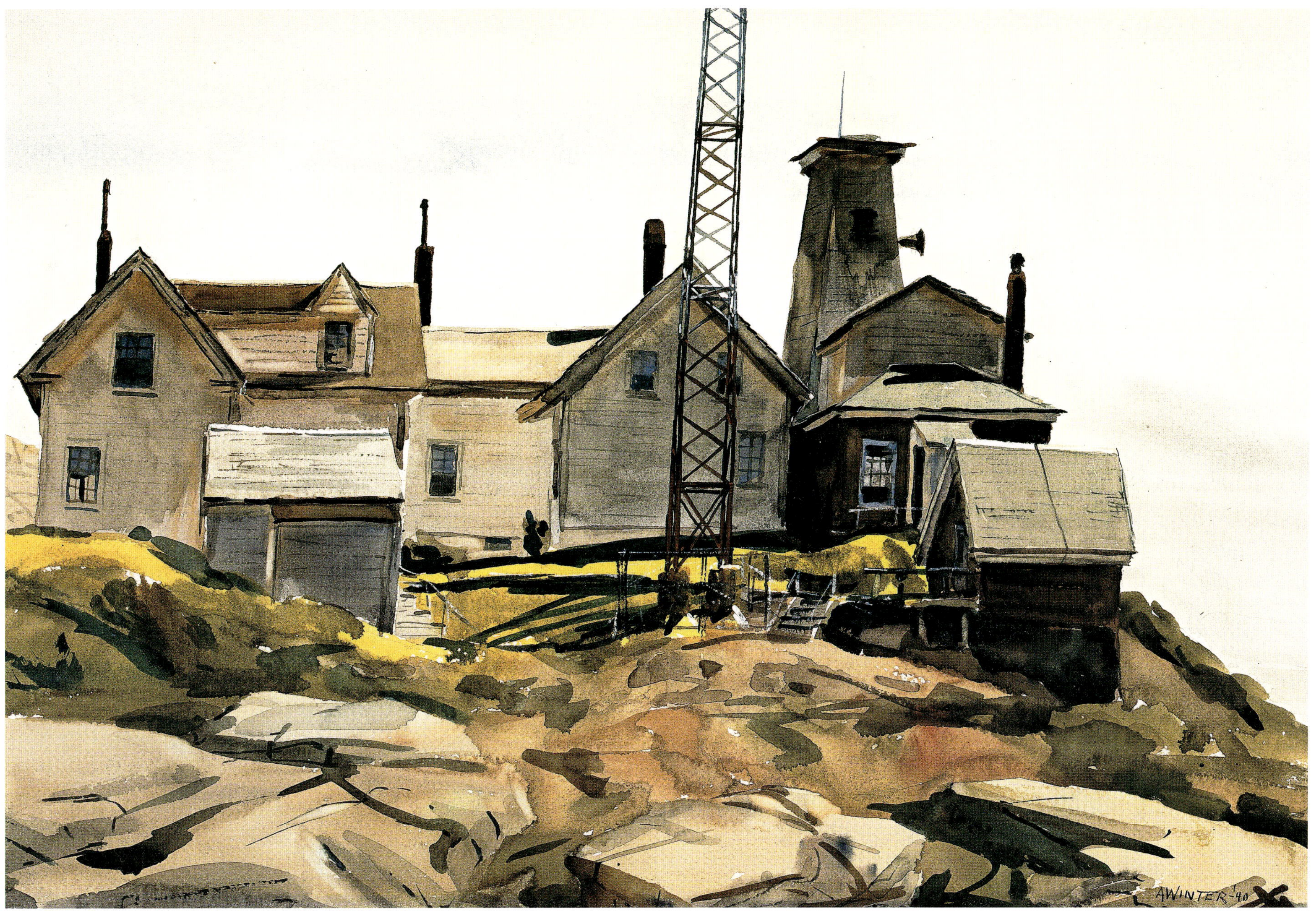

Andrew Winter, *Coast Guard Station, Manana*, 1940, watercolor on paper, 14 x 20 in., courtesy of Spanierman Gallery, LLC, New York

15

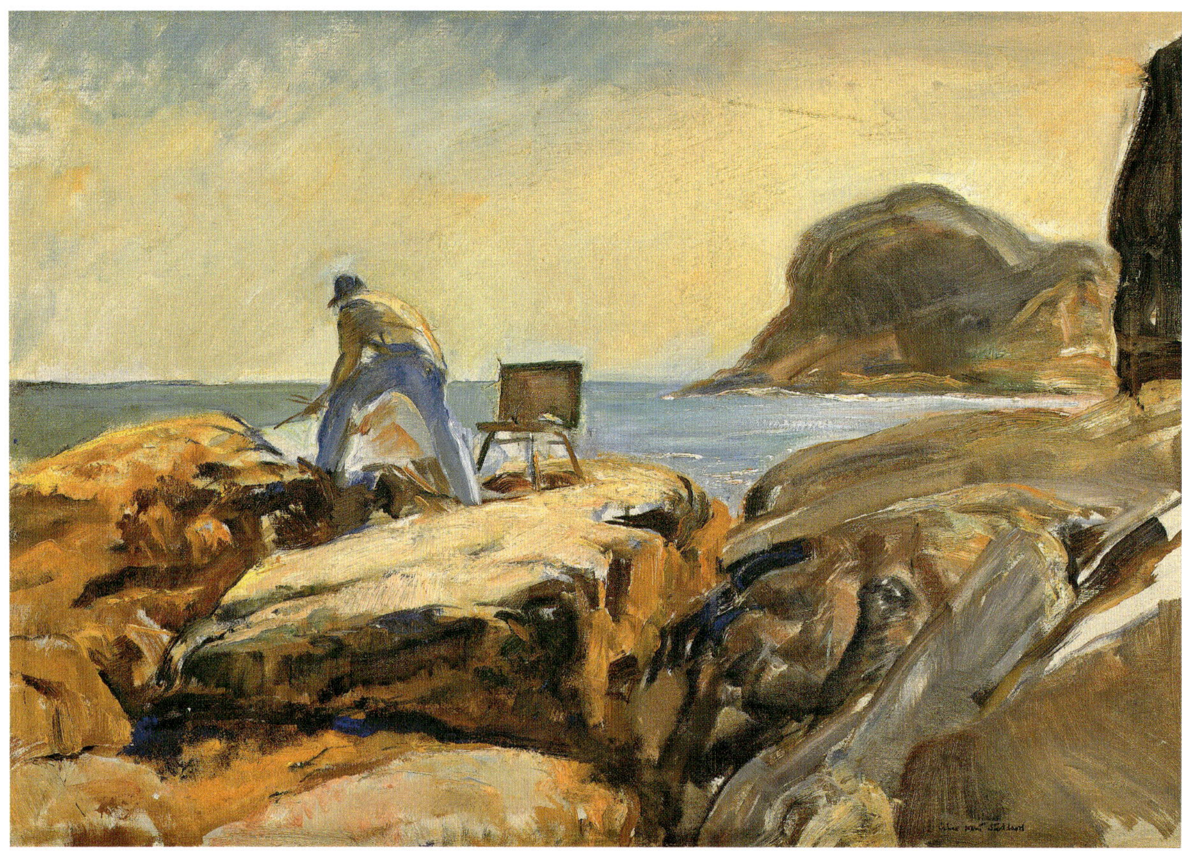

the long line of artists who have painted the island. In a fit of whimsy and revelation, he decided it might be simpler, in his words, "to send postcards."

Just about everyone "enters" the island by way of the town dock. In the painting *At the Dock (p. 8)*, Robert Van Vorst Sewell (1860–1924) captured the wonderful bustle of arrival and departure at the island wharf, which had been rebuilt in 1908 to accommodate the *May Archer*, an eighty-foot steamer that brought passengers and freight to the island from Thomaston on the St. George River *(p. 11)*. "The *May Archer* was anything but luxurious," Alta Ashley, a longtime islander, recalls, "although she did boast of a few staterooms, a heated salon and card room, wide decks and boat deck which we [children] were not supposed to explore."[4]

The wharf itself makes for a resonant motif, as shown in a handsome study by Remak Ramsay (b. 1937), who has been visiting Monhegan since 1993 *(p. 11)*. Whether viewed from higher ground, as in an oil *(p. 12)* by Margaret Morris Hoskins (1886–1955), or from sea level, as in an atmospheric rendering *(p. 13)* by Jay Hall Connaway (1893–1970), this epicenter of island comings and goings is a visually stimulating subject.

The English-born artist Henry "Harry" Fenn (1845–1911), who made a name for himself as an illustrator of such popular armchair travel books as *Picturesque America* (1872), adds a sparkle to the waterfront in an 1895 watercolor *(p. 14)*. Richard Knapp Fletcher (1885–1965)—an architectural draftsman from Boston, who designed the west portal of the Cathedral of St. John the Divine in New York City—took along his sketchbook on a trip to Monhegan and turned out a finely detailed view of a sailboat in the harbor *(p. 20)*.

To get to the dock, travelers must often navigate an assortment of moored vessels, such as those represented in Hayley Lever's

Alice Kent Stoddard, *Andrew Winter Painting Gull Rock*, c. 1938, oil on canvas, 20 x 27 in. Schwartz Family Collection. photo courtesy of David David Galleries, Philadelphia, PA

lively view of the harbor *(p. 10)*. Influenced by Impressionism, Lever (1876–1958), who was a native Australian, came into contact with Robert Henri, Bellows and other painters in New York. He specialized in marine subjects, many of which he found along the New England coast.

Lever painted his view of the village from Manana where the Coast Guard Station once stood. When Andrew Winter (1893–1958) made his watercolor of the station in 1940, the complex was at its height of activity, with World War II in the offing *(p. 15)*. A year-round islander for many years, Winter, who was born in Estonia, was a plein air painter of the first rank, known to brave bitter temperatures in his pursuit of a motif. The portrait of him by Alice Kent Stoddard (1883–1976) catches him in action *(p. 16)*, painting a view of Gull Rock on a sunny island day.

Many artists on Monhegan work outdoors. "Where in years gone by sheep clambered," wrote Charles Francis Jenney in *The Fortunate Island of Monhegan*, "easels of artists now stand."[5] The portrait of painters Alice Swett (1846–1916) and Maud Briggs Knowlton (1870–1956) by Eric Hudson (1862–1932) shows the women painting side by side in full dress, seated beneath umbrellas that protect them from the sun. Hudson himself may have been dressed to a tee while painting this canvas. A photo of him on the island circa 1900 shows a mustachioed man perched on a folding chair before a tripod easel, garbed like a businessman: full suit with vest and tie.[6]

By contrast, Rockwell Kent looks relaxed in a partial self-portrait that shows him sketching in his one-room house on Monhegan in 1907 *(p. 18)*. He described his happy existence in his autobiography:

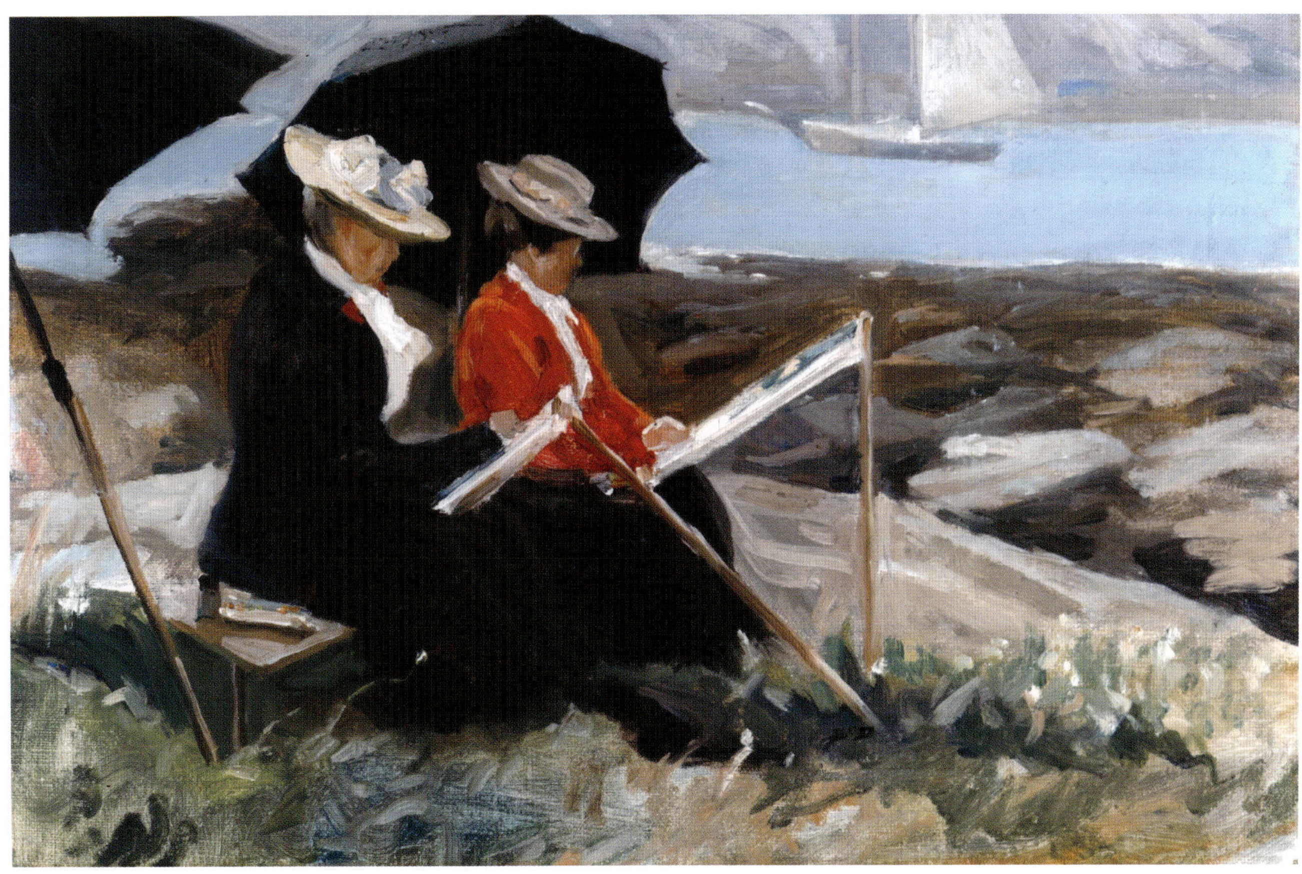

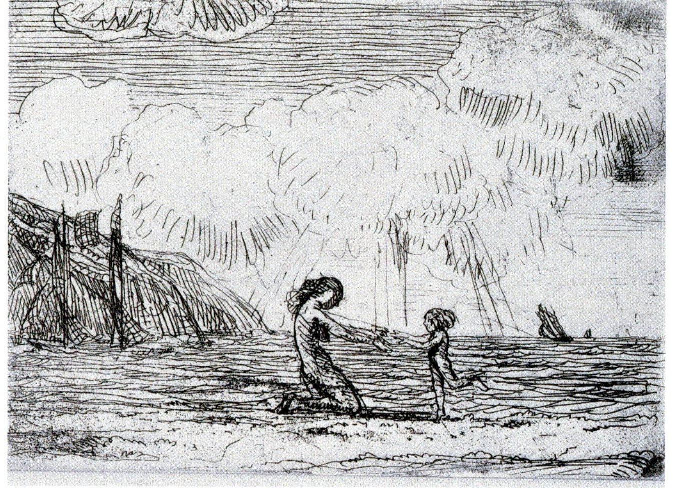

ROCKWELL KENT, *MOTHER AND CHILD AT MONHEGAN*, 1910
ETCHING ON COPPER, 2 $^{11}/_{16}$ x 3 $^{11}/_{16}$ IN.
SCHWARTZ FAMILY COLLECTION

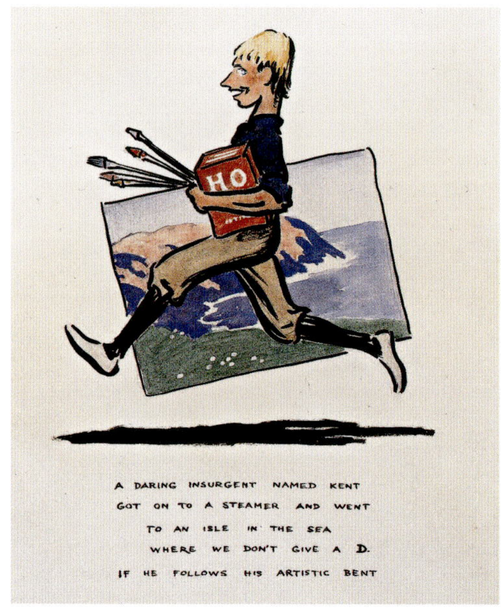

FREDERICK DORR STEELE
THE YOUNG KENT, 1910
INK AND WATERCOLOR ON PAPER, 22 x 16 $^1/_4$ IN.
COLLECTION OF EDWARD L. DECI
INCLUDES THE DOGGEREL
"A DARING INSURGENT NAMED KENT
GOT ONTO A STEAMER AND WENT
TO A PLACE IN THE SEA
WHERE THEY DON'T GIVE A D
IF HE FOLLOWS HIS ARTISTIC BENT."

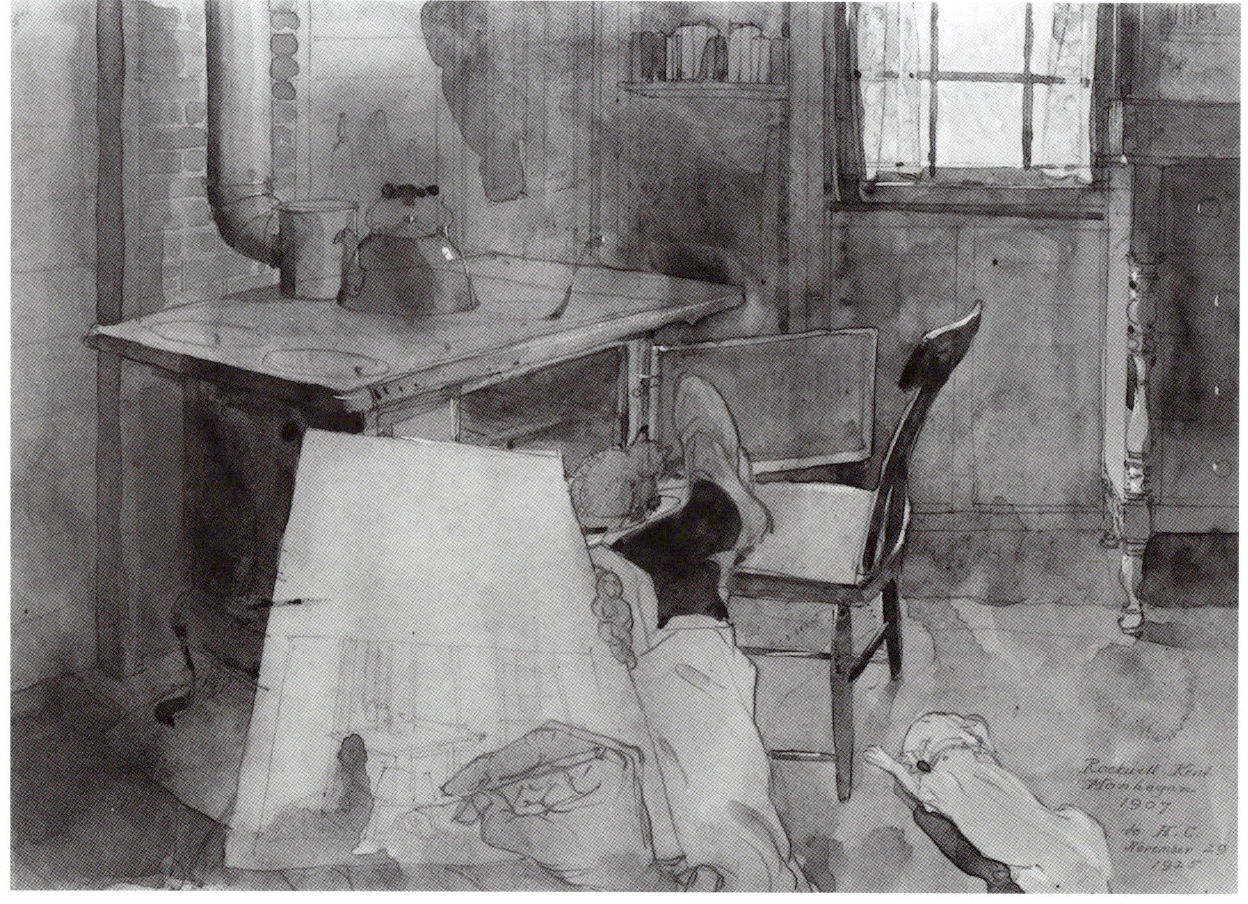

ROCKWELL KENT, *INTERIOR OF A COTTAGE, MONHEGAN ISLAND*, 1907, WATERCOLOR ON GRAPHITE TOUCHED WITH WHITE
PHILADELPHIA MUSEUM OF ART: PURCHASED THROUGH THE LOLA DOWNIN PECK FUND FROM THE CARL AND LAURA ZIGROSSER COLLECTION, 1971

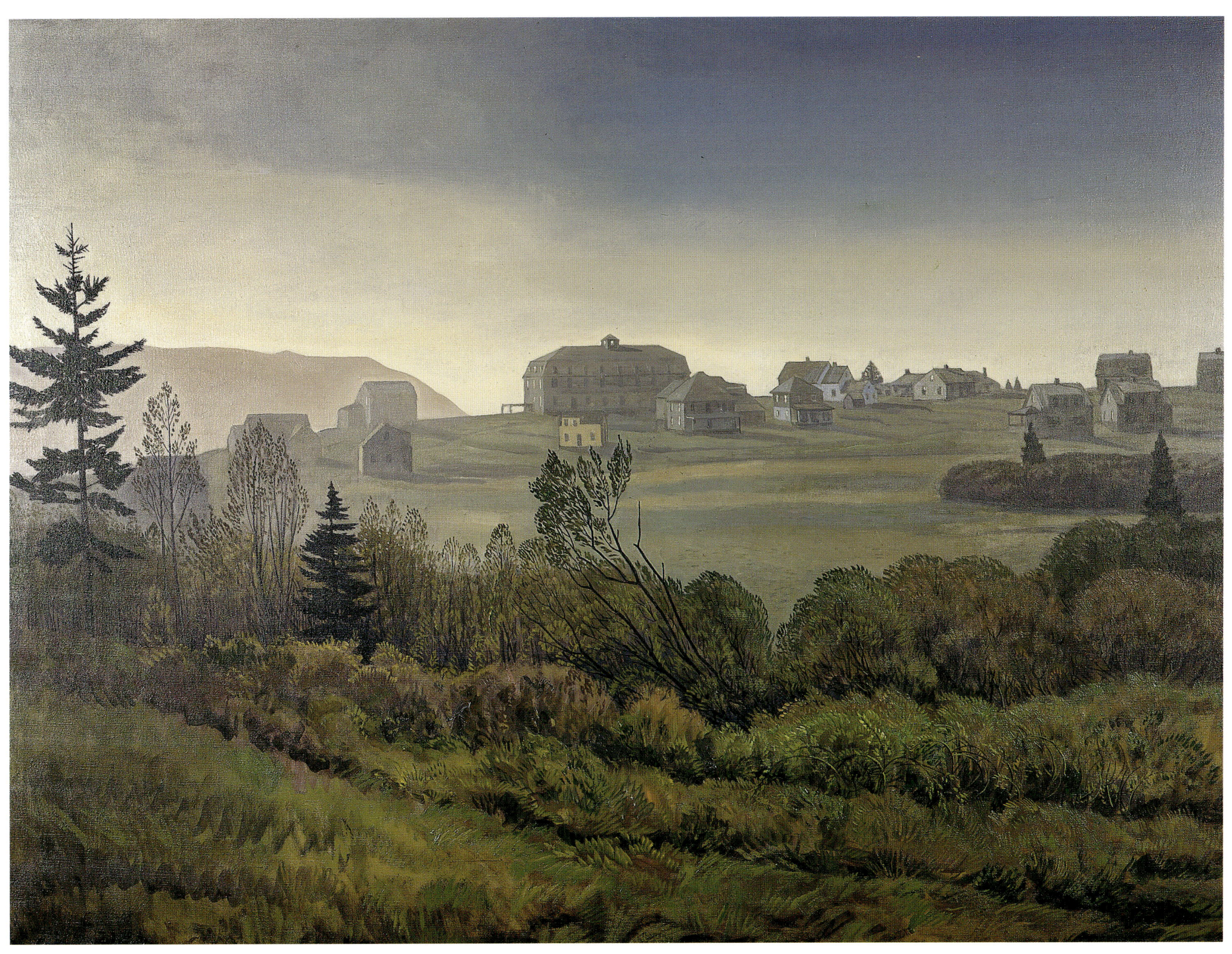

Rockwell Kent, *Maine Fog: Monhegan,* 1955, oil on canvas, 34 x 44 in., Pushkin Museum, St. Petersburg, Russia

by permission of Plattsburg State Art Museum, Plattsburg College Foundation, Rockwell Kent Gallery and Collection, Bequest of Sally Kent Gordon

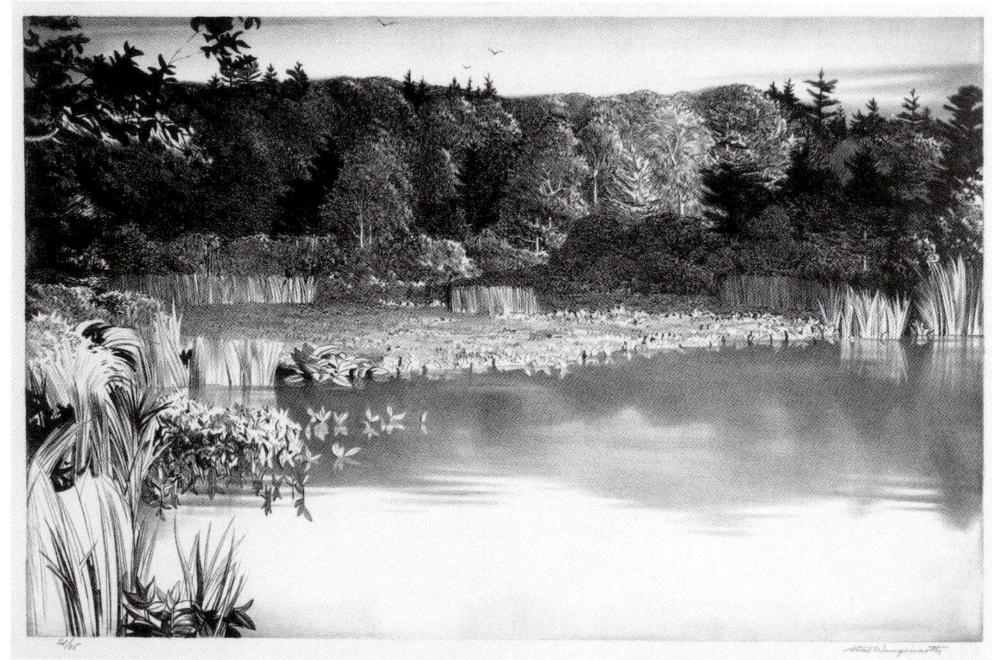

STOW WENGENROTH, *QUIET POND, MONHEGAN, MAINE*, 1946
LITHOGRAPH, 10 3/16 X 15 7/16 IN., EDITION OF 85, PRIVATE COLLECTION

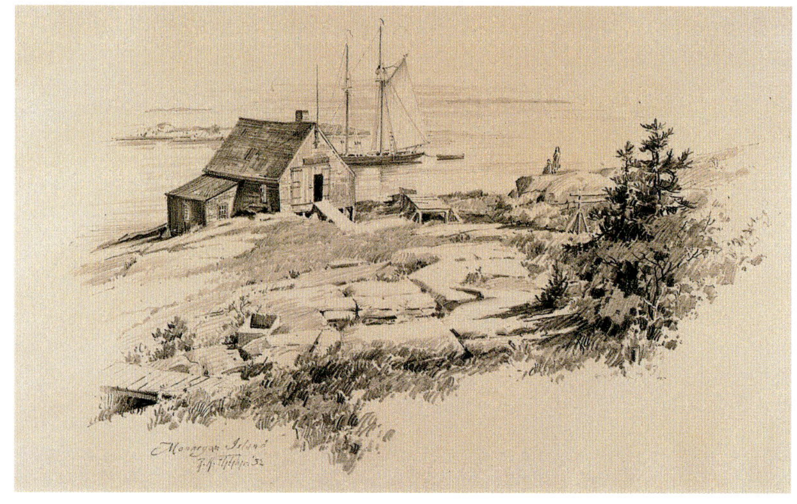

RICHARD KNAPP FLETCHER, *MONHEGAN ISLAND*, 1932
PENCIL, 8 1/2 X 13 1/2 IN., PRIVATE COLLECTION

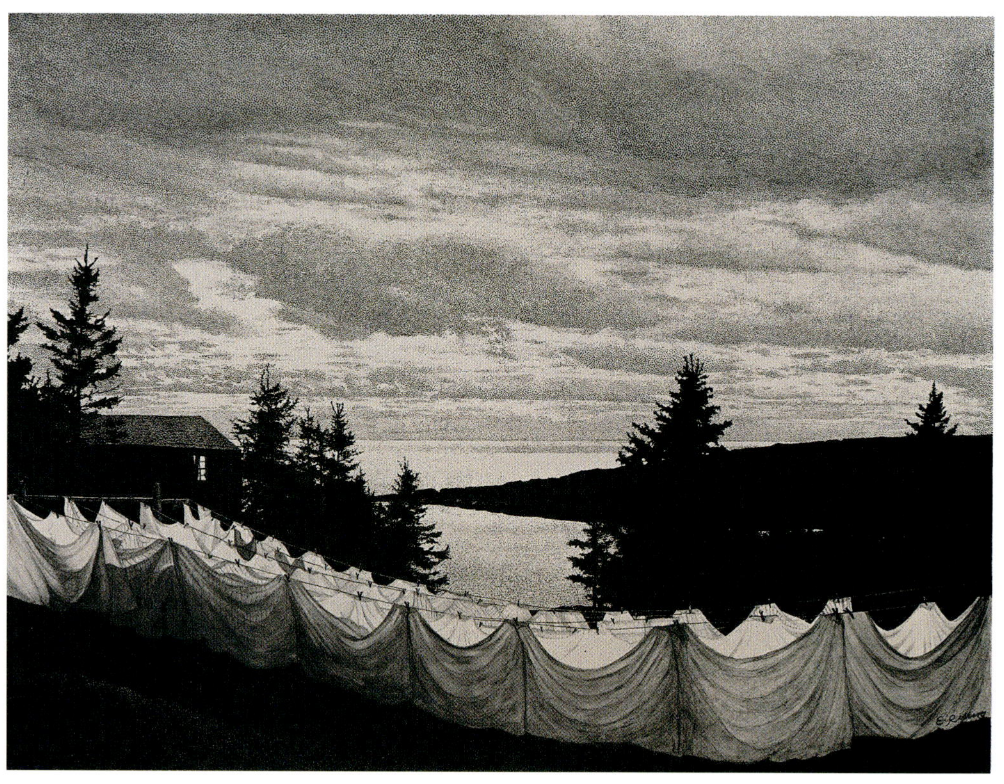

ELMER RISING, *MONHEGAN HANGUP*, 1975
PHOTO LITHOGRAPH, 10 3/4 X 14 IN., PRIVATE COLLECTION

"Seated in my rocker, my feet at the oven door, the lamp at my elbow, my curtains drawn to shut out the night's immensity, my purring cat for living company, I'd read."[7]

The island library wasn't built until 1930, constructed in memory of an 11-year-old girl who was swept off the edge of the island in a storm, and the 15-year-old boy who tried to save her. The well-known etcher and illustrator (of the Sherlock Holmes series) Frederick Dorr Steele (1873–1944) designed the plan for the structure, which today can barely contain its collection of books. It was Steele who made the wonderful caricature of Kent striding off to the island *(p. 18)* — brushes and turpentine under one arm, one of his classic Monhegan headland canvases under the other.

When William Kienbusch (1918–1980) visited Monhegan in 1948, he chose as a subject the ubiquitous kerosene lamp *(p. 4)* for one of his semi-cubist caseins — ubiquitous because electricity was only sparingly available from generators. Kerosene lamps also appear in Sarah McPherson's intimate view of her room at the

If you were with me we could tramp the wild places all day and night and be alone together again; and sit by the sea in the night wind; and watch the moon lay a silver carpet over the ocean. We could slip over the velvet covered rocks down at the Sea's brink and watch the waves reach for us, and you could laugh at me for being timid and afraid of those crystal green hands which are so clean and cold. . . . And everything I spoke of to you would be about Love and beauty and love again and the greatness of this nature which is in us. We two and the great sea and the mighty rocks greater than the sea, and we two greater than the rocks and the sea. Four eternities.

—George Bellows, letter to his wife, Emma, from Monhegan

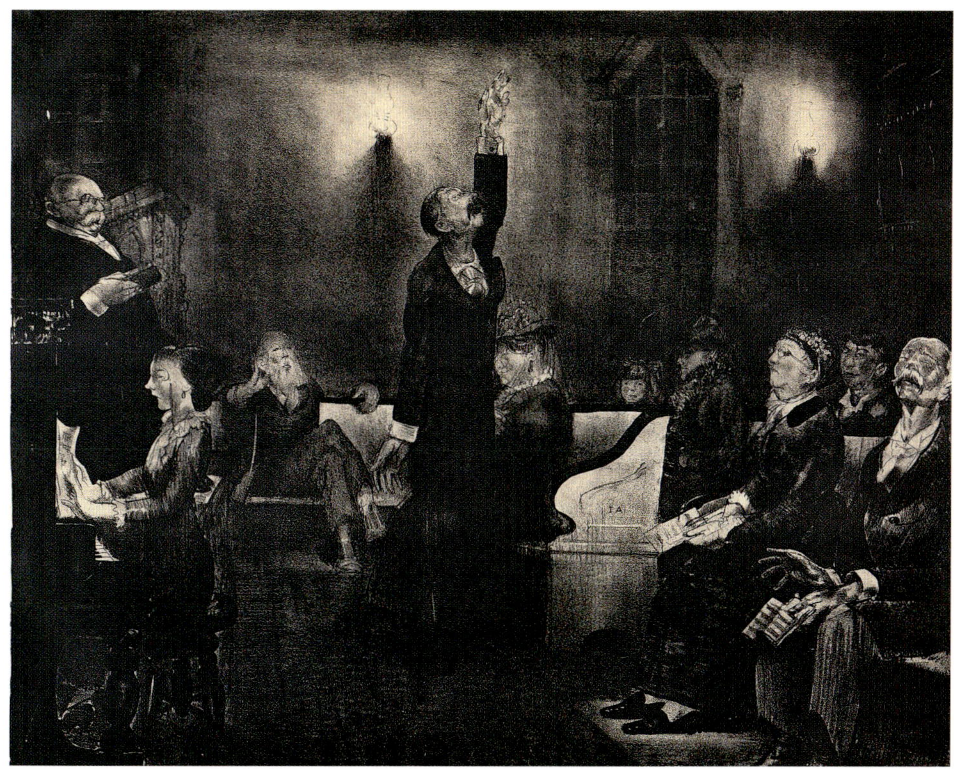

George Wesley Bellows, *Prayer Meeting*, 1916
lithograph, 18 1/4 x 22 1/4 in., Schwartz Family Collection
photo courtesy of Owen Gallery, New York, NY

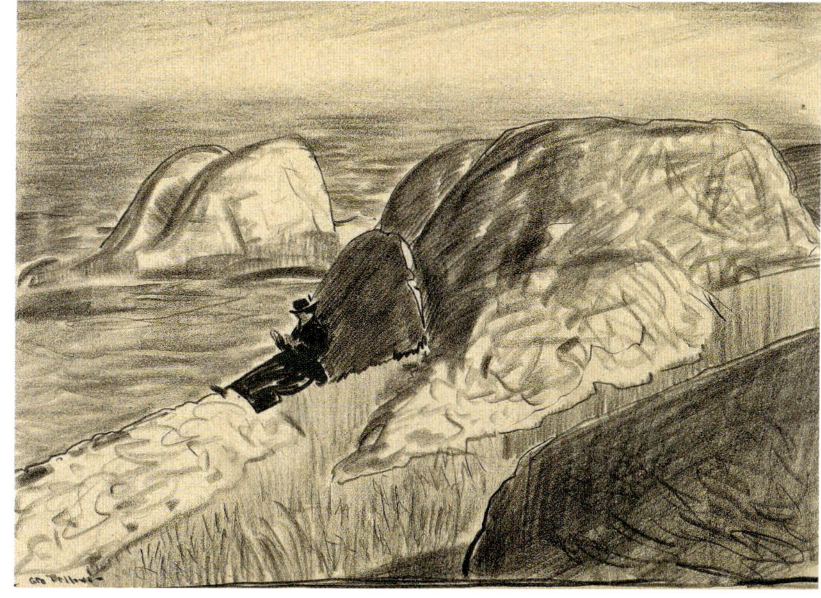

George Wesley Bellows, *Emma on Gull Rock*, 1913
conte crayon on paper, 6 3/4 x 8 1/2 in.
Schwartz Family Collection
photo courtesy of Adelson Galleries, Inc.

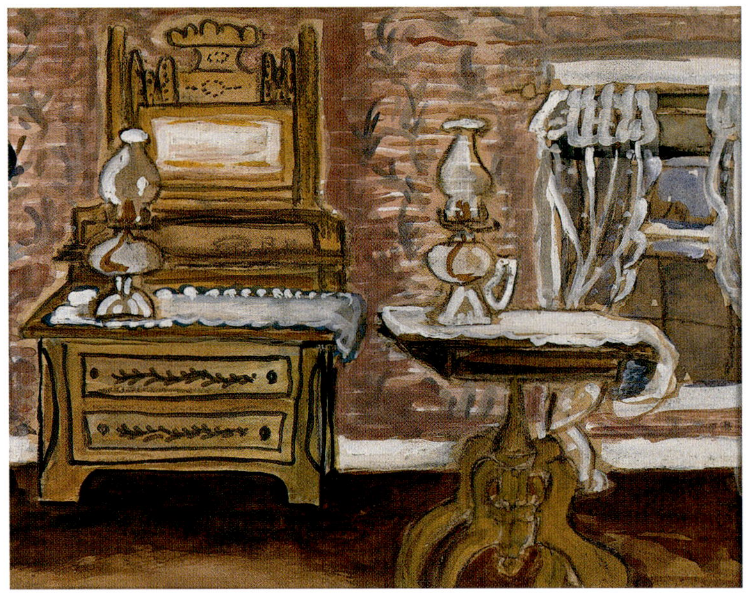

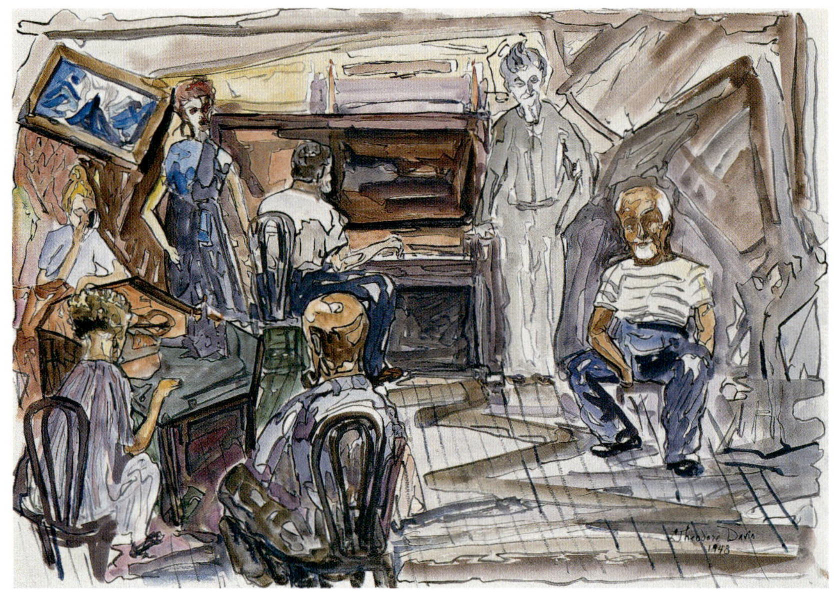

Trailing Yew. A student of Robert Henri, McPherson (1894–1978) spent her first summer on the island in 1928. She was known to hang her miniature paintings by clothespins at the back of the Periwinkle coffee shop, "where anyone could take his pick and replace it with a $5 bill." For the writer, behaviorist and island visitor B. F. Skinner, McPherson was "as much a part of Monhegan as Burnt Head or White Head."[8]

A clothesline hung with billowing white sheets stretched between two Monhegan rooming houses (the Mooring Chain on the left, the Anchorage on the right) caught the eye of Rockland, Maine, native Elmer Rising (1906–1987), who first visited the island in 1973 *(p. 20)*. "I always went over in the fall, after most of the summer people had gone," he once wrote. "After three days, you wouldn't know what day it was, you wouldn't have a care in the world."[9]

Master lithographer Stow Wengenroth (1906–1978) spent one summer on Monhegan, gathering material for a half dozen or so prints, including a lovely view of the ice pond—the major source of freshwater on the island *(p. 20)*. This sheltered watering hole with its cattails, frost flowers, arrowhead and pond lilies, where skaters figure-eight in winter and where ice was harvested until 1972, was Wengenroth's favorite spot, the place "where sea gulls come to wash salt from their wings."[10]

A list of island activities might include a dip at Swim Beach—a pastime for the more hearty individual, as the water is quite cold. In what is thought to be his first etching, created with the help of his friend and fellow painter John Sloan, Kent sketched a mother and child frolicking in the chilly waters *(p. 18)*. Other entertainment might include an impromptu musicale in the lobby of the Monhegan House, as depicted in a wonderful watercolor by Theodore "Ted" Davis (1908–1995), or a serious game of cribbage, which appealed to the German-born Emil Holzhauer (1887–1986) as a subject for one of his oils *(p. 25)*. Islanders also organized costume balls, gymkhanas and baseball games.

Churchgoing has also been popular on the island. In an article in the *Boston Evening Transcript* (August 21, 1897), a travel writer described the Advent preacher "who sails over from 'the main' every third or fourth Sunday, to hold a service in the little meeting-house [on Monhegan]." The preacher "deals out to the people the harsh doctrine that the world—and in particular their island—is growing more and more wicked, and will soon come to an end, in fulfillment of God's prophecy—and the people believe it."[11]

George Bellows (1883–1925) captured such a rousing prayer meeting *(p. 21)* in a dramatic lithograph from 1916, the first he ever made. The painter, who had traveled to the island at the behest of his teacher Robert Henri, contributed to the island community by playing snare drums in the Monhegan Marching Band. His wife, Emma, chose a more tranquil diversion, as shown in a 1913 crayon drawing of her taking the air on Gull Rock *(p. 21)*.

Nearly a century later, Adirondack chairs arranged on a bit of lawn provide a comfortable spot from which to view the harbor *(p. 112)*, as depicted in an oil by Peter Poskas (b. 1935). "What intrigues me about Monhegan Island," says the artist, who has been painting there since the early 1990s, "is the light in all its facets: at times subtle and caressing and at others harsh and penetrating."[12] Such effects of light draw artists to Monhegan like moths to a flame.

NOTES

1. Charles McLane, *Islands of the Mid-Maine Coast, Muscongus Bay and Monhegan Island* (Rockland, Maine: Island Institute, 1992), 215–216.
2. Rockwell Kent, *It's Me O Lord* (New York: Dodd, Meade, 1955), 120.
3. Kent, *It's Me O Lord*, 117–118
4. Alta Ashley, *Under the Grey Gull's Wing* (Monhegan: Grey Gull Publications, 1983), 97.
5. Charles Francis Jenney, *The Fortunate Island of Monhegan* (Worcester: Davis Press, 1922), 69.
6. Photograph reproduced in Earle G. Shettleworth and W. H. Bunting, *An Eye for the Coast: The Maritime and Monhegan Island Photographs of Eric Hudson* (Gardiner, Maine: Tilbury House, 1998), 5.
7. Kent, *It's Me O Lord*, 150.
8. Both quotes from Robert Karen, "The Lost Art of Sarah McPherson," *New York*, 17 August, 1981, 52.
9. Elmer A. Rising, *The Pen Renderings of Elmer Rising: New England in Black and White* (Belmont, Mass.: Friends of Elmer Rising Publishing Company, 1986), 17.
10. Ronald and Joan Stuckey, *The Lithographs of Stow Wengenroth, 1951–1972* (Boston: Boston Public Library, 1974), 286.
11. Cited in Shettleworth and Bunting, *An Eye for the Coast*, 159.
12. *Peter Poskas: A Sense of Place*, exhibition catalogue, Spanierman Gallery, 2004, 12.

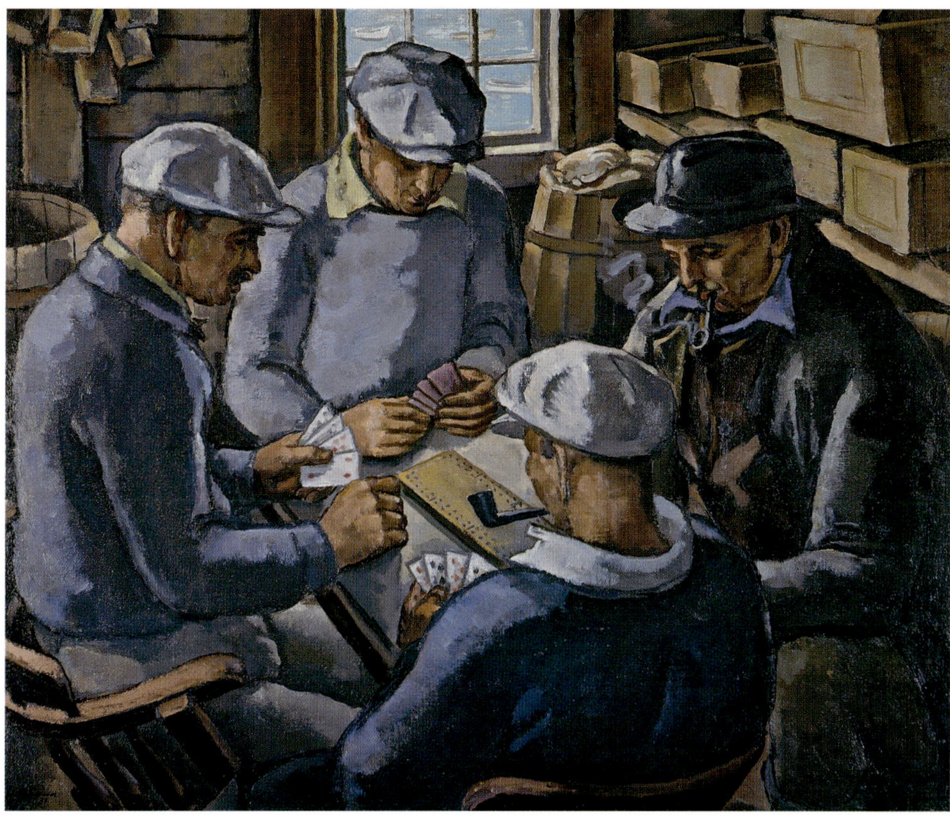

EMIL HOLZHAUER, *FISHERMEN AT CRIBBAGE*, 1931, OIL ON CANVAS, 36 X 44 IN. SCHWARTZ FAMILY COLLECTION. PHOTO COURTESY OF GUARISCO GALLERY, WASHINGTON, DC

The beach itself is formed of about equal parts of sand, shells and fish-bones. One man ventured the assertion that if all the fish-bones that had been thrown into the harbor could be gathered together into one heap, they would reach as high as Monanis [Manana] — not so incredible a statement as it would at first seem, since they have been cutting up fish here and tossing the bones about for some two hundred and eighty years or more.

—SAMUEL ADAMS DRAKE, *THE PINE-TREE COAST*, 1891

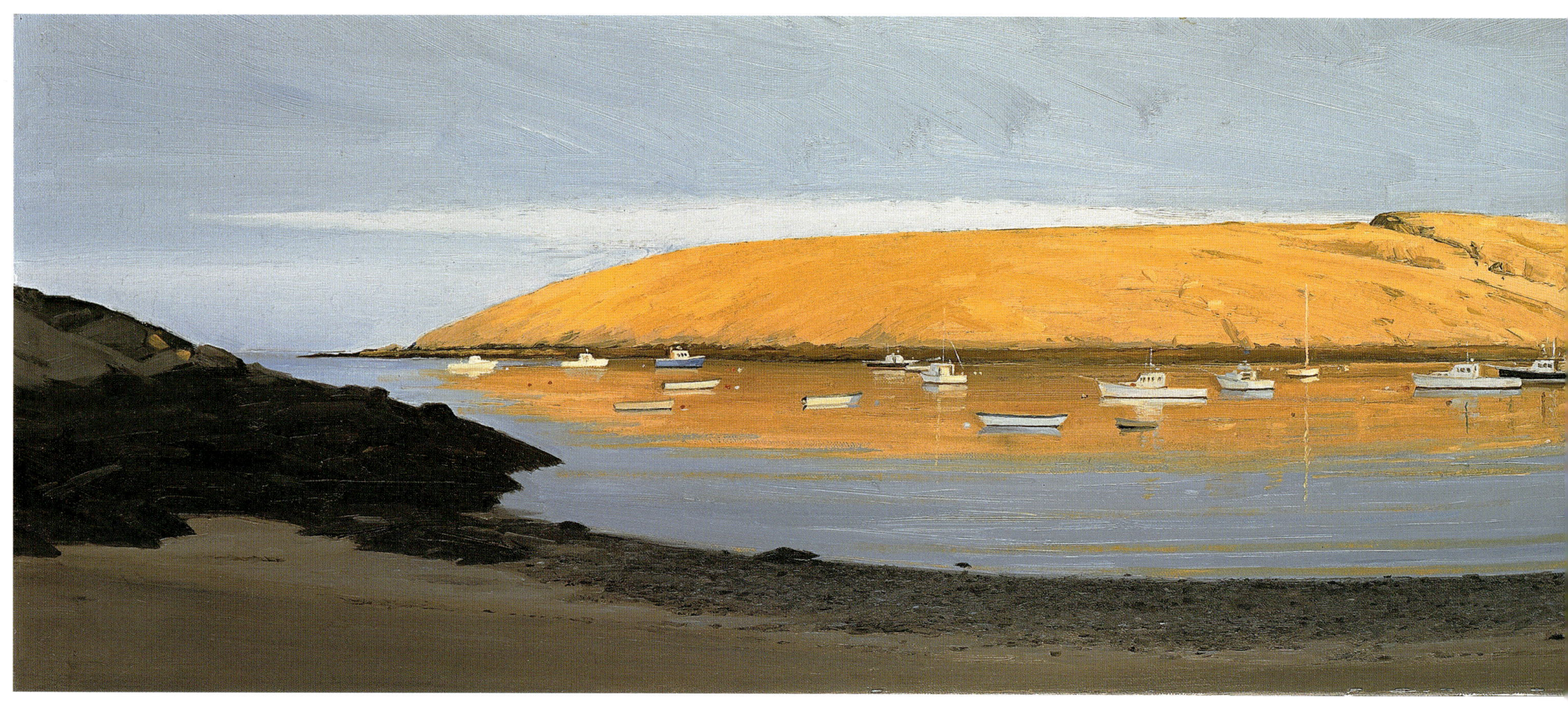

24   KEVIN BEERS, *ORANGE MANANA PANORAMA*, 2001, OIL ON CANVAS, 11 X 38 IN., COLLECTION OF JIB AND JOY FOWLES

Harbor and Work

Trap Day is much more than the opening of a season. This is Monhegan's day, and the culmination of a social contract that involves honor, justice, fairness, patience, and frank fellow-feeling. It represents a lot of hard work ashore, so that a lot more hard work can be performed at sea. It is all the traditional Yankee values rolled into one—delayed gratification, honest labor, dogged persistence, and the rest of the inventory—combined with manifest individual prowess and community elan. It is a very, very special and fine time, and these people are not crazy.
—GEORGE PUTZ, *ISLAND JOURNAL*

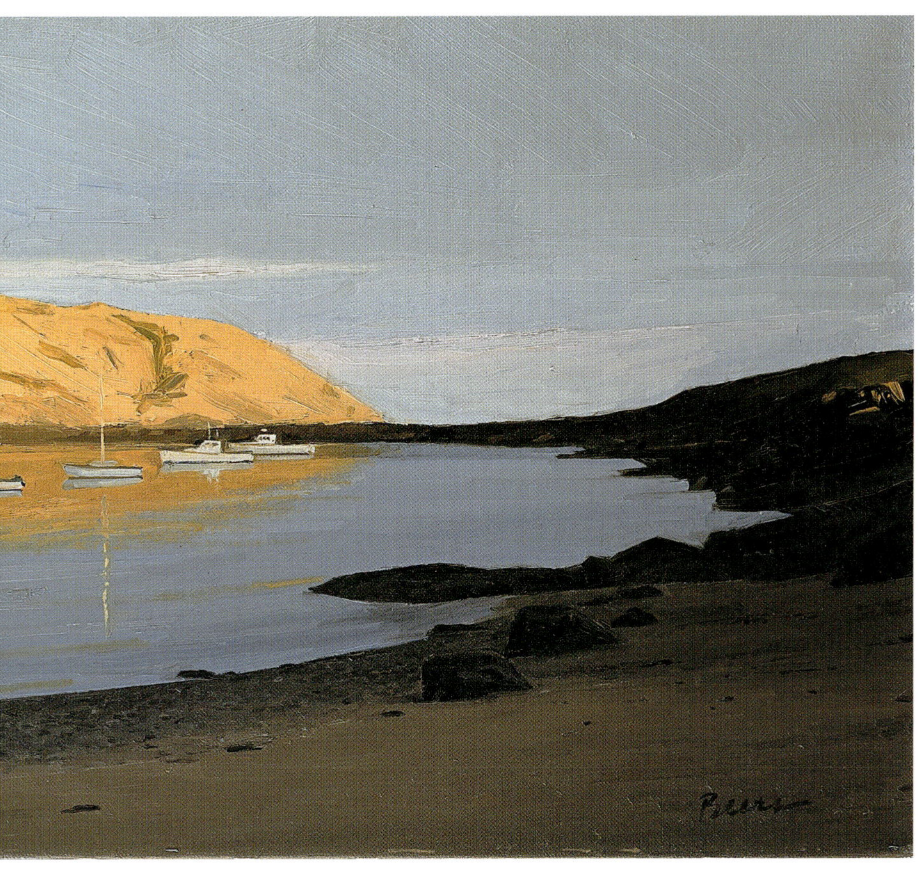

Writing about a visit to Monhegan in the *Saturday Evening Post* in 1953, Charles Rawlings fittingly titled his article "Lobster Town."[13] Lobstering and an assortment of other fishing activities, from purse seining to tuna harpooning, have represented the core "industry" of the island, going back to the earliest visitors. "By hooke and line with 15 men at most, 60,000 cod were tooke in lesse than one month," reported Captain John Smith in a record of his visit to the island in 1614.[14]

Such bounty in the Gulf of Maine has diminished through overfishing, but the lobster harvest on Monhegan has remained steady, thanks to its closed season on lobstering, established by state law in 1909 to conserve the supply of *Homarus americanus*. The season runs from January 1, Trap Day, to June 25, when the "toilers of the sea," as Rockwell Kent called them, take in their lobster pots, repair traps and pursue other pastimes till the season starts up again.

Fred Boynton, a lobsterman from New Harbor on the mainland, expressed his admiration for the hardiness of his Monhegan counterparts. "They do their lobstering in the winter," he noted, "when you get all the bad storms. They catch lobsters right in the shallow waters, but they take awful chances to get them and sometimes they get caught with quite a loss of gear."[15] In *Lobstermen, Maine Coast (p. 26)*, James Floyd Clymer (1893–1982) depicts men recovering traps driven onto the shore of Monhegan by a storm.

This winter harvesting is not crazy behavior, as George Putz avers, for the lobsters are bigger at this time of the year and the market tends to be at its most lucrative. Yet winter lobstering has

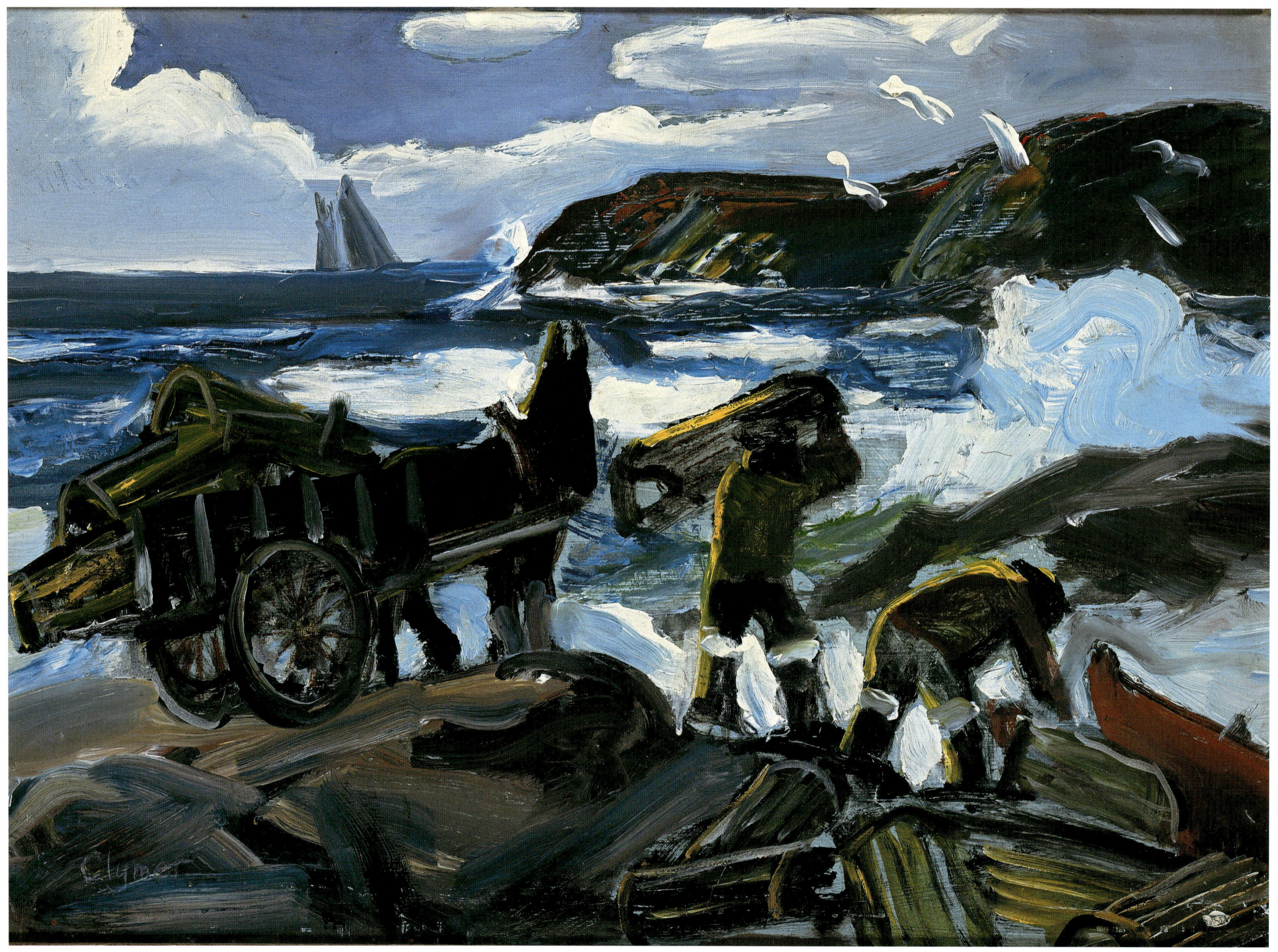

JAMES FLOYD CLYMER, *LOBSTERMEN, MAINE COAST*, N.D., OIL ON BOARD, 18 x 24 IN., COLLECTION OF WISCASSET BAY GALLERY, MAINE

On the Monhegan shore of the harbor, and mainly clustered around the wharf and two small beaches, stood the fish-houses, most of them two-storied structures with runways leading to their lofts. Unpainted and weatherbeaten, they proclaimed to eyes—and nose!—the island's industry. So too did every foot of intervening ground occupied, as it was in summer, by drying-flakes for cod, and by the pyramids of lobster traps and heaps of painted buoys withdrawn for the season.

—ROCKWELL KENT, *IT'S ME O LORD*, 1955

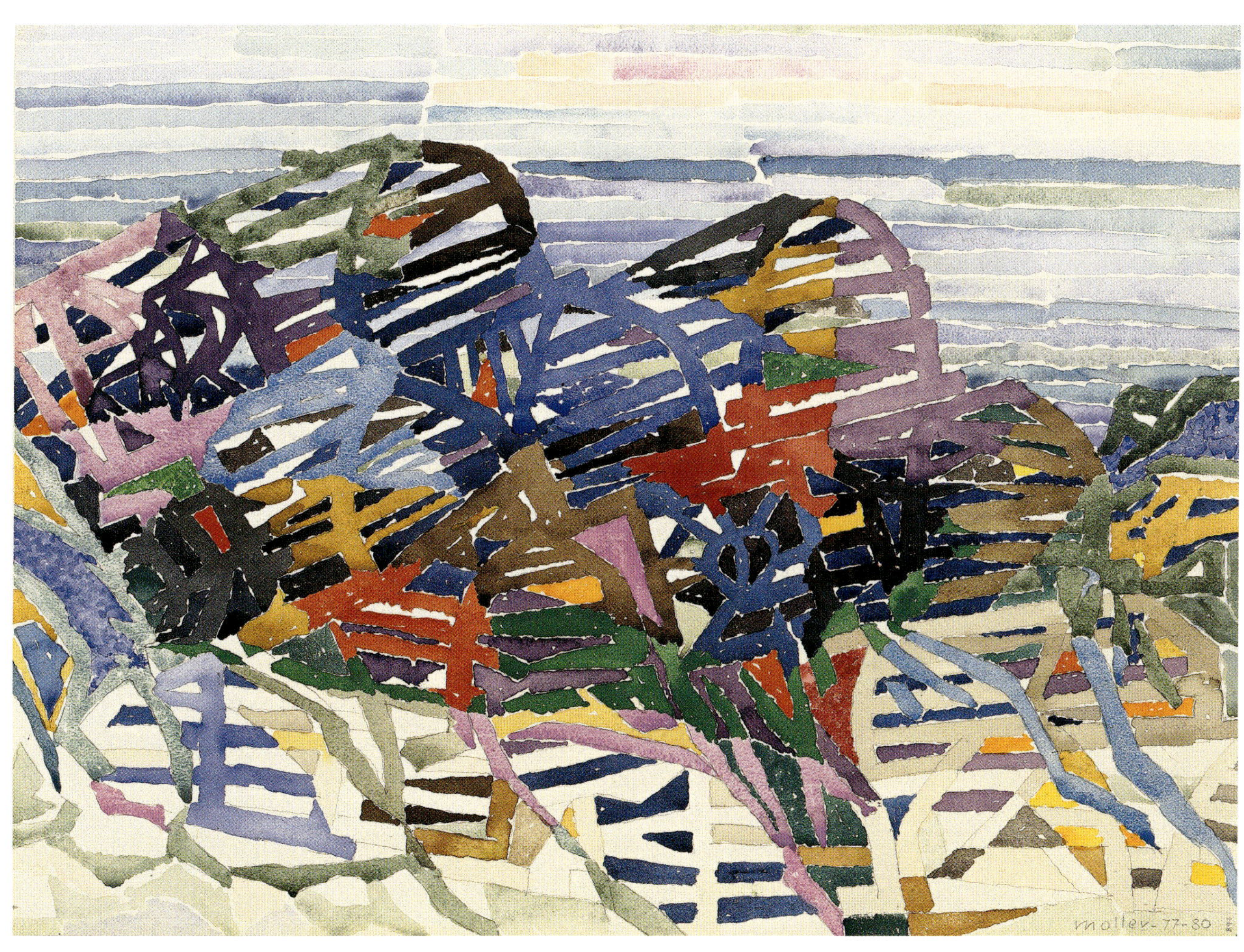

HANS MOLLER, *LOBSTER TRAPS I*, 1977–80, WATERCOLOR ON PAPER, 18 X 24 IN., COLLECTION OF KAROLYN VREELAND BLUME
PHOTO BY ROBERT WALCH, COURTESY OF LORE DEGENSTEIN GALLERY, SUSQUEHANNA UNIVERSITY

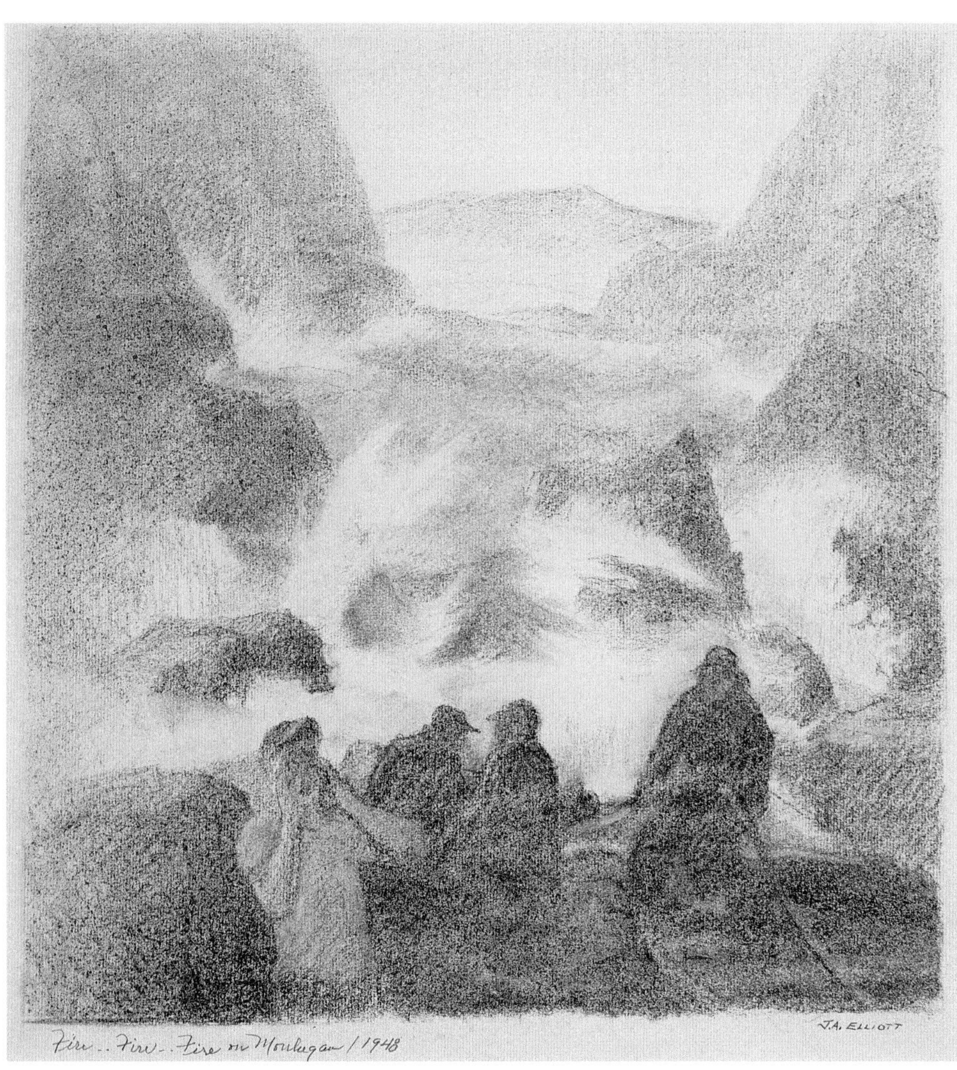

JAMES ELLIOTT, *FIRE FIRE FIRE ON MONHEGAN*, 1948
CHARCOAL ON PAPER, 18 X 16 IN.
RIVER GALLERY COLLECTION, DAMARISCOTTA, MAINE

its risks. In her writings about Monhegan, Elizabeth Coatsworth offered several accounts of the perils associated with this livelihood, including the story of a drowned fisherman whose grieving widow threw into the sea "his family Bible, his old pair of carpet slippers, and his cat," as her offerings, when his body was not found.[16]

The island has experienced its share of wrecks. The destruction of the Gloucester fishing schooner *St. Christopher* on the rocks at Squeaker Cove in 1949 inspired several dramatic canvases *(p. 29)* by Joseph DeMartini (1896–1984). A Mobile, Alabama, native who studied with Leon Kroll, DeMartini first arrived on Monhegan around 1946 and became a regular visitor for the rest of his life. He is one of a line of formidable abstract-leaning artists who have found aesthetic sustenance on the island.

The hardworking islanders have been a favorite subject for painters going back well over a hundred years. Boston-born James Fitzgerald (1899–1971), who first visited Monhegan in 1925 and ended up moving to the island for good in 1942, paid homage to their island livelihoods in many works. In one of his brilliant water-colors, fishermen in yellow oil clothes haul nets onto the beach, their bodies straining with exertion *(p. 31)*. He endows the islanders with vigor and grace.

Jay Hall Connaway, who hailed from Liberty, Indiana, also paid homage to islanders in his paintings. Living on the island year-round from 1933 to 1947, he came to know and respect the travails of island life, which were especially intense in the winter, as shown in the canvas *Snow on Black Head (p. 30)*. He also recognized the importance of his own vocation, affixing a sign to his studio door that read, "I am working. Go thou and do likewise."[17]

Connaway directed an art school on the island in the 1940s. One of his students, Maine-born James A. Elliott (b. 1919), felt a similar empathy for the islanders. In his haunting charcoal drawing titled *Fire Fire Fire on Monhegan*, the artist depicted islanders pumping water from the ocean to put out a wildfire on the back side of the island. (The island has always maintained strict rules against smoking or building fires of any kind.)

A native of Minsk, Russia, Abraham J. Bogdanove (1888–1946) first went to Monhegan in 1918; he purchased a studio cottage on the island two years later. A painting of fishermen cleaning their catch on Fish Beach *(p. 33)* displays his bold style—what critics of

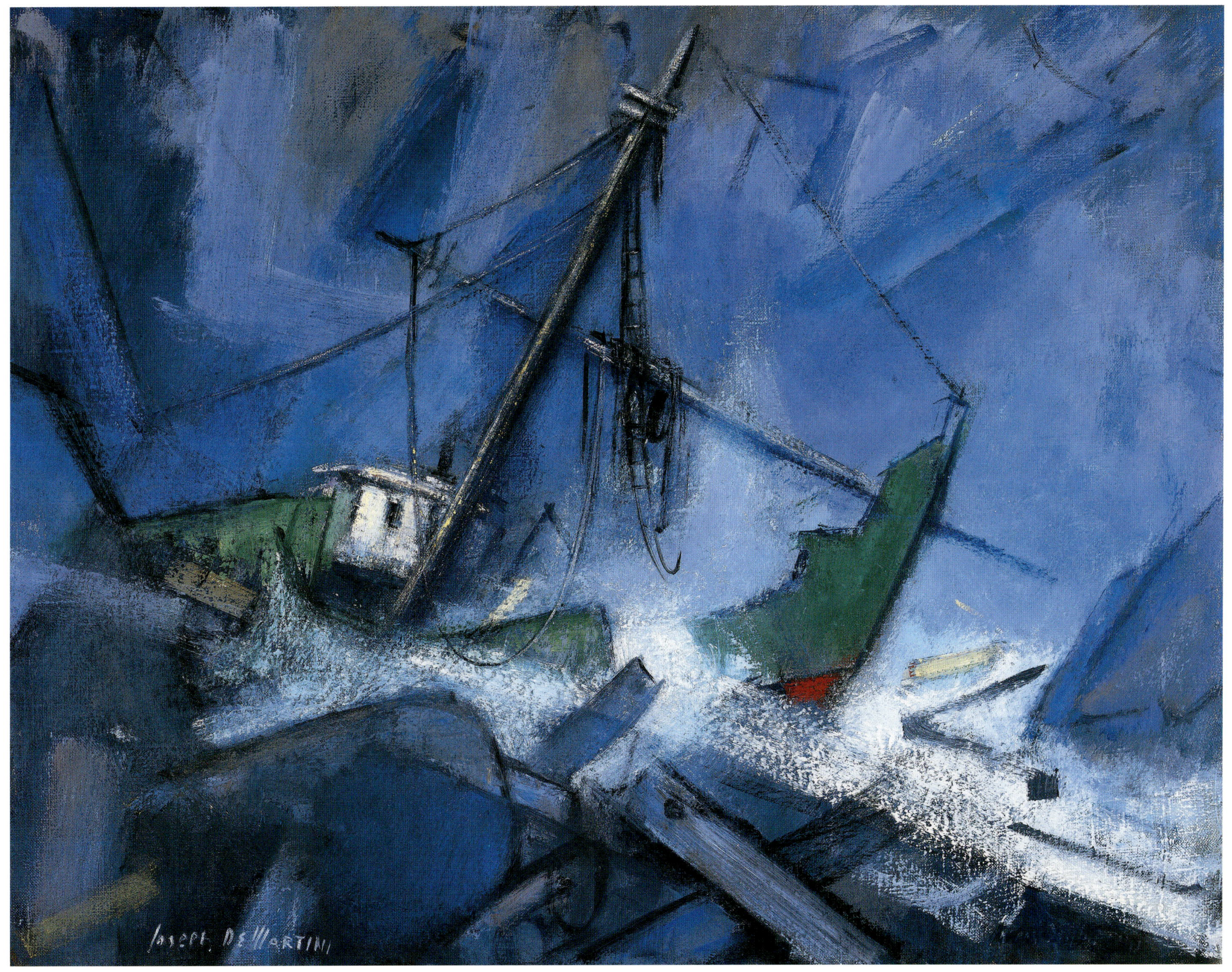

Joseph DeMartini, *Wreck in Squeaker Cove*, n.d., oil on canvas, 24 x 30 in., River Gallery Collection, Damariscotta, Maine

29

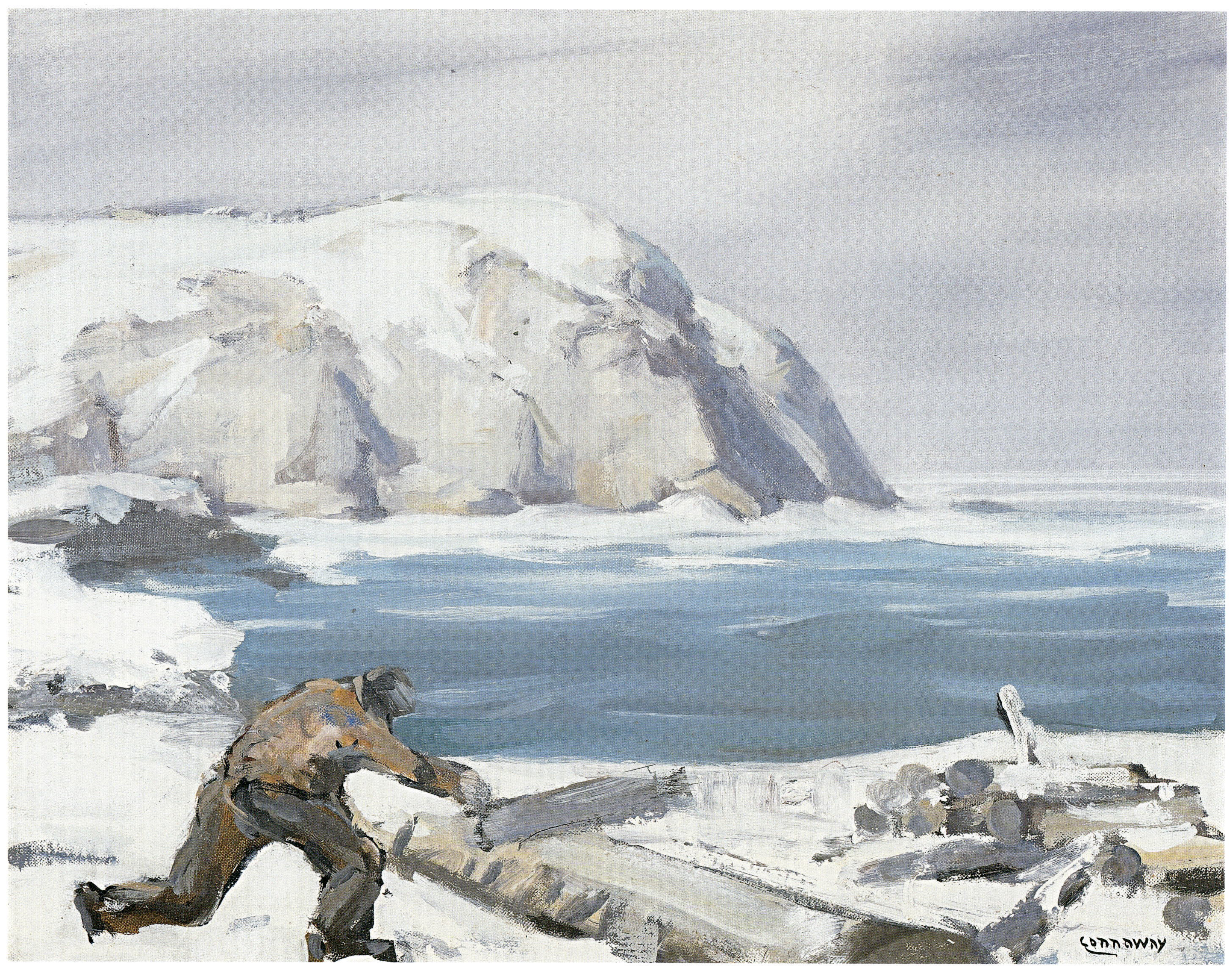

JAY HALL CONNAWAY, *Snow on Black Head*, N.D., OIL ON ARTIST BOARD, 16 x 20 IN., ROBERT AND CAROL STAHL COLLECTION

He calls the island "Munhiggin" and tells me he's lived on it most of his life. He tried the mainland once, some time back, but gave it up and returned to the island. "A man gets by with less here. He don't need an auto or a fancy wardrobe. And he's free of responsibilities for all those possessions. And free of the pressures of shoreside living."

"Islands have pressures," I say.

"Not so much. In cities when people want spiritual comfort they flock to churches and psychiatrists and have to pay high for it. Here you pray when you want, where you want, in solitude. You're free. And you're handsomely rewarded"— he gestured with a sweep of his big rough hand—"wherever you turn."

— HENLEY DAY IN CONVERSATION WITH MARTIN DIBNER

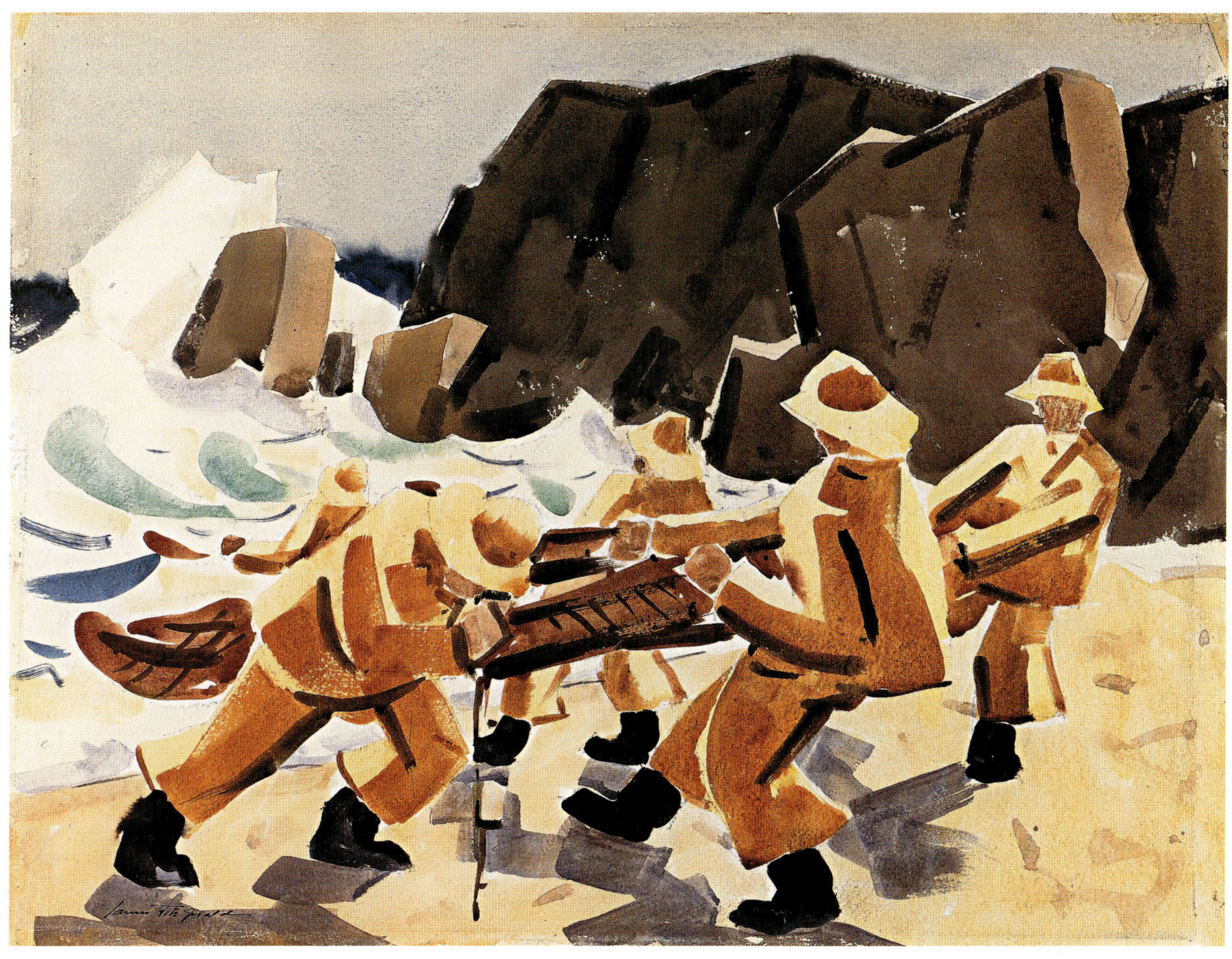

JAMES FITZGERALD, *FISHERMEN*, C. 1938, WATERCOLOR ON PAPER, 19 $^{7}/_{16}$ X 25 $^{1}/_{8}$ IN.
COLLECTION OF THE FARNSWORTH ART MUSEUM. MUSEUM, PURCHASE, 1945

It is thru these men and women that this tiny isle of the seas has been made familiar to artlovers, at least, the world over. Thru them it is true to-day, in the big galleries of this country and of Europe, may be found portrayals of Monhegan scenery and native types, so that, tho the world may not come to Monhegan, the inner life and beauty of the place have gone forth upon canvas to fascinate and enthrall men here and abroad.

—CHARLES F. JENNEY, *LEWISTON EVENING JOURNAL*, AUGUST 6, 1914

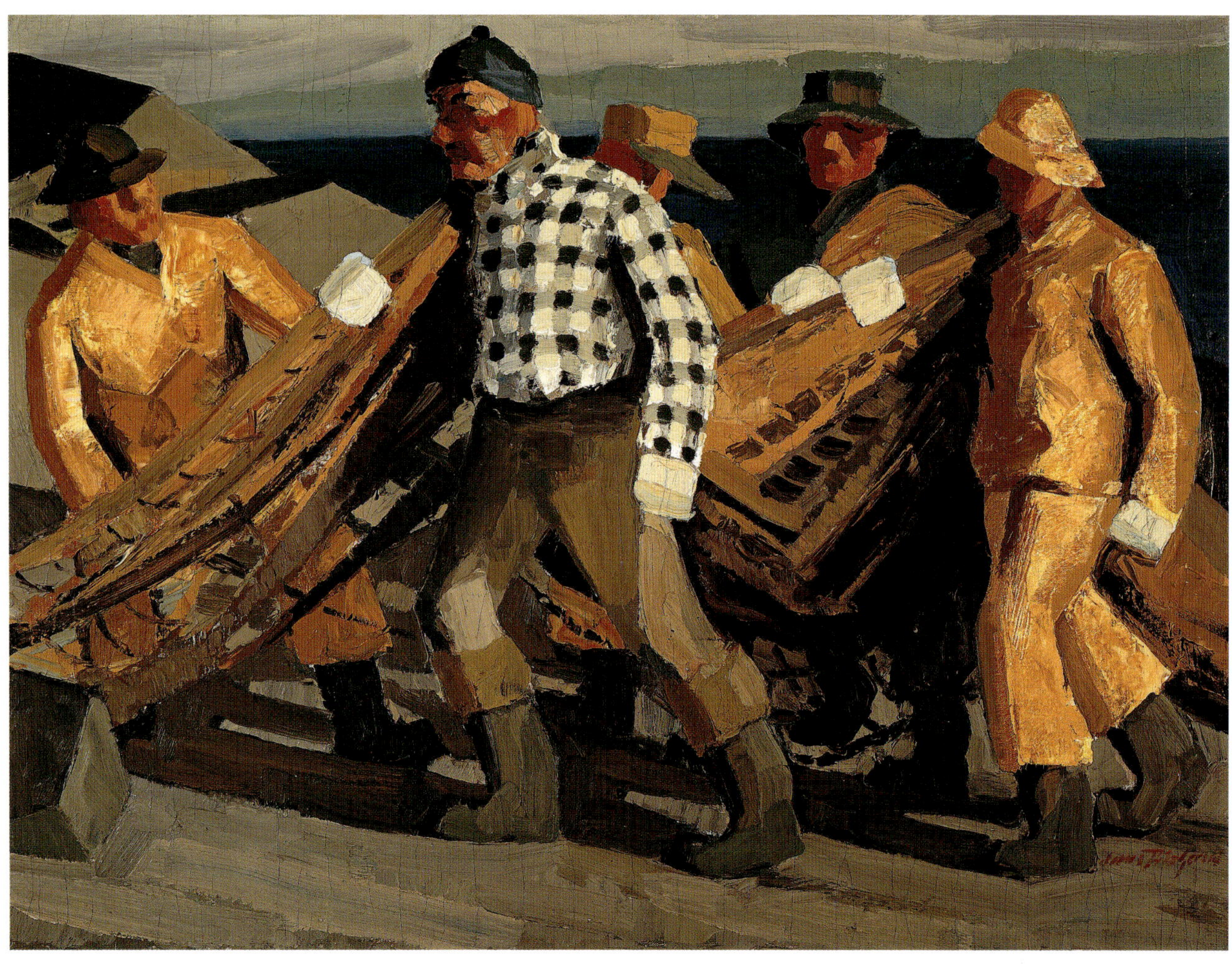

JAMES FITZGERALD, *HAULING THE NETS*, N.D., OIL ON CANVAS, 26 x 34 IN.
SCHWARTZ FAMILY COLLECTION. PHOTO COURTESY OF GLEASON FINE ART, BOOTHBAY HARBOR, MAINE

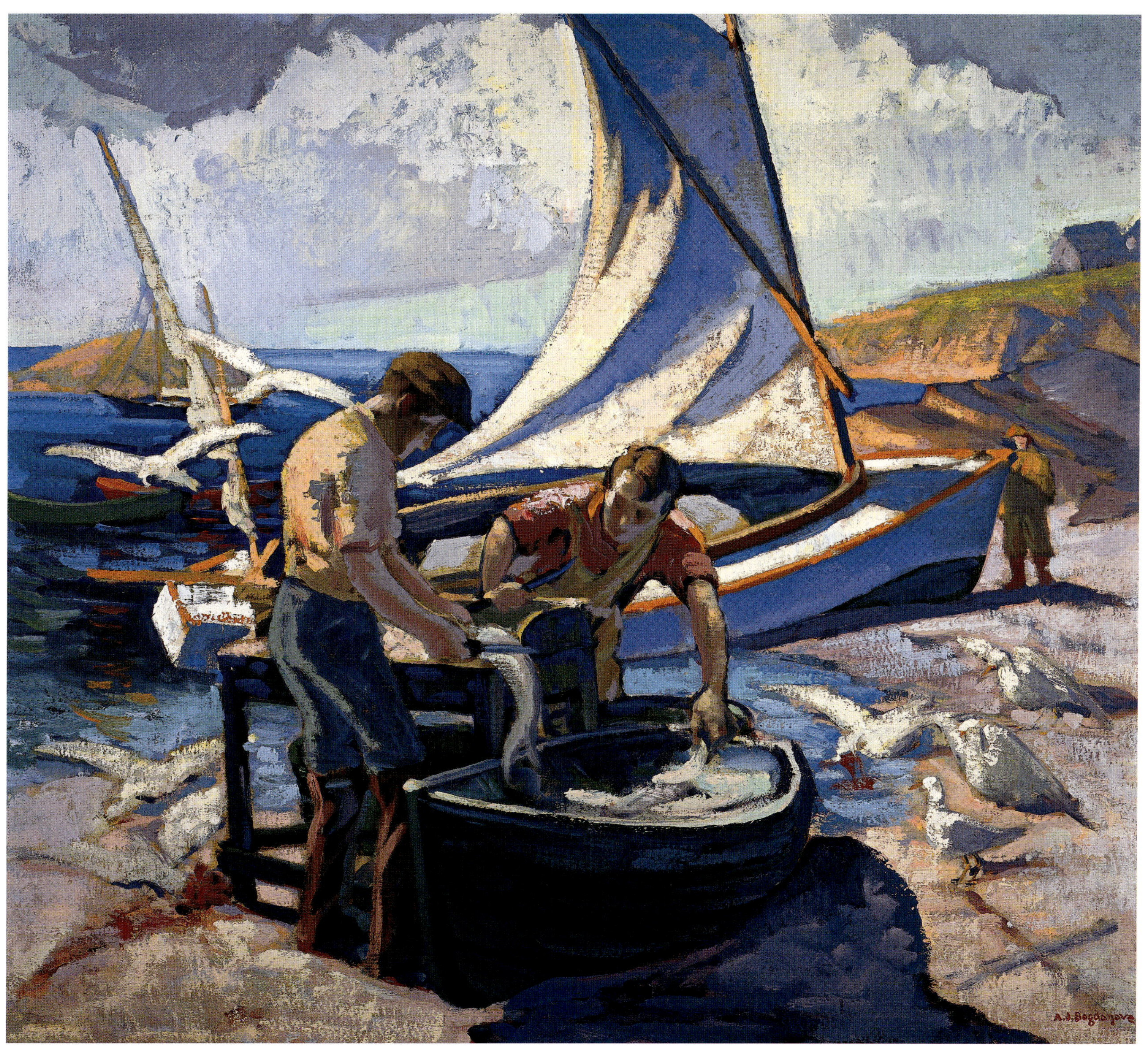

Abraham J. Bogdanove, *On the Beach*, n.d., oil on canvas, 36 x 40 in., River Gallery Collection, Damariscotta, Maine

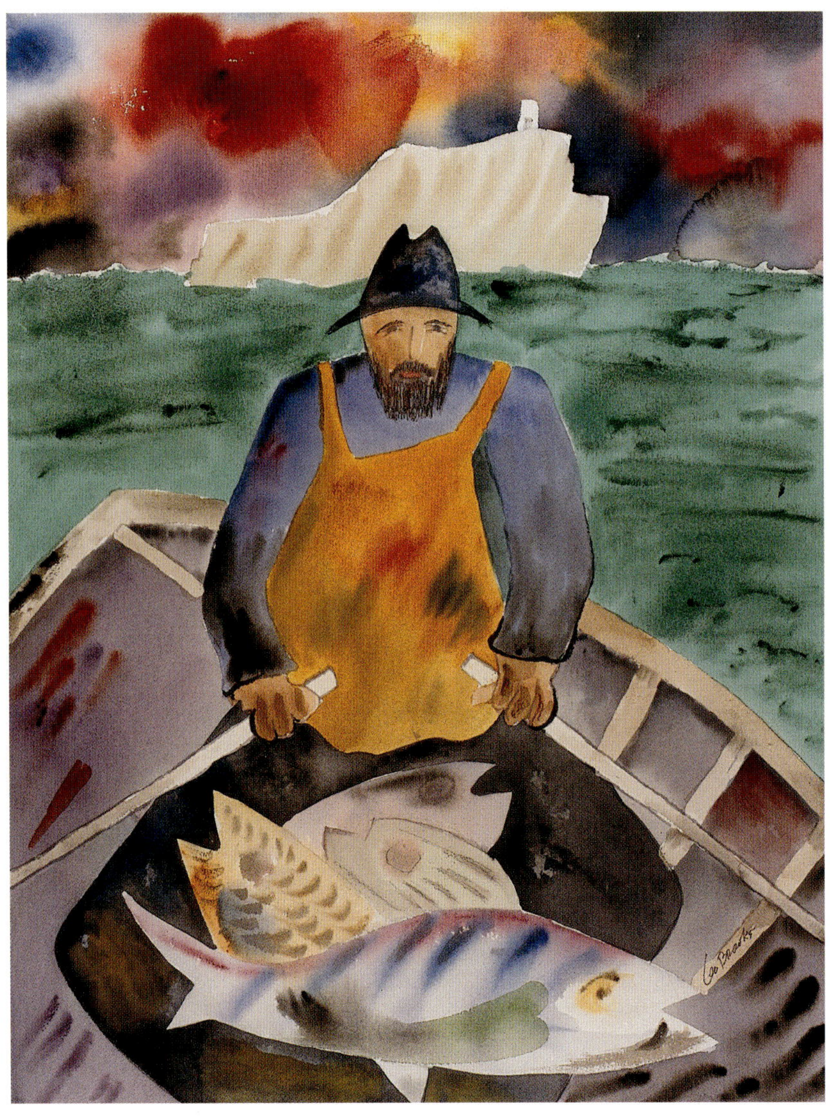

another era would have called virile. Writing about the beach in a 1891 travelogue, Samuel Adams Drake reported the assertion of one islander "that if all the fish-bones that had been thrown into the harbor could be gathered together into one heap, they would reach as high as Monanis [Manana]."[18]

More recently, artists like Leo Brooks (1909–1996) and Thomas R. Barrett (b. 1927) have depicted island fishermen *(pp. 34, 35)*. A son of Jewish Russian immigrants from the Bronx, Brooks didn't paint till he was in his 60s, but he hit his stride on Monhegan, inspired by the people and the environment. Brooks always said painting was like fishing. "You never know what you're going to have on the end of the line," he told his friend and fellow island painter John Hultberg.[19]

For Castine, Maine, painter Barrett, a four-month immersion in the life of Monhegan in 1949 determined the course of his artistic sensibility. "Here the island people confront risks of sea, of weather, of economic stringency with warmth and wit in the microcosmic dimensions of this quintessential place—cliffs, beaches, ledges, foaming surf, tangled forests," the artist has written. In his dynamic canvas *Monhegan Lobsterman*, Barrett offers a bird's-eye view of a solo islander gaffing a buoy line.

Fishing boats have had great appeal to artists. Eric Hudson (1862–1932), who first came to Monhegan in the late 1800s, painted the various smacks and dories in the harbor, drawn to the shapes and the geometry of sails *(p. 36)*. Hudson's boats, wrote the prominent art critic Royal Cortissoz, "ride the waves not like birds, lightly skimming them, but like the heavily built craft that they are, full of strength and character."[20]

The painter's daughter Jacqueline Hudson (1910–2001) also favored harbor subjects, including a handsome clutch of lobster buoys *(p. 37)*. The "grand dame" of Monhegan's cultural and social life, Hudson spent many of her ninety-one summers on the island. She and her sister, Julie, helped build the Monhegan Historical and Cultural Museum into the significant institution it is today.

"In front and to the south was the little harbor filled with gently rocking dories and larger fishing craft," W. D. Quint wrote in the *Boston Herald* in October 1900. "On the right stretched the grand Manana, a huge ledge rising over a hundred feet from the water like a great rampart guarding the boats below."[21]

Leo Brooks, *Coming Home II*, c. 1987
watercolor on paper, 31 x 22 in.
Gallery-by-the-Sea/Sally MacVane, Port Clyde, Maine

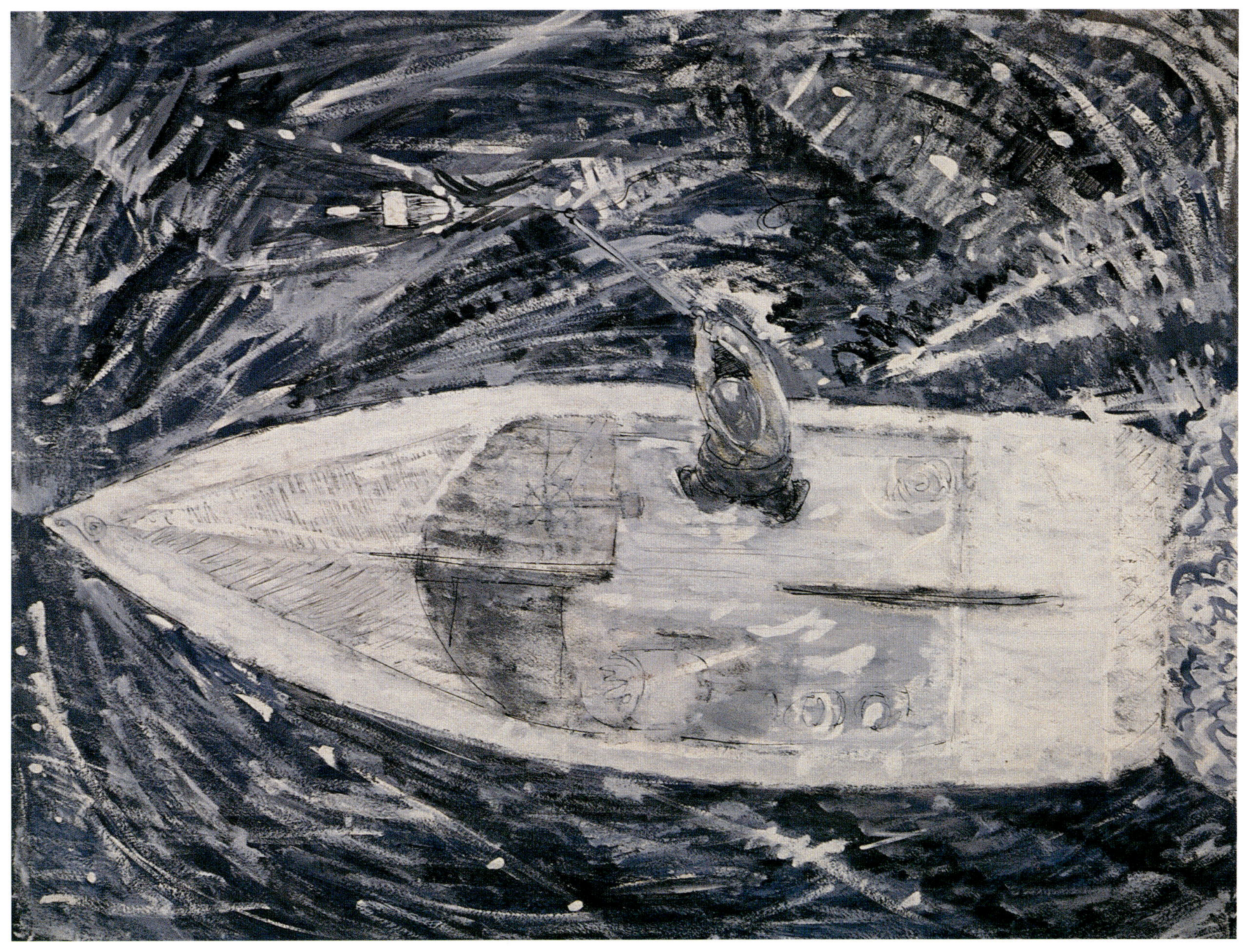

Thomas R. Barrett, *Monhegan Lobsterman*, 1949, casein on paper, 10 x 26 in., collection of John M. Day

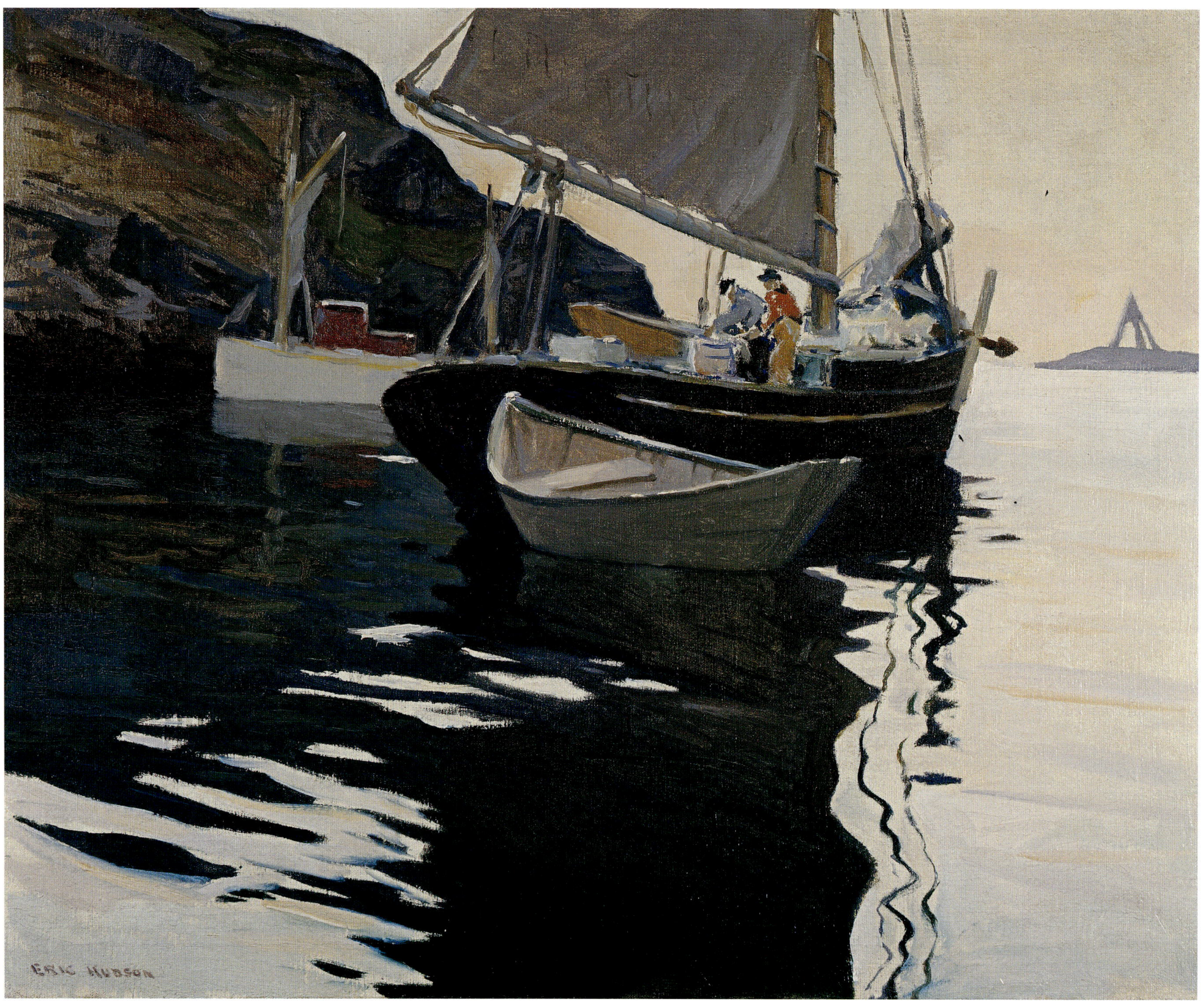

  ERIC HUDSON, *THE END OF THE DAY*, N.D., OIL ON CANVAS, 28 x 34 IN., SCHWARTZ FAMILY COLLECTION

This picturesque scene hasn't changed much over the centuries, and it has been a continual favorite subject for artists. Kevin Beers (b. 1952) offers a luminous, wide-angle view of the harbor from Fish Beach *(pp. 24–25)*. In one of his watercolors, Ted Davis, who was a student of the great abstractionist Hans Hofmann, employs a lively style to represent the harbor and its boats *(p. 38)*.

In a similarly modern manner, the German-born artist Hans Moller (1905–2000) brings a quality of mosaic work to his view of the boat-filled waters. Moller, who purchased a summer cottage on Monhegan in 1959, was also fascinated by the patterns made by the hoops of wooden lobster traps *(p. 27)*. "During my first visit to Monhegan, many years ago," the painter wrote in 1977, "I looked at nature in a new way again. The light, sky, horizon, and colors have inspired me to paint some of my most successful canvases in a style I still hope to develop further."[22]

Like Moller, the Philadelphia-born, New York-trained painter Henry Kallem (1912–1985) practiced a singular aesthetic in his Monhegan landscapes, painting during summer visits in the years following World War II *(p. 110)*. Using a kind of loose pointillistic approach, he turned a view of the island harbor into a dynamic and colorful patchwork of brushstrokes.

In their delightful and fanciful diorama representing Fourth of July on Monhegan in 1899, the French artists Anne-Emmanuelle Marpeau (b. 1962) and Bernard Lagny (b. 1947) offer a distinctly patriotic vision of the island, with flags flying from houses and boat masts *(p. 39)*. The image brings to mind a poem cited in A. J. Pettingill's travel piece about the island, published in *New England Magazine* in September 1898:

> Monhegan is a pleasant isle,
> As fair as fair can be,
> The sweetheart of the summer sun,
> The jewel of the sea.

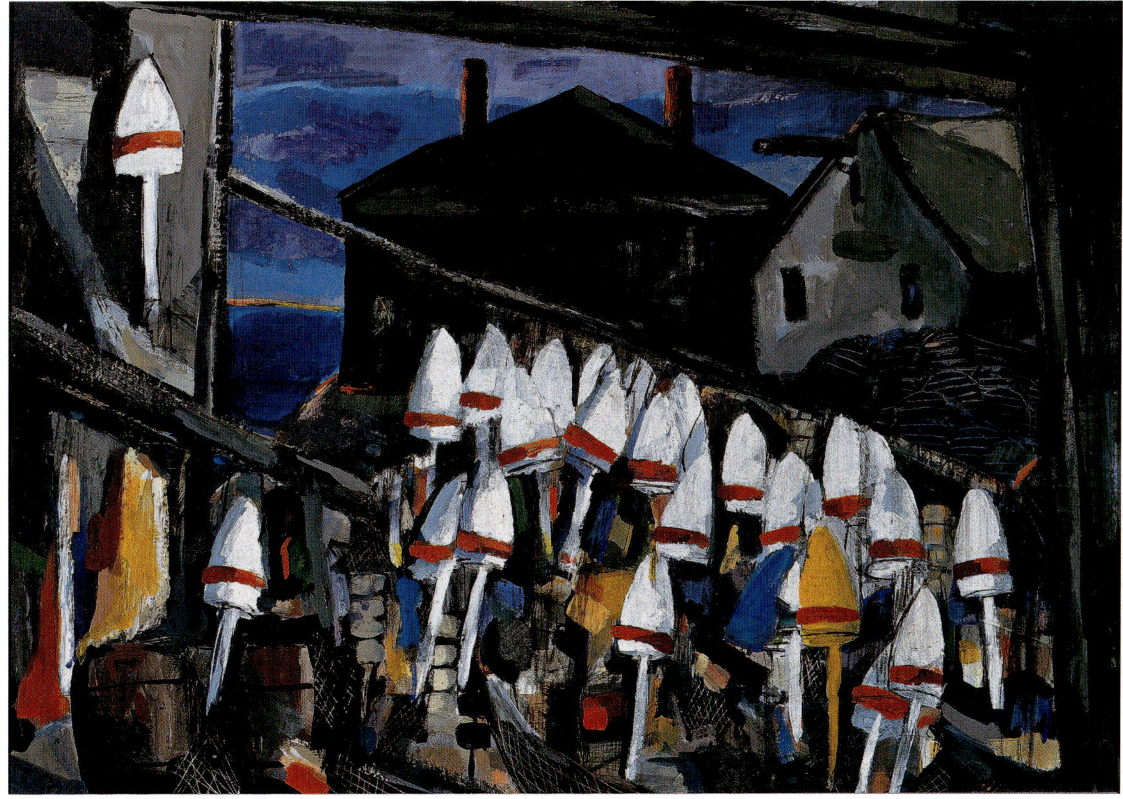

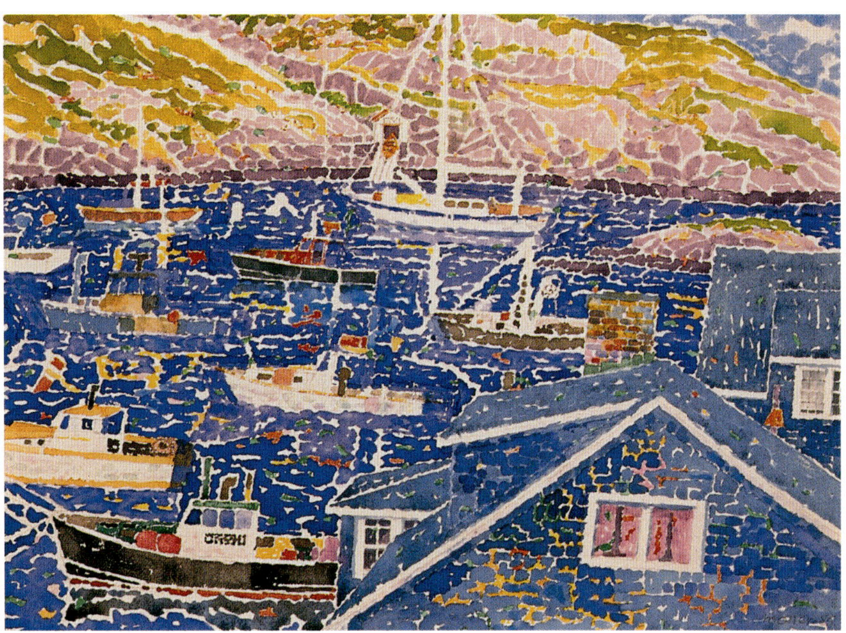

HANS MOLLER, *MONHEGAN HARBOR*, 1985
WATERCOLOR ON PAPER, 18 X 24 IN.
COLLECTION OF MRS. ANNE L. VARTABEDIAN

NOTES

13. Charles Rawlings, "Lobster Town," *Saturday Evening Post*, 15 August 1953, 32–33.

14. McLane, *Islands of the Mid-Maine Coast*, 216. The author notes that Smith probably exaggerated his fishing claim in order to "promote settlement."

15. Ted Van Winkle, *Fred Boynton, Lobsterman, New Harbor, Maine* (Camden, Maine: International Marine Publishing Company, 1975).

16. Elizabeth Coatsworth, *Maine Memories* (Brattleboro, VT: The Stephen Greene Press, 1968), 146.

17. Edward Feit, *Jay Hall Connaway—American Artist*, exhibition catalogue, Vose Galleries of Boston, April 1986, 7.

18. Cited in Shettleworth and Bunting, *An Eye for the Coast*, 145.

19. "Leo Brooks," tribute by John Hultberg, Gallery-by-the-Sea, 1986 (photocopy).

20. Cited in Shettleworth and Bunting, *An Eye for the Coast*, 9. According to Shettleworth, Hudson once advised the aspiring artist James Fitzgerald that to render "convincing" boats, "he must sketch them on the beach first and then fill in the ocean" (p. 49).

21. Ibid., 112.

22. Valerie Livingston, *Hans Moller: Purveyor of Color 1905–2000* (Selinsgrove, Pennsylvania: Susquehanna University, 2002), 63.

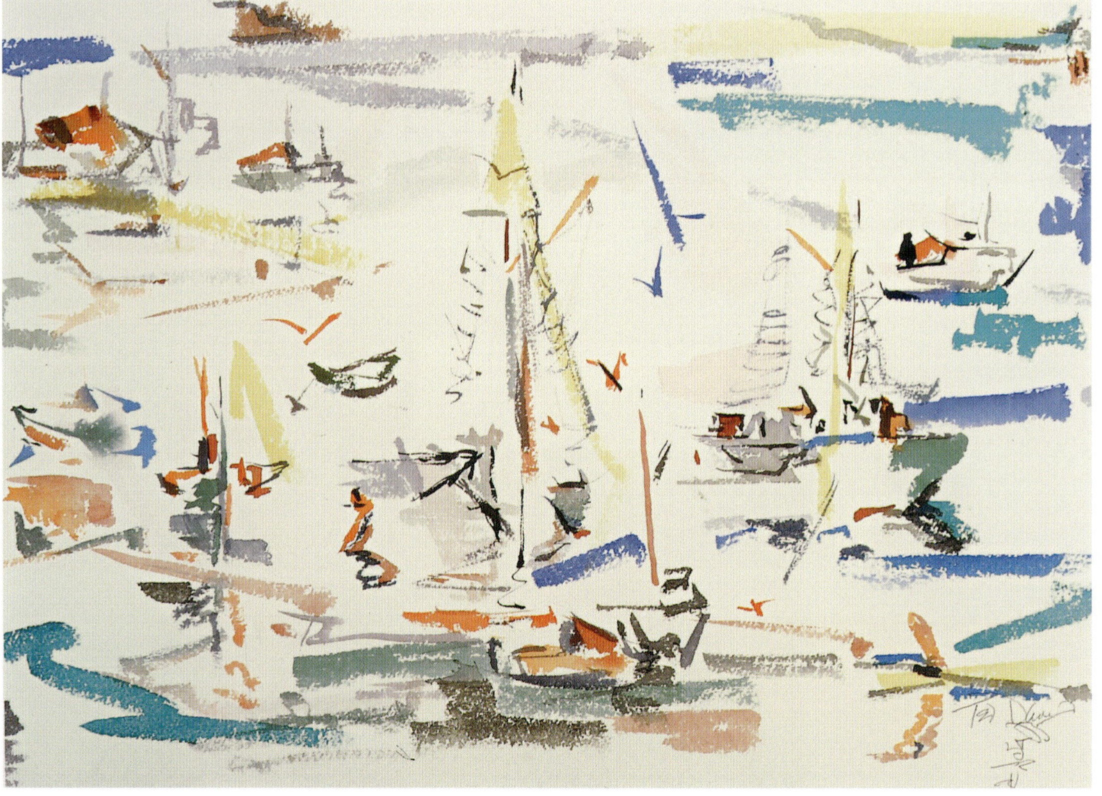

TED DAVIS, *MONHEGAN HARBOR*, 1958, WATERCOLOR ON PAPER, 9 X 12 IN., COLLECTION OF JOHN M. DAY

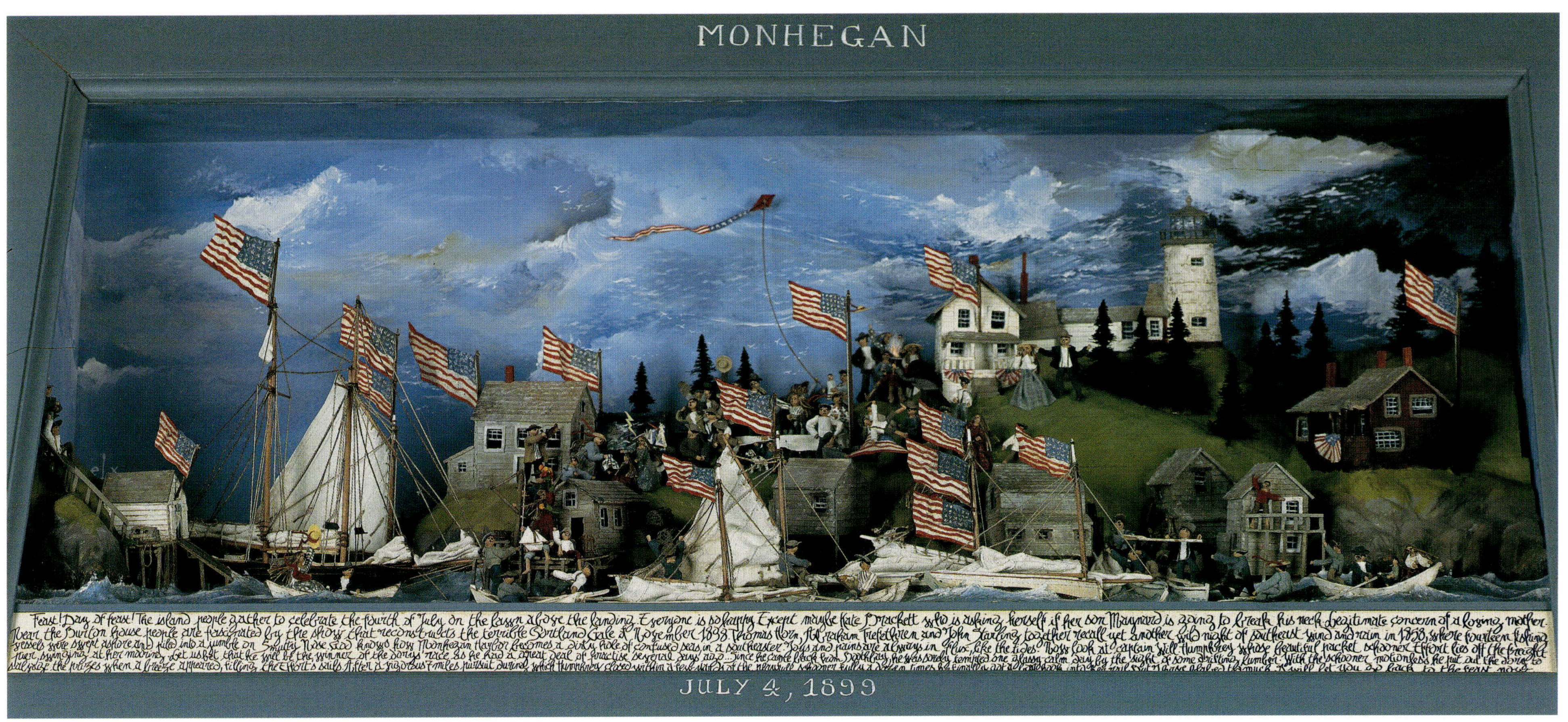

Anne-Emmanuelle Marpeau and Bernard Lagny, *Monhegan — July 4, 1899*, 1999, ex-voto box
PRIVATE COLLECTION. photo courtesy Gleason Fine Art, Boothbay Harbor, Maine

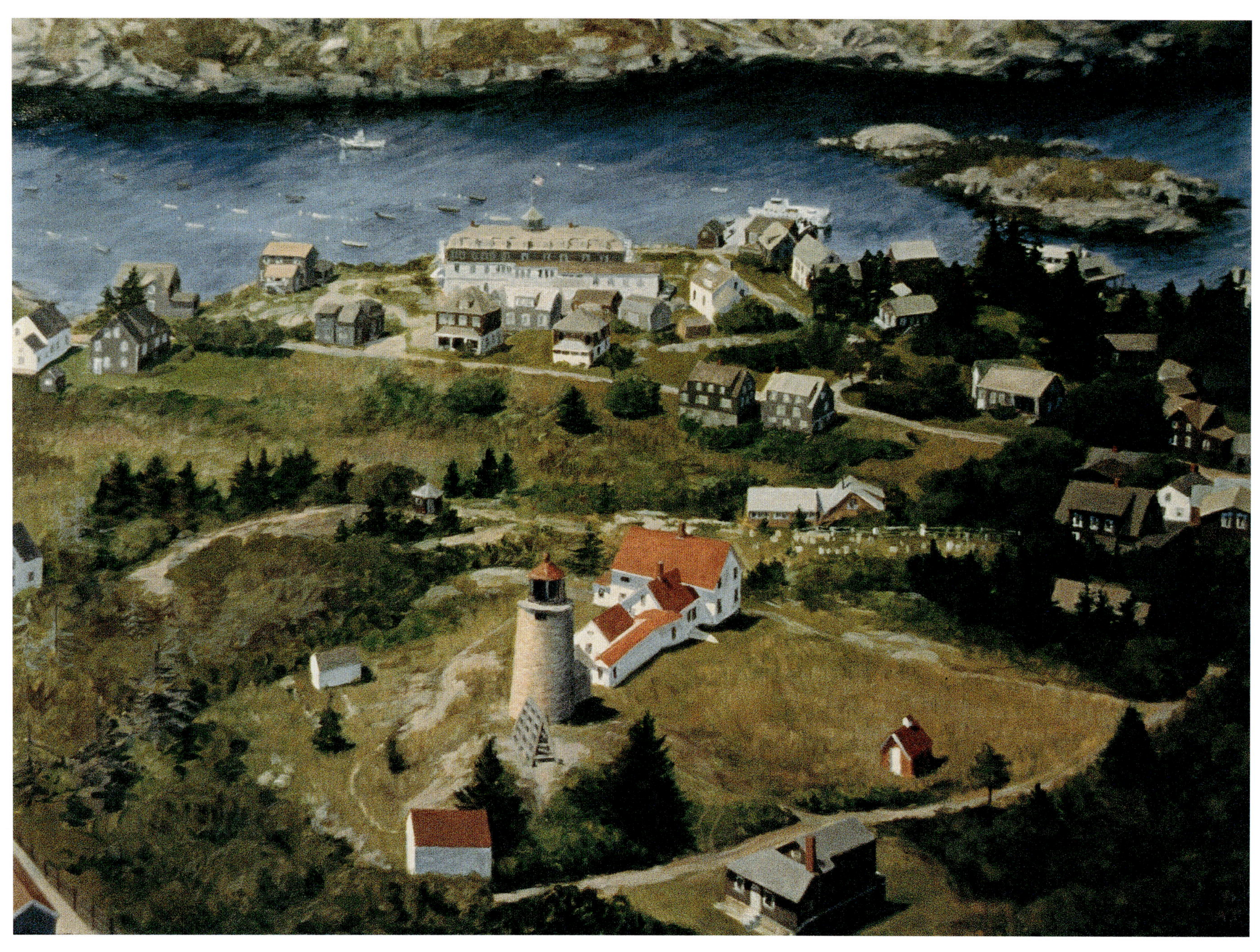

ALEXANDRA TYNG, *AERIAL VIEW, MONHEGAN (AFTER A PHOTOGRAPH BY CHARLES FEIL)*, 1999, OIL ON LINEN, 38 X 58 IN. PRIVATE COLLECTION. PHOTO COURTESY OF FISCHBACH GALLERY, NEW YORK

The Village

One stony, grassy lane twists about among the buildings, sometimes sending off a footpath toward the straggling cots out among the hillocks. The zig-zag fences and capsized stone walls were once built to keep the wandering cows from the little gardens, where the flowers are of unusual beauty and brilliancy, acquired from the salty atmosphere.

—Joseph W. Smith, *Gleanings from the Sea*, 1887

Monhegan had a glorious open out-look, somewhat too rare in the other Maine islands, where impertinent satellites, of which the map gives little idea, are continually cropping up to destroy the desirable effect of space. From an elevated point Middleton could follow the sea all around, and shoreward a distant blue island or two lay in the high-lifted horizon like a cloud over the tops of the pines.

—William Henry Bishop, "Mackerel Fishing off Monhegan," *Harper's*, 1880

In the aerial view of Monhegan by Alexandra Tyng (b. 1954), based on a photograph by Charles Feil, one can make out some of the pathways that follow the island's rugged topography. These humble unpaved thoroughfares are an enduring charm, leading resident and visitor around the inns and houses of the village, past the pond and cemetery, over Lighthouse Hill, hither and yon through the rough-and-tumble island landscape.

In his painting *Gram Richards' House*, the American impressionist painter Charles Ebert (1873–1959) depicts the grassy lanes of earlier days when the terrain had fewer trees and a distinctly pastoral feel *(p. 43)*. Ebert first came to Monhegan in 1909 to convalesce from a bout of malaria.

Ebert's contemporary Mary Townsend Mason (1886–1964), who began visiting Monhegan in the 1920s, also chose a warm palette to render a view of spread-out houses and one of the island's splendid gardens, planted among rock outcroppings *(p. 42)*. "There are flowers everywhere," the writer Louise Dickinson Rich observed about Monhegan, "and the little gardens of the island women, surrounded by picket fences, simply boil with prim, old-fashioned varieties."[23]

Darker in vision is the crepuscular view presented in *A Stroll on Monhegan Avenue* by the Toronto-born modernist painter Henrietta Shore (1880–1963). A student of Robert Henri, Shore practiced the vigorous brushwork encouraged by her professor. Painting on the island nearly a century later, Marguerite Robichaux (b. 1950) offers a sunny view of a tree cascading over a picket fence *(p. 45)*, throwing midday shadows across the lane.

Robichaux numbers among nearly thirty artists who have been awarded a prestigious Carina House residency since the program

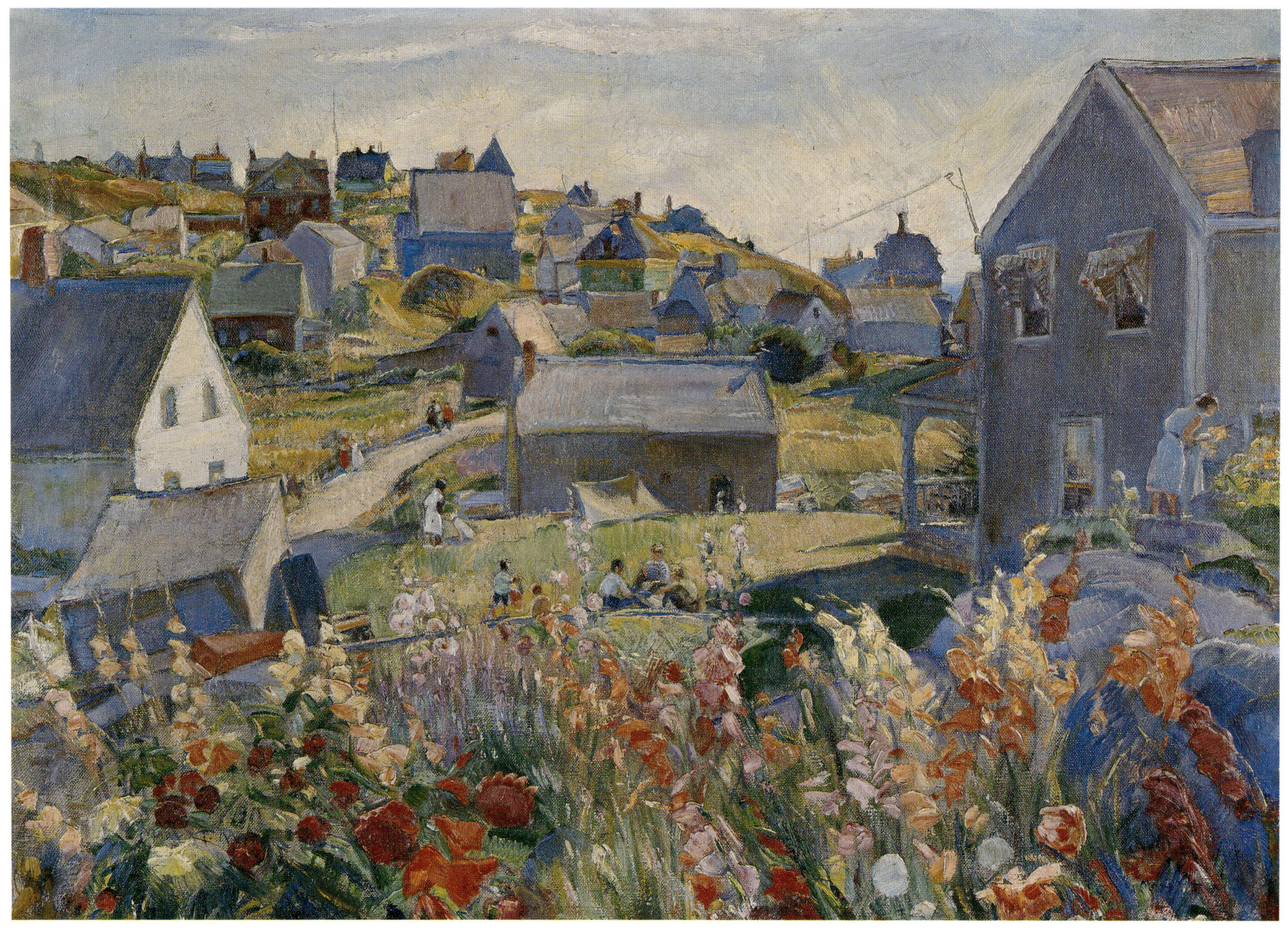

42 MARY T. MASON, *SIDNEY'S GARDEN,* N.D., OIL ON CANVAS, 22 x 30 IN., COLLECTION OF MONHEGAN MUSEUM, GIFT OF THE HUDSON AND DICKSON FAMILIES

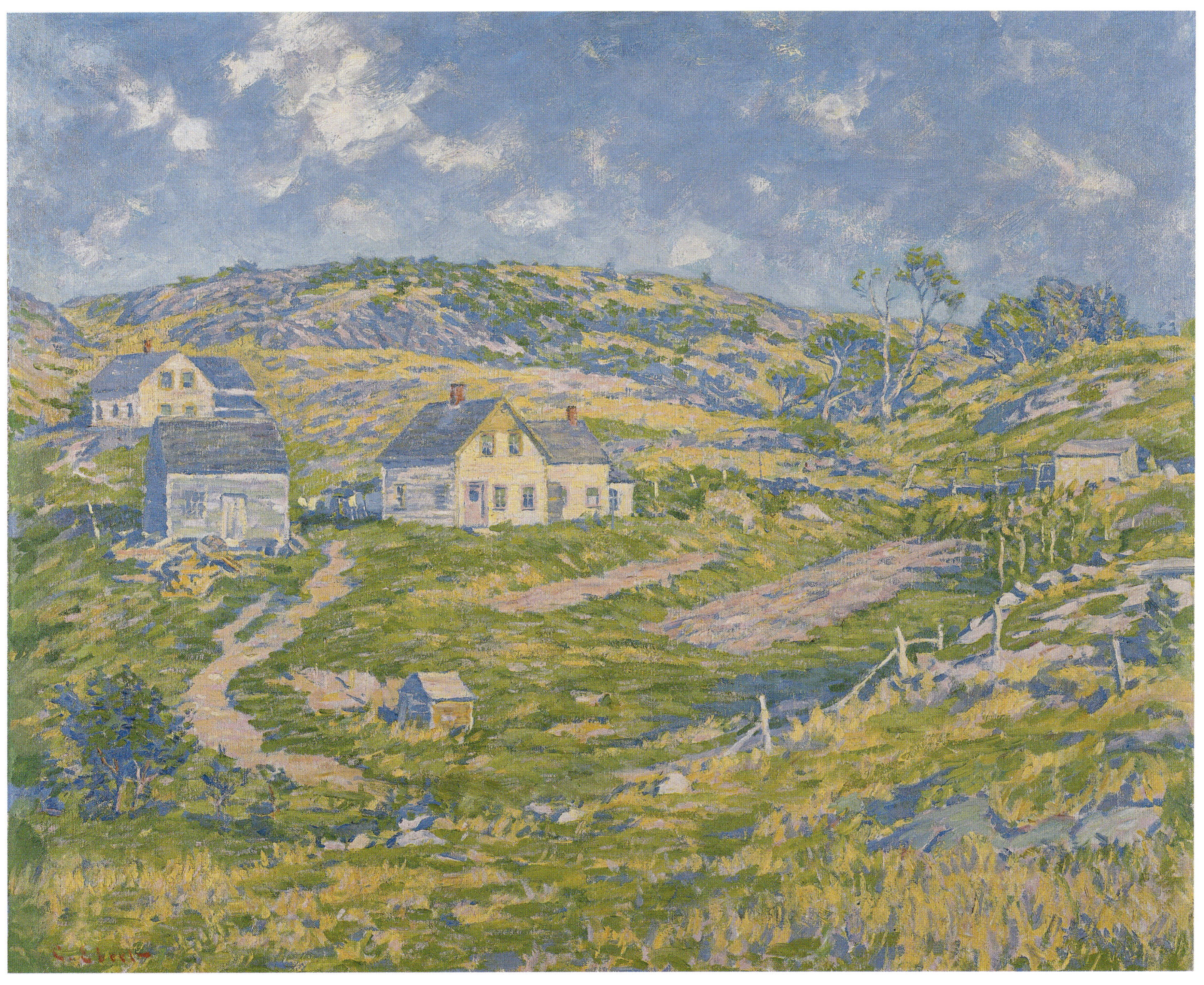

Charles Ebert, *Gram Richards' House*, c. 1915, oil on canvas, 30 $^1/_{16}$ x 36 in., collection of Monhegan Museum, gift of Elisabeth R. Ebert

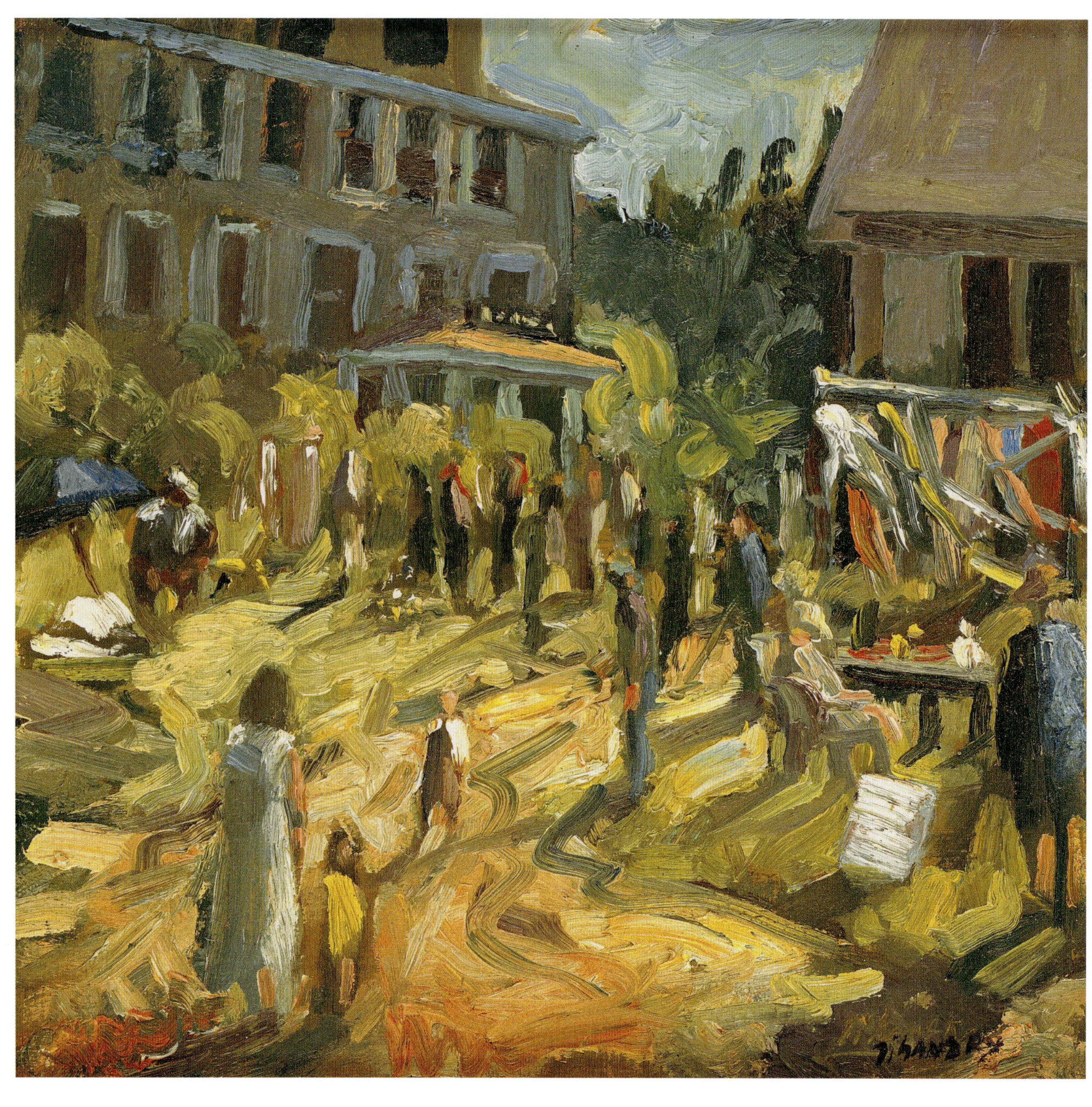

TED TIHANSKY, *THE ARTISTS' SHIRTS,* 2001, OIL ON BOARD, 13 X 13 IN., SCHWARTZ FAMILY COLLECTION.
PHOTO COURTESY OF LUPINE GALLERY, MONHEGAN, MAINE

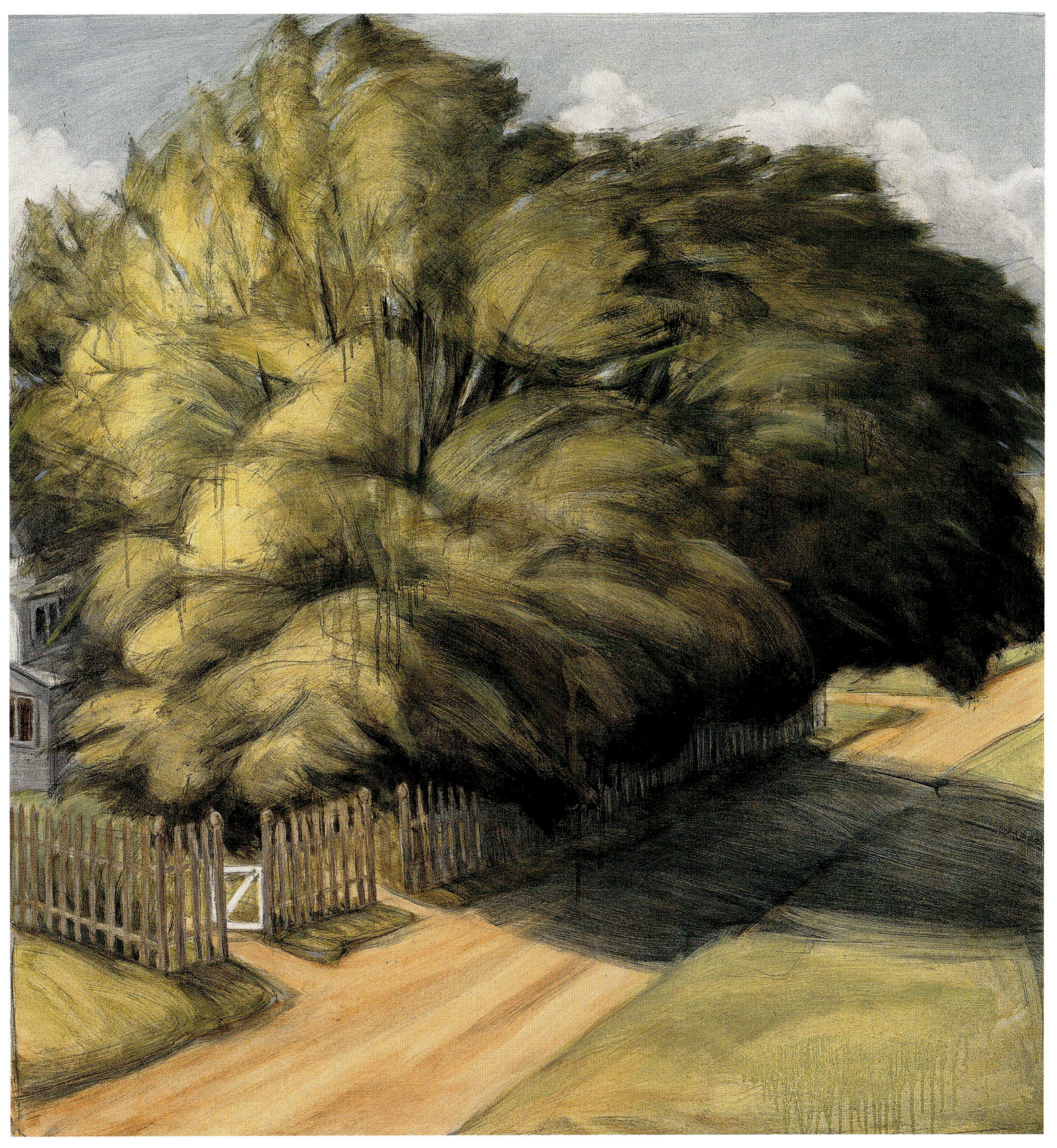

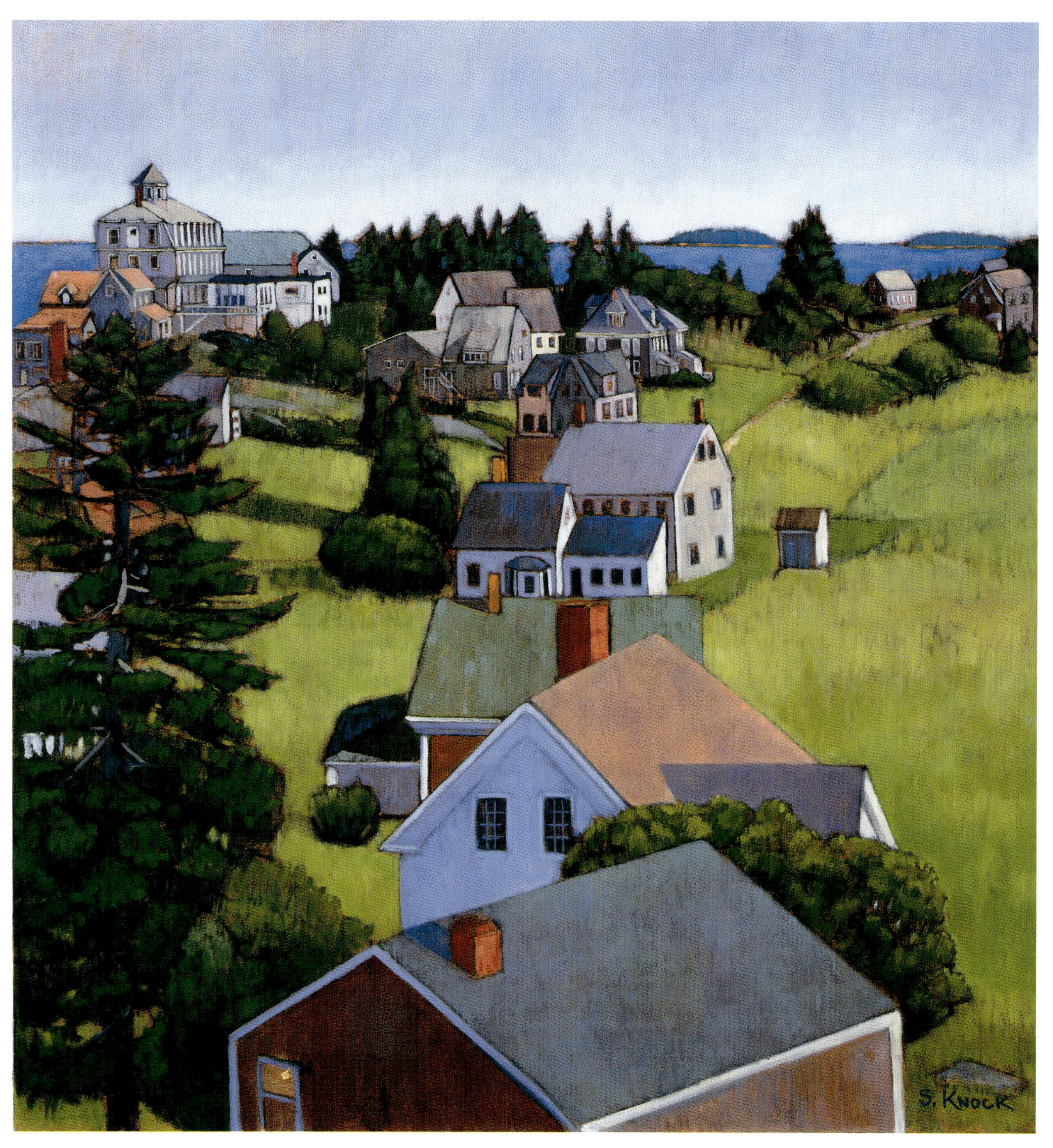

SARAH KNOCK, *MONHEGAN ROOFTOPS*, 1994, OIL ON CANVAS, 33 x 30 IN.
PRIVATE COLLECTION. PHOTO COURTESY OF WISCASSET BAY GALLERY, MAINE

was established in 1989. Each year two artists are selected to spend five weeks on Monhegan. Property values on the island are out of sight and rentals on the island can be quite steep—long gone are the $15-a-month converted fish shacks. Artists who would otherwise not be able to afford an extended stay on the island are encouraged to apply for the residency.

Another past Carina House fellow is Sarah Knock (b. 1947) from Freeport, Maine. "The residency set up an intense passion for the coast," she has written. "When I returned home, which was inland, I found myself longing to be on or near the water on a daily basis."[24] In the painting *Monhegan Rooftops*, the viewer's eye is drawn into the island landscape via a line of distinct geometric shapes (*p. 46*). No two houses seem to be oriented in quite the same way, which speaks to the individuality of the householders.

Connie Hayes (b. 1952) was awarded a Carina House residency in 1991. "Monhegan offered brilliant light, storms, drama, houses stacked on hillsides, and a community of artists," Hayes has written of her stay that summer.[25] While there, she produced several striking portraits of island houses, capturing their character and countenance in rich oil paint.

The architectural landscape of Monhegan consists of a mix of vernacular styles common along the Maine coast. There are capes and saltboxes, shingle-style and colonial. An inventory of the structures would include a lighthouse (built in 1824), fish houses, a chapel, a school and such landmark buildings as the Island Inn.[26]

The Island Inn's distinctive cupola rises over the village and appears in many paintings of the island, including a clean-lined depiction of a pickup truck parked at the Monhegan Store (*p. 49*) by Mary Alice Treworgy (b. 1936). In the fifteen or so years she has been going to the island, Treworgy, who lives in Brunswick, Maine, has produced what amounts to a virtual catalogue of images of Monhegan's buildings, from the humble fire station to the lighthouse.

Rockwell Kent described the island dwellings this way: "Many of the houses, though not of great antiquity, had inherited the character and fine proportion of New England architecture at its best—although, in keeping with the island's windswept situation, they were simple and unadorned to the point of austerity."[27] Kent added to the inventory during his sojourns to the island between 1905 and 1910. He built the houses that appear in Jamie Wyeth's

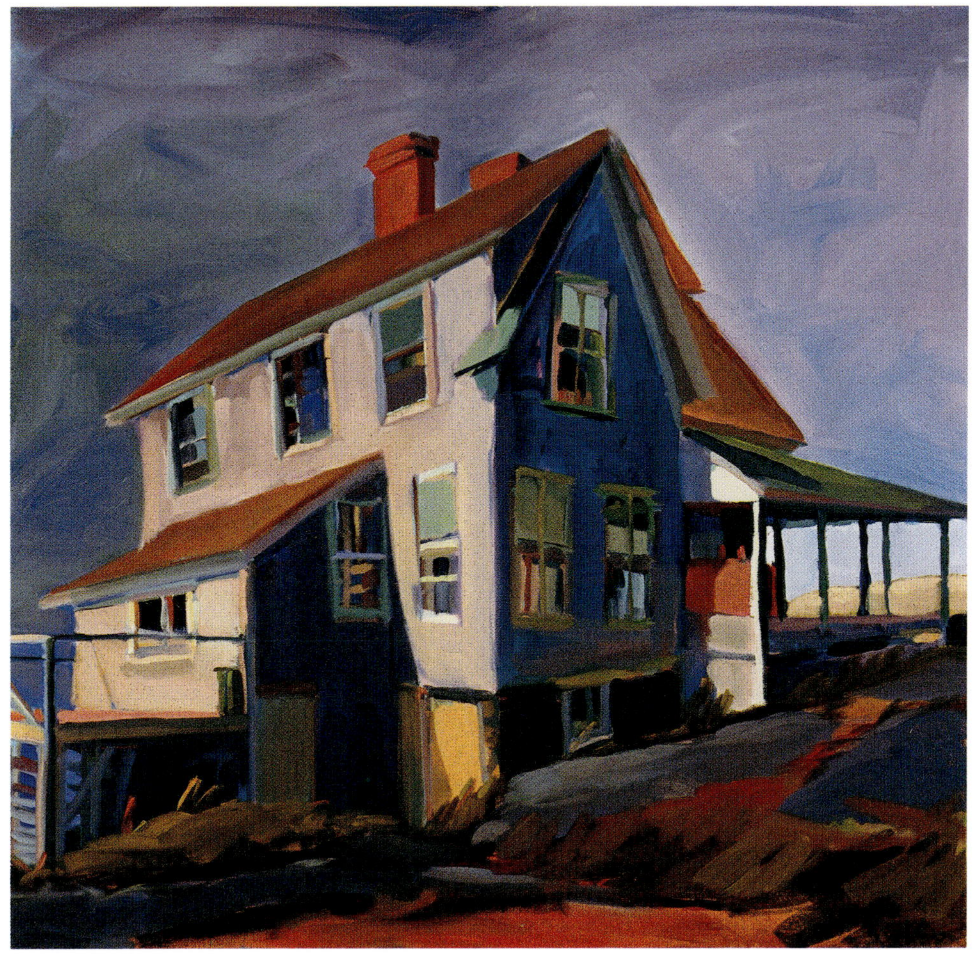

Connie Hayes, *Baldwin House, Monhegan*, 1991
OIL ON CANVAS, 20 X 20 IN., PRIVATE COLLECTION

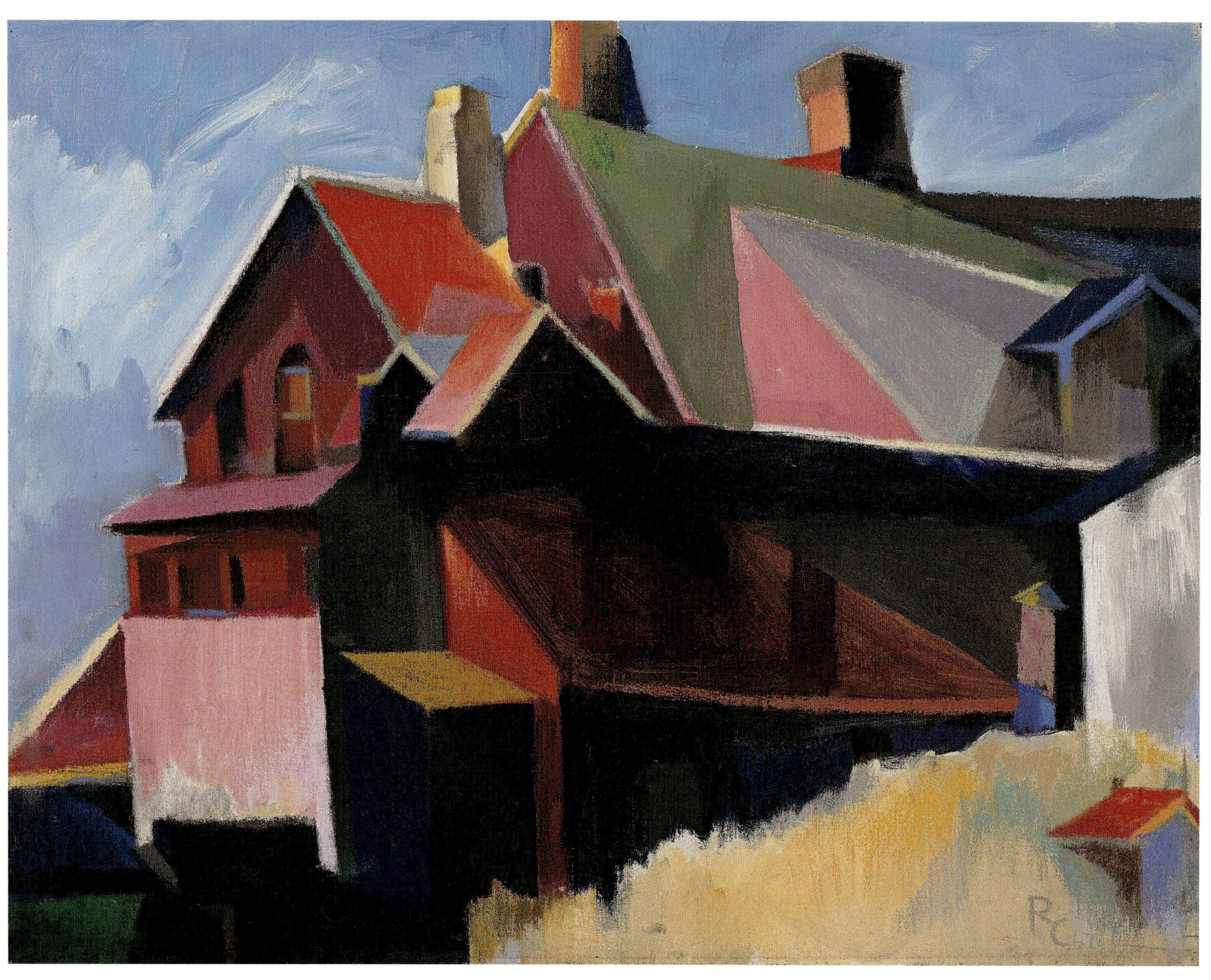

ROBERT CASPER, *RED HOUSE*, 1967, PASTEL AND ACRYLIC WITH PUMICE ON CANVAS, 24 X 30 IN., COLLECTION OF JOHN M. DAY
PHOTO BY MELVILLE MCLEAN, COURTESY OF THE BATES COLLEGE MUSEUM OF ART

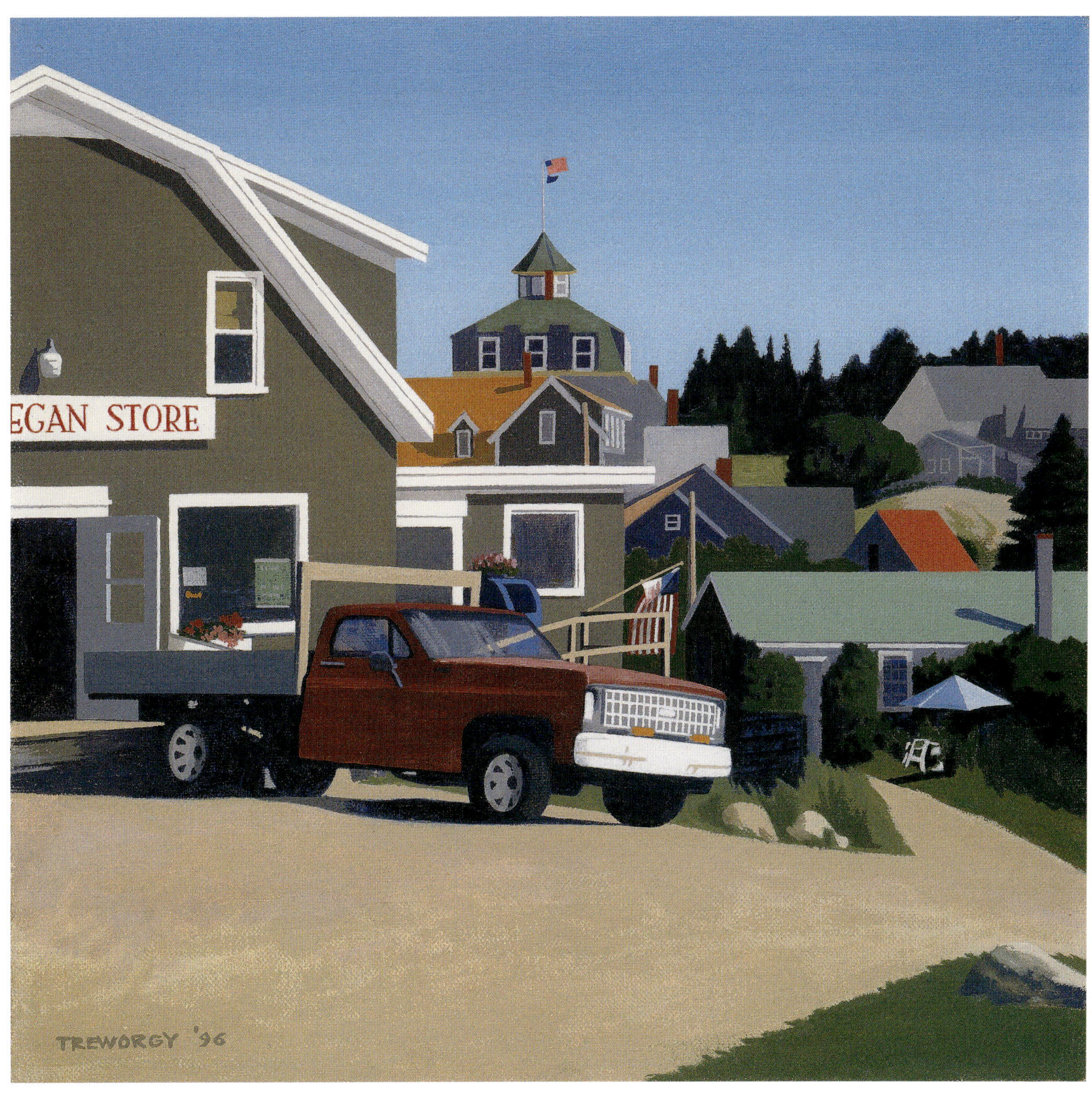

Mary Alice Treworgy, *Monhegan Store*, 1996, oil on linen canvas, 12 x 12 in., collection of Bruce and Sandra Davis

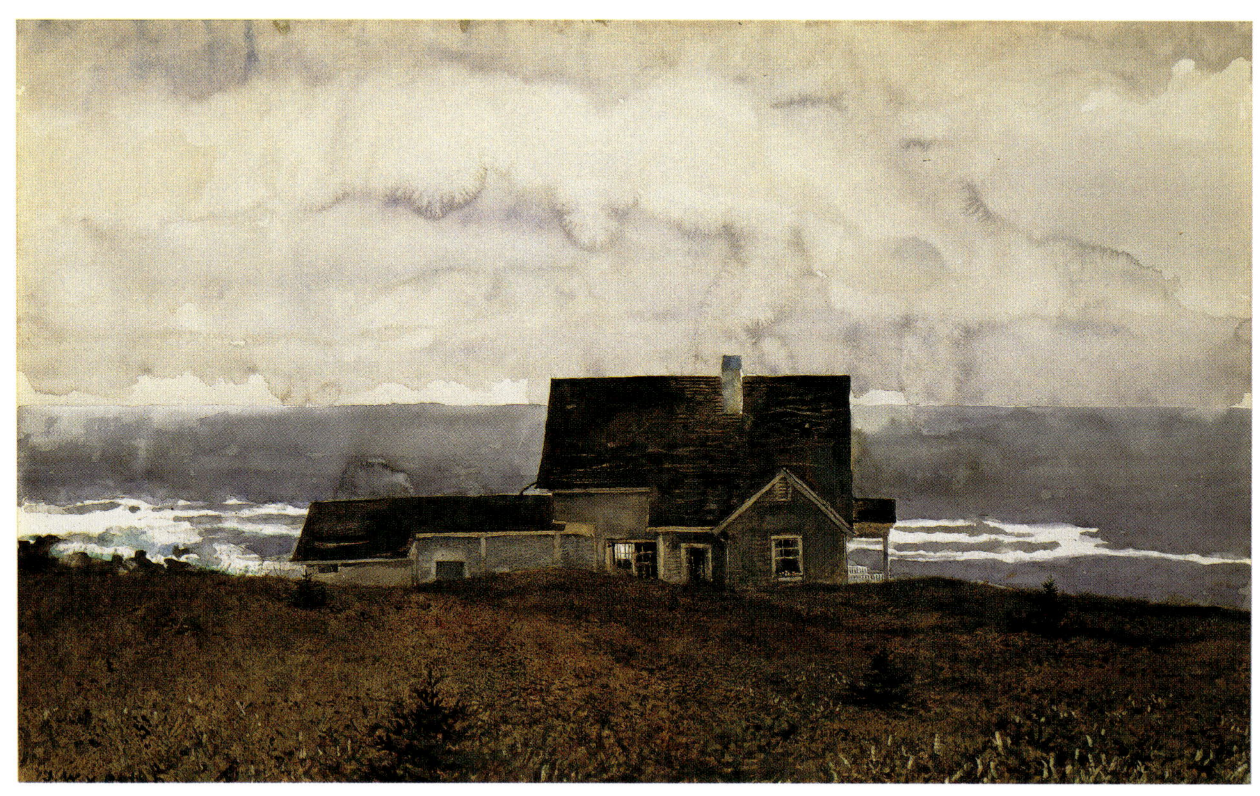

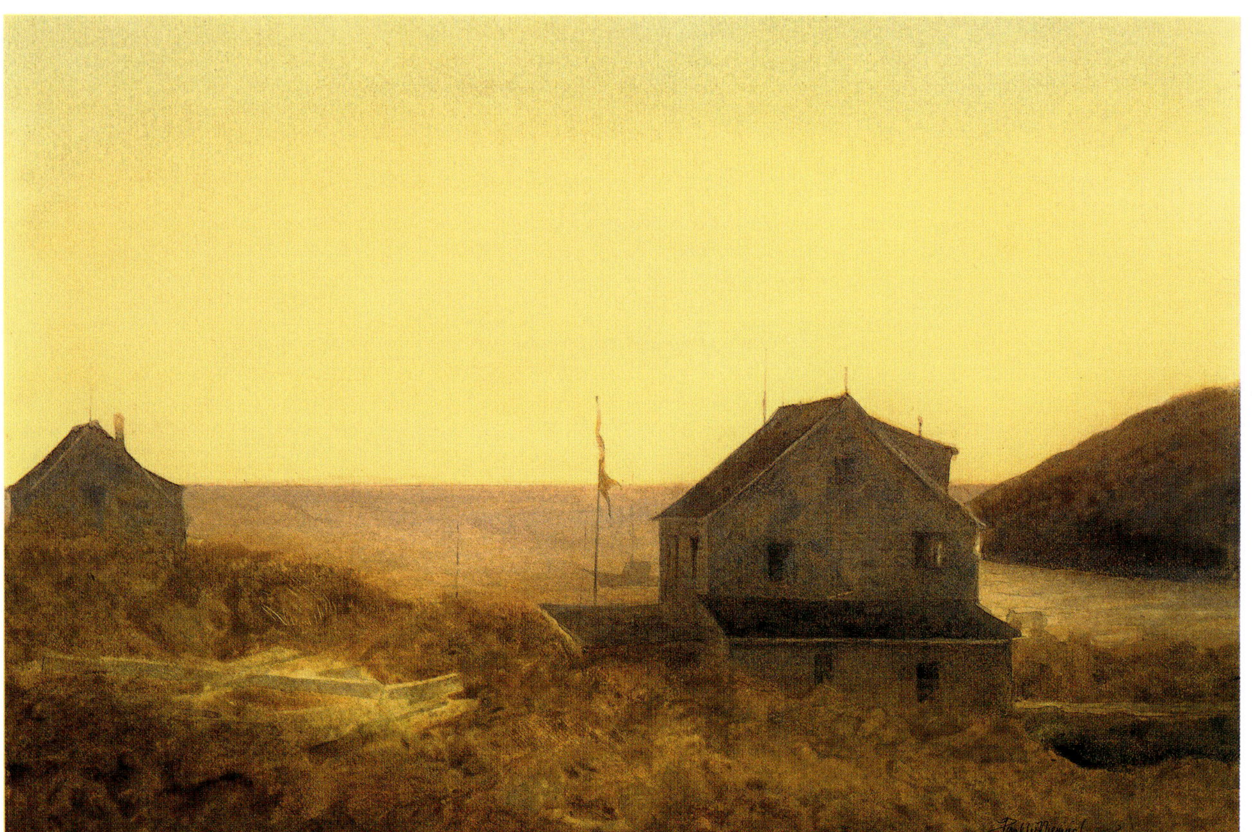

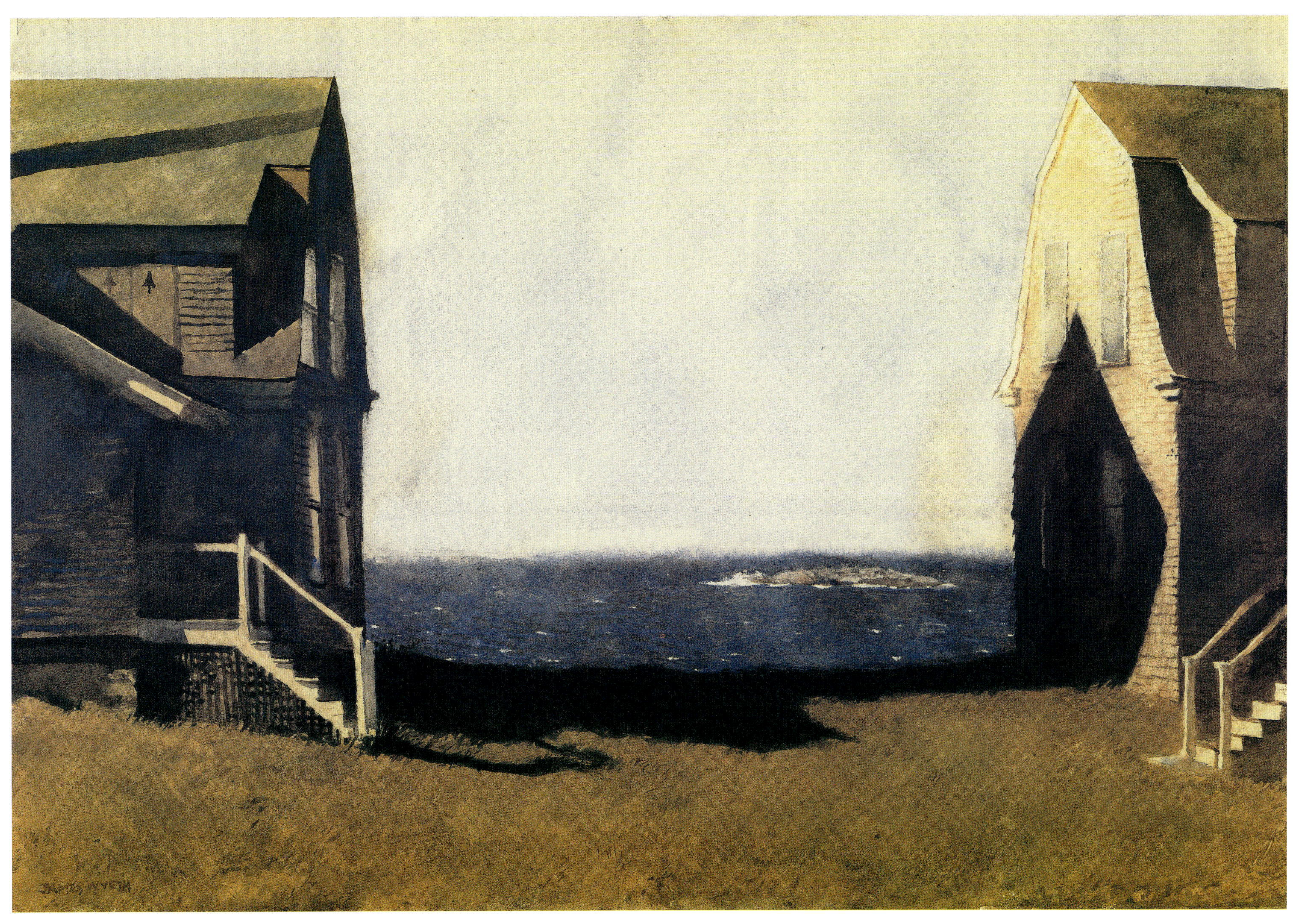

(opposite above) Jamie Wyeth, *The Kent House*, 1972, watercolor on paper, collection of Remak Ramsay

(opposite below) Paul Niemiec, *Harbor South*, 1998, combined mediums, primarily watercolor, 7 3/4 x 11 in., collection of Remak Ramsay

(above) Jamie Wyeth, *Summer House, Winter House*, 1975, watercolor on paper, 21 3/4 x 30 in.
collection of the Farnsworth Art Museum, gift of MBNA America, 2003

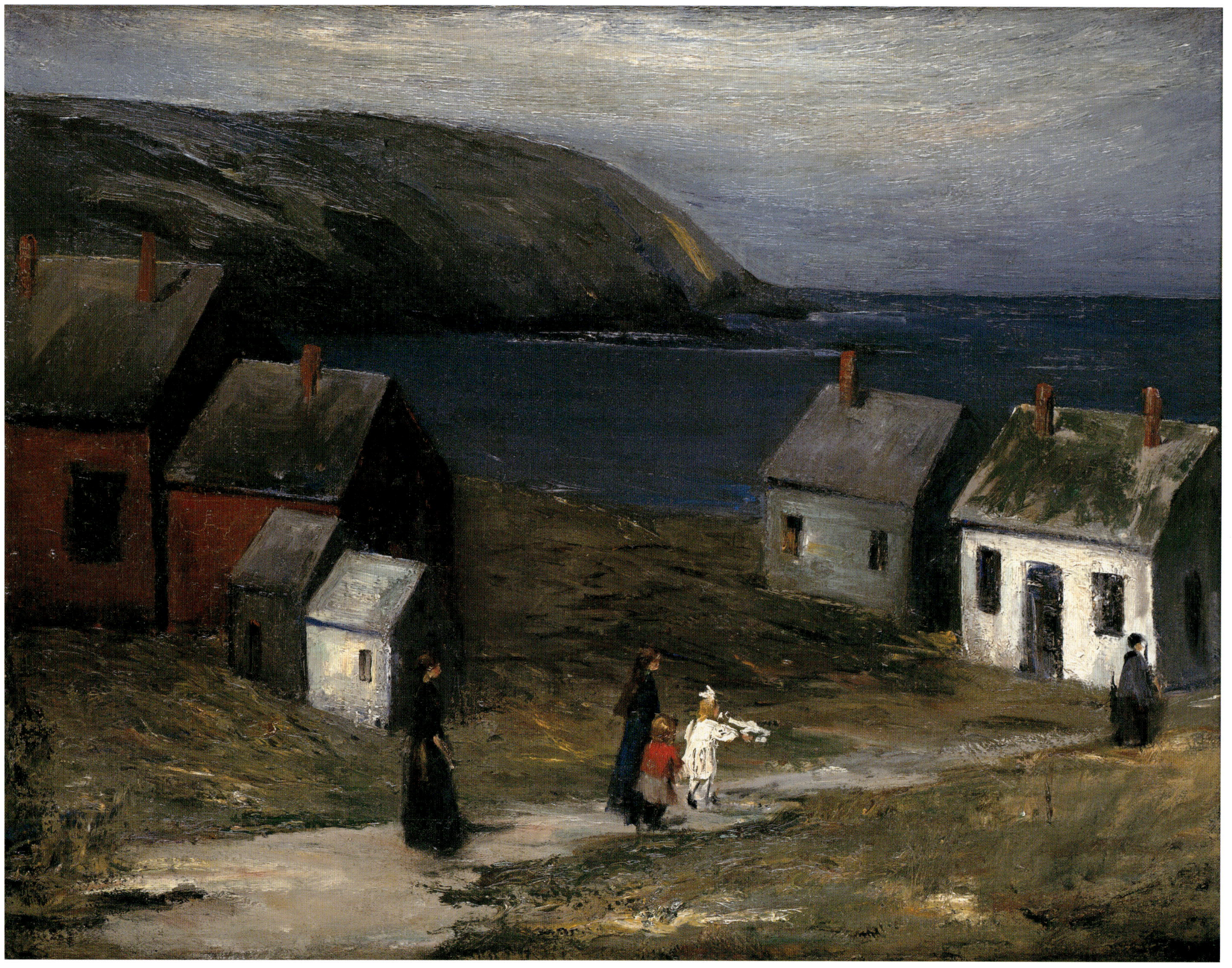

Henrietta Shore, *A Stroll on Monhegan Avenue*, c. 1911, oil on canvas, 26 x 32 in., Schwartz Family Collection

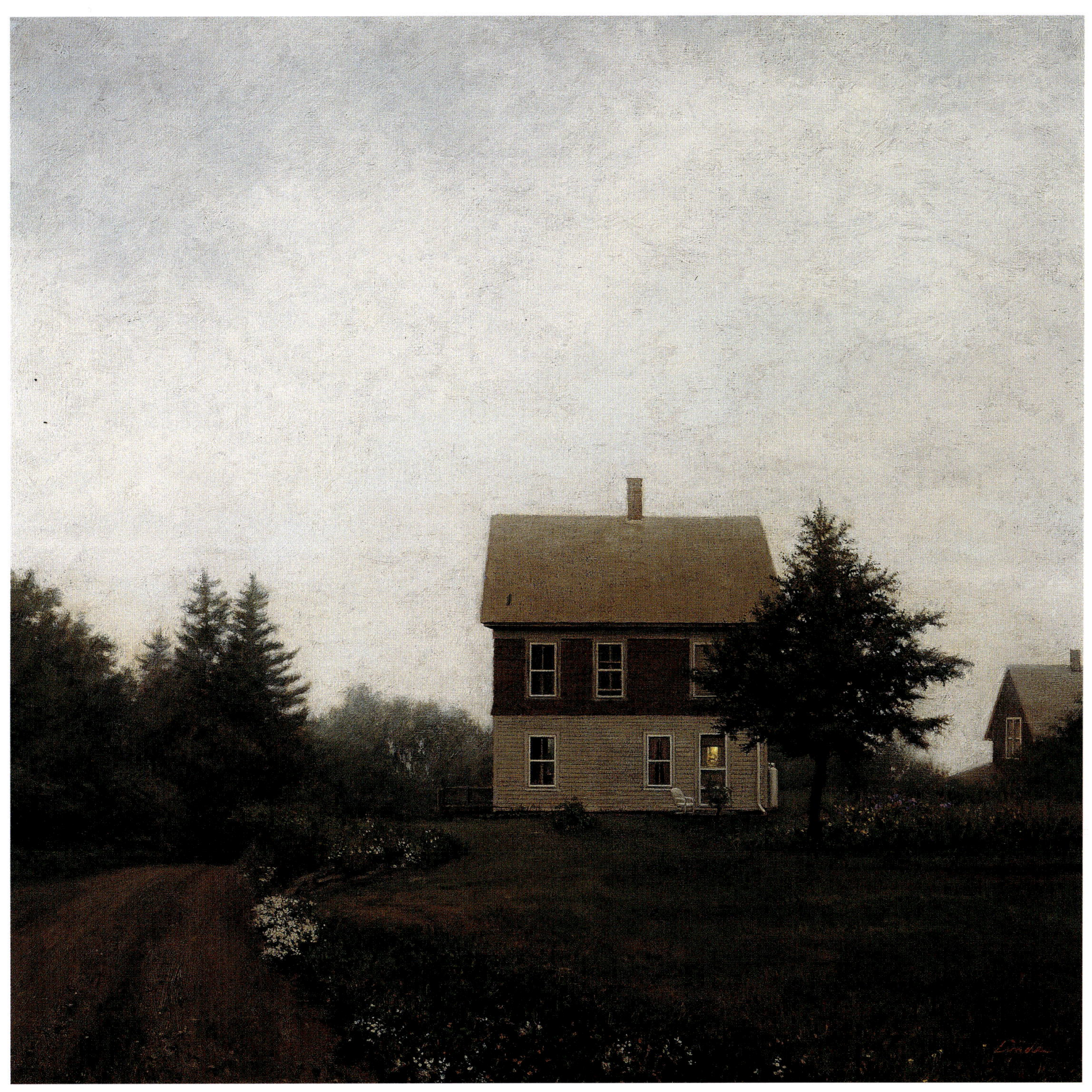

Linden Frederick, *Islander*, 1998, oil on linen, 24 x 24 in., collection of Joe Higdon and Ellen Sudow

canvases *The Kent House (p. 50)* and *Summer House, Winter House (p. 51)*.

"Kent has had such an influence on my life, in all sorts of ways," Wyeth (b. 1946) has said, "but the houses [in *Summer House, Winter House*] particularly fascinated me because they are mirror images of themselves. Everything is reversed," he noted. "I think they're wonderful—the architectural whimsy."[28] Wyeth's houses bring to mind the final lines of Wesley McNair's poem "Flying on Monhegan Island":

On land gray cottages,
their wings of roof half-raised,
decide for now to stay.[29]

Wyeth once referred to his paintings of Monhegan houses as "portraits"—"the houses have taken on a whole kind of life out there," he says.[30] This sense of structural personality comes through in paintings by Paul Niemiec (b. 1948) and Linden Frederick (b. 1953). While both artists *(pp. 50 and 55)* owe allegiance to the realistic tradition in American art, each captures a special quality of light and atmosphere. Their portraits of island houses go beyond representation, depicting a mood of solitude and survival.

A number of artists have painted "the Red House" *(p. 48),* originally the Henry Trefethren Homestead built in the late 1700s. Robert Casper (b. 1928), a student of Hans Hofmann in New York, chose a semi-cubist approach to encompass the angular complexity of the structure.

Among the most imposing buildings on Monhegan is the Island Inn, which started out as "the Pink House" around 1816 and then was added on to between 1906 and 1910. In James Fitzgerald's dramatic oil, the beam from the lighthouse's powerful Fresnel lens illuminates the inn as it sweeps across the island. The inn, in turn, is reflected in a watery meadow. Fitzgerald reduced the scene to broad shapes representing night, sky and paths of light.

Caleb Stone (b. 1966) chose to paint a view of the Island Inn as seen from below, near the wharf, its wide façade lit by bright sunlight. Stone, who lives in Ipswich, Massachusetts, first visited Monhegan as a child and has returned regularly ever since, occasionally offering art workshops on the island. The artist had a distinct advantage tackling island motifs: Don Stone, his father, has been painting on the island since the late 1950s.

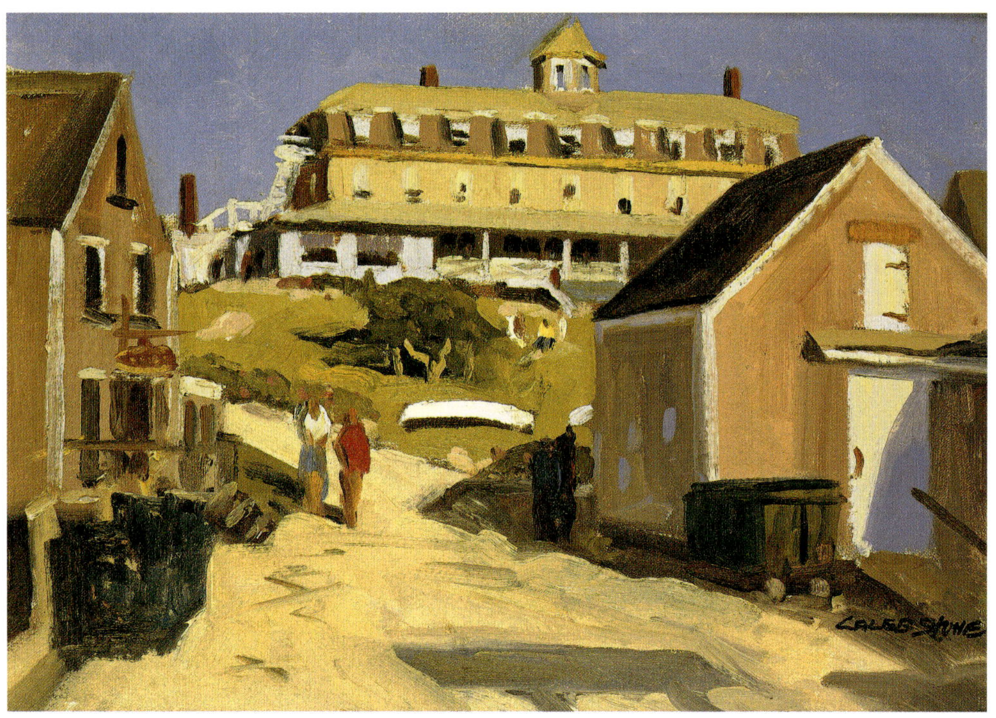

CALEB STONE, *ISLAND INN, FROM THE WHARF,* 1998
OIL ON LINEN MOUNTED ON BOARD, 12 1/4 x 16 IN.
COLLECTION OF REMAK RAMSAY

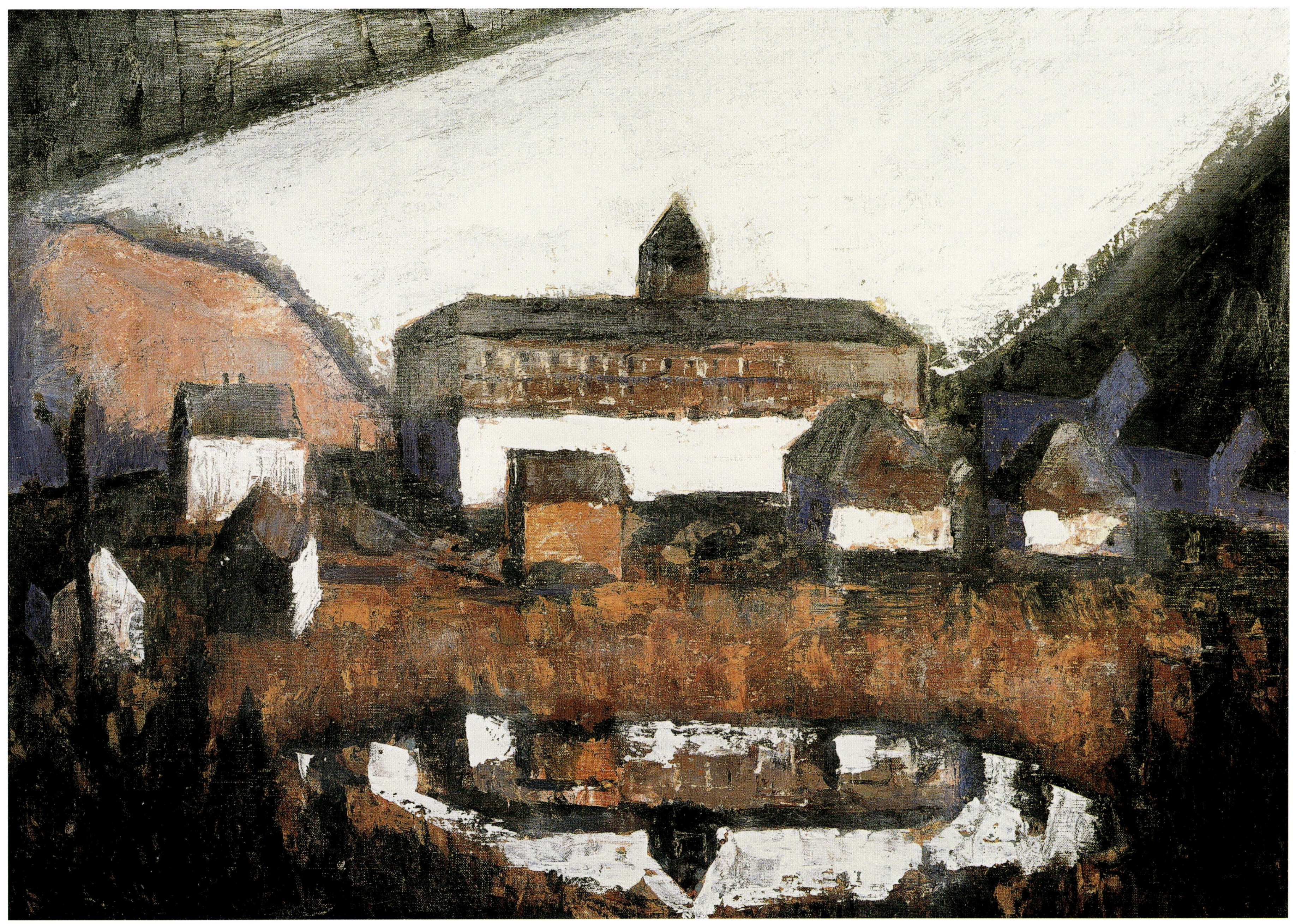

James Fitzgerald, *Reflections of the Old Monhegan Beam*, n.d., oil on canvas, 30 x 40 in., Schwartz Family Collection

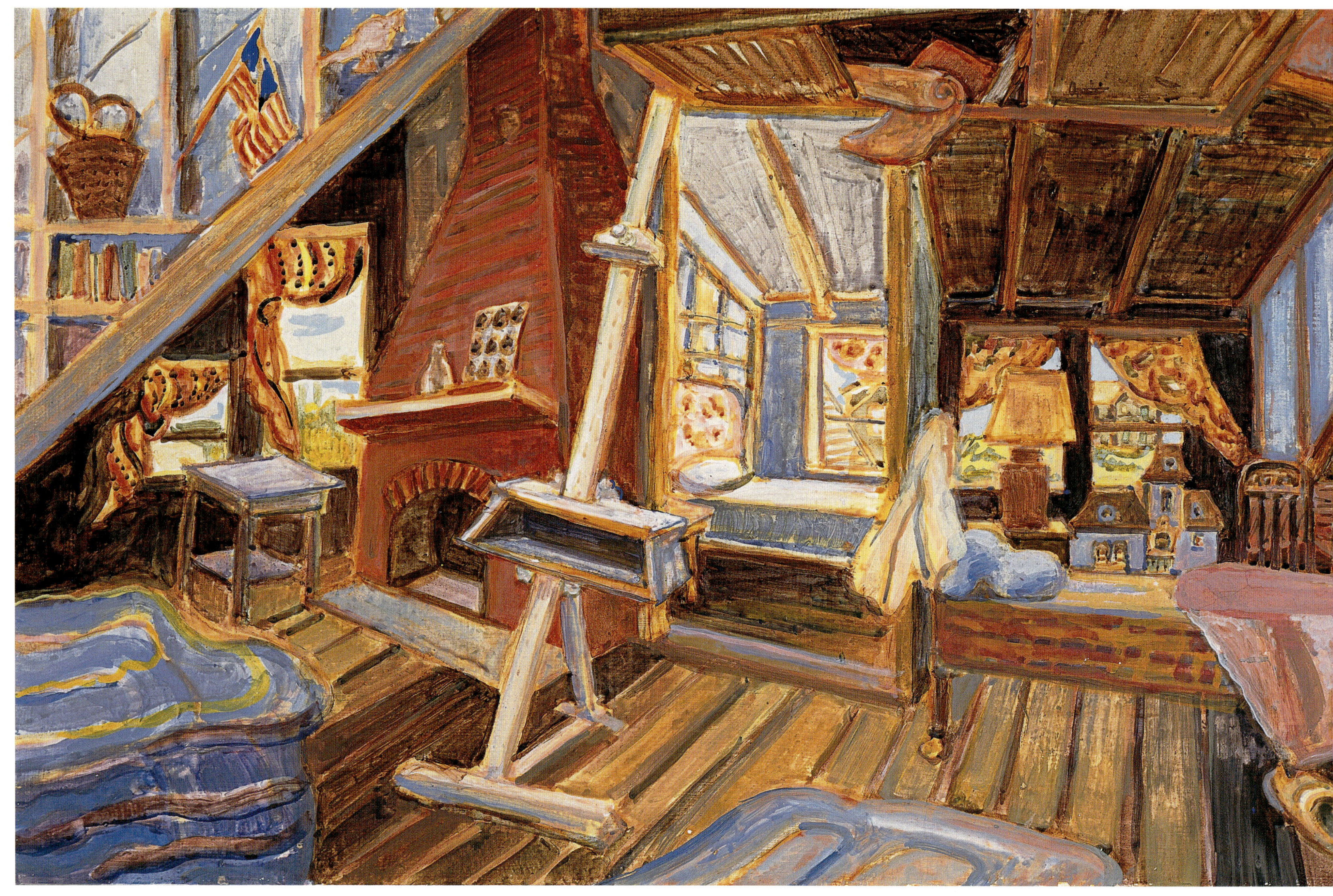

 DIANA YOUNG, *ARTIST'S ATTIC*, 2001, EGG TEMPERA ON GESSO PANEL, 16 X 36 IN., COURTESY OF CLARK HOUSE GALLERY, BANGOR, MAINE

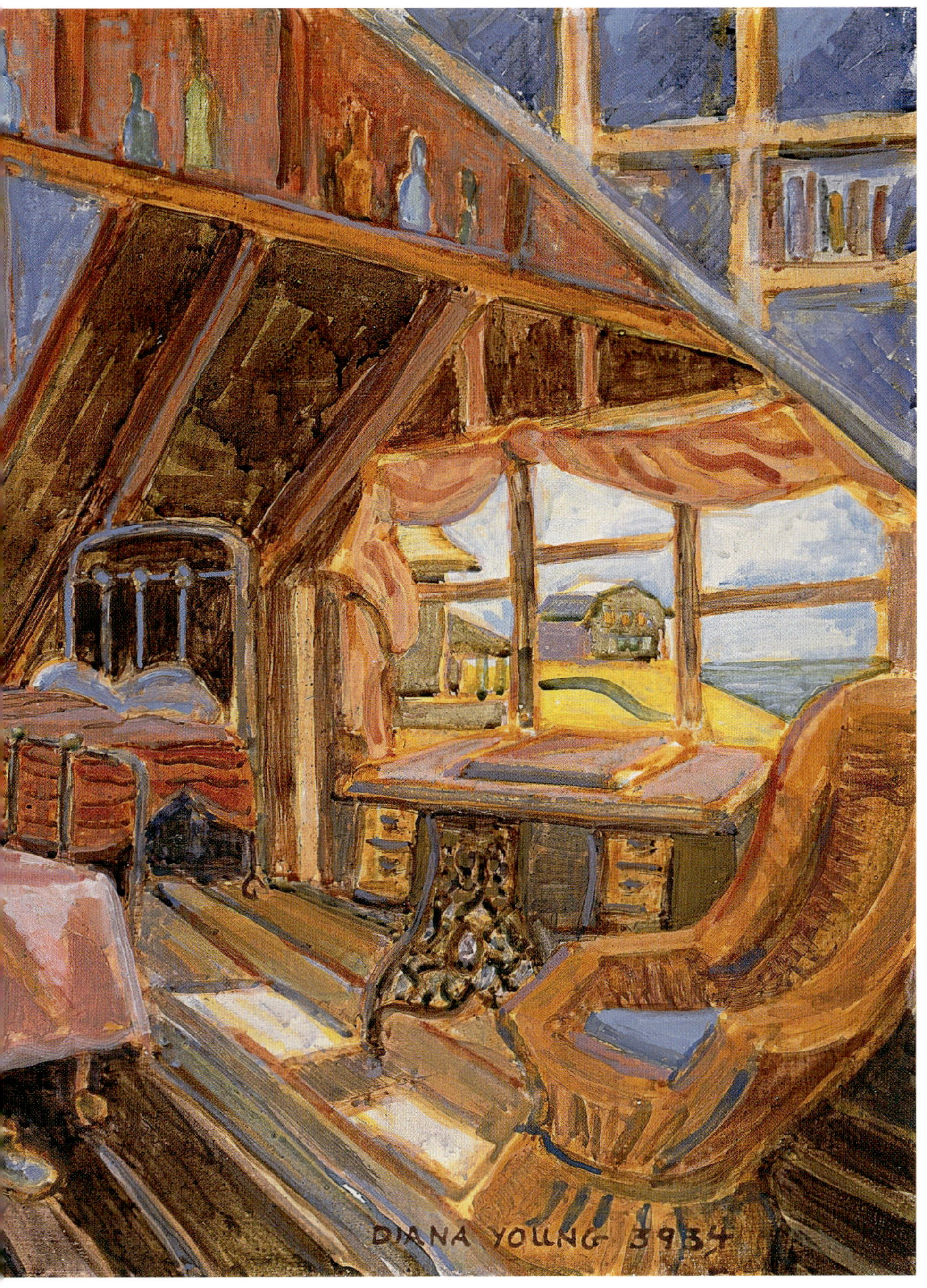

Another venerable island hostelry, the Monhegan House, appears in a wonderfully unbridled oil by Ted Tihansky (b. 1953). The painting shows racks of shirts painted by island artists *(p. 44)*. The shirts were auctioned off as a fundraiser for the Monhegan Emergency Rescue Service in 2001. While many artists are seasonal visitors, they often contribute to community life.

Among the more unusual structures on Monhegan is the Dead Cat Museum, the creation of islander Kyle Murdock, who is shown proudly presenting his special attraction in a painting by Jamie Wyeth *(p. 7)*. Wyeth's Monhegan work includes a remarkable gallery of portraits of island residents, from the caped Kyle to the school-teacher toweling off before a wintry morning view of the harbor and Manana *(p. 65)*.

Diana Young (b. 1936) painted the "dormitory" attic of the three-story Eider Duck Cottage on Fish Beach. Her view presents a delightful jumble of easels, beds, and odds and ends of beach-combings *(pp. 56–57)*. "Every year for the past ten or so, a dirty dozen of artists, the 'Plein-air Heads' from Bangor, invade Monhegan for a week in June," Young explains, all of them piling into the cottage.

A host of artists have painted the village as seen from the slopes and heights surrounding the harbor. These panoramas often include Manana Island, whose bare flank offers a solid backdrop to a landscape dotted with houses. A clear autumn day proved perfect for Sarah Knock's view *(p. 59)*, while James Wolford (b. 1958) presents a summery prospect *(p. 60)*. In an unfinished canvas by Alice Kent Stoddard (1885–1976), some of the houses seem to melt into the landscape *(p. 58)*. By contrast, the buildings depicted in *On Monhegan Island* by William Beebe (b. 1956), a marine painter from Williamsburg, Virginia, stand out sharply in the shimmering sunlight *(p. 61)*.

Evelina Hollins Kats (1936–1999) and Dyan Fitzpatrick (b. 1945) bring a fresh approach to their views of the village *(p. 111)*. Kats, who painted on Monhegan in 1985, captures the island on a day of scudding clouds and fresh breezes. In her winter landscape, Fitzpatrick, a former resident of the island, shows the village tucked in a covering of snow.

In Jamie Wyeth's watercolor *Obelisk (p. 6)*, the view of the village is partially obstructed by the 2,500-pound bell that once served as

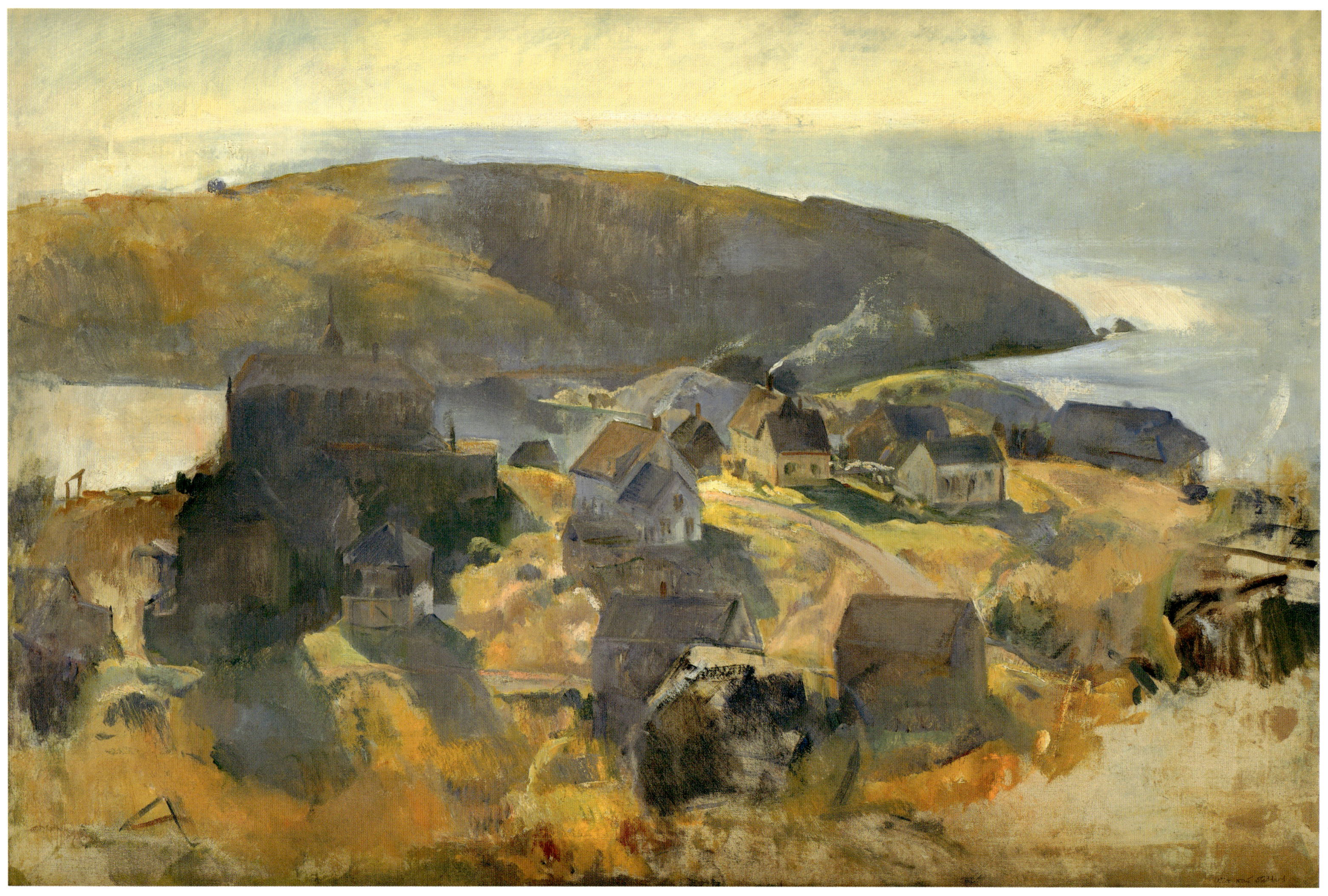

ALICE KENT STODDARD, *A View of Monhegan*, c. 1942, oil on canvas, 26 x 36 in., SCHWARTZ FAMILY COLLECTION

the fog signal on Manana (it was rung by hand). The bell was trans-
ported by helicopter to its current site on Lighthouse Hill in 1972.

The village cemetery is often featured in landscapes painted
from atop Lighthouse Hill. In his haunting 2001 canvas *First Light,*
Ronald Frontin (b. 1962) provides us with a view of the village as
seen from the graveyard *(p. 62)*, with headstones leaning slightly
here and there in the uneven ground. The yellow gold of dawn is
descending on the island, lighting up Manana and distant win-
dows, but it has not yet driven the morning chill from the final
resting place of the islanders.

NOTES

23. Louise Dickinson Rich, *The Coast of Maine: An Informal History and Guide*
    (Camden, Maine: Down East Books, 1993), 245.
24. *Carina House: The First Decade, 1989–1999,* exhibition catalogue, Farnsworth Art
    Museum, 1999–2000, 13.
25. Ibid., 10.
26. See Ruth Grant Fuller, *Monhegan: Her Houses and Her People 1780–1970* (Melrose,
    Mass.: Mainstay Publications, 1995).
27. Kent, *It's Me O Lord,* 119.
28. Jamie Wyeth, interview by Christopher Crosma, in *Jamie Wyeth: Islands,* exhibi-
    tion catalogue, Farnsworth Art Museum, June 27–August 22, 1993, 12.
29. Wesley McNair, *Twelve Journeys in Maine* (Portland, Maine: Romulus Editions, 1992).
30. Jamie Wyeth, interview.

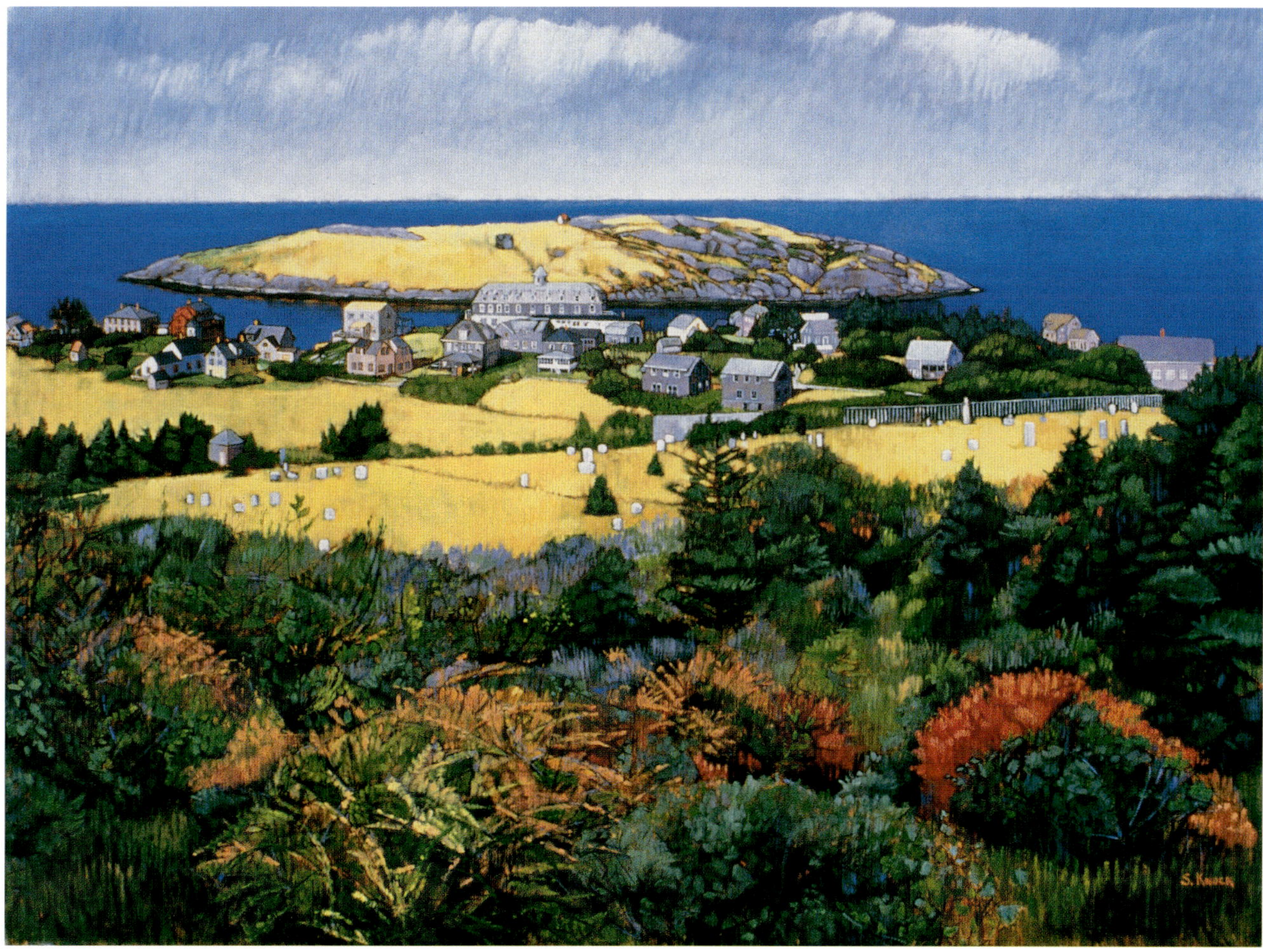

SARAH KNOCK, *MONHEGAN AND MANANA ISLAND — FALL,* 1994, OIL ON CANVAS, 42 X 56 IN., PRIVATE COLLECTION

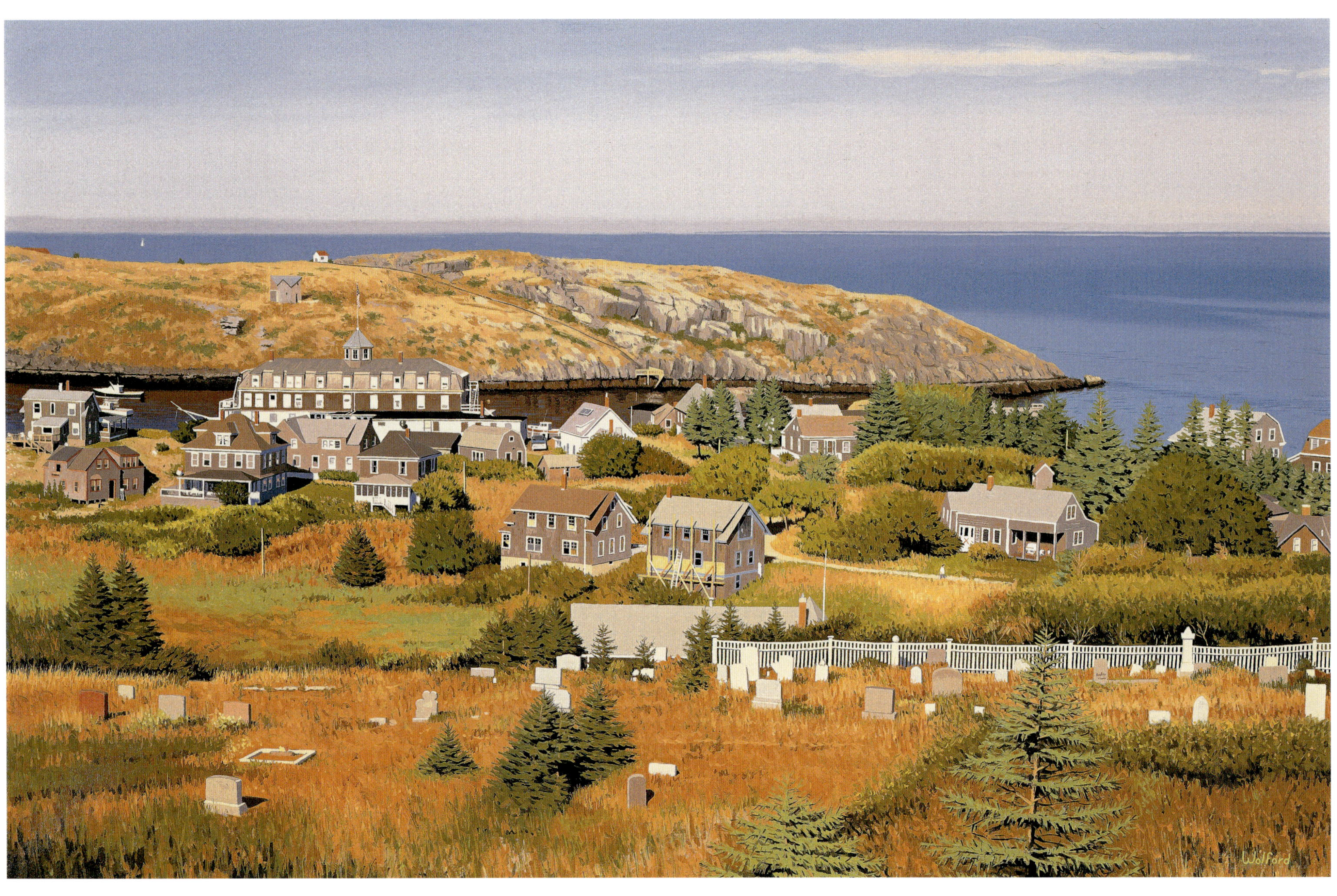

  JAMES WOLFORD, *Monhegan Summer II*, 2001, OIL ON CANVAS, 32 x 48 IN., BAYVIEW GALLERY, CAMDEN, MAINE. PHOTO BY WILLIAM THUSS

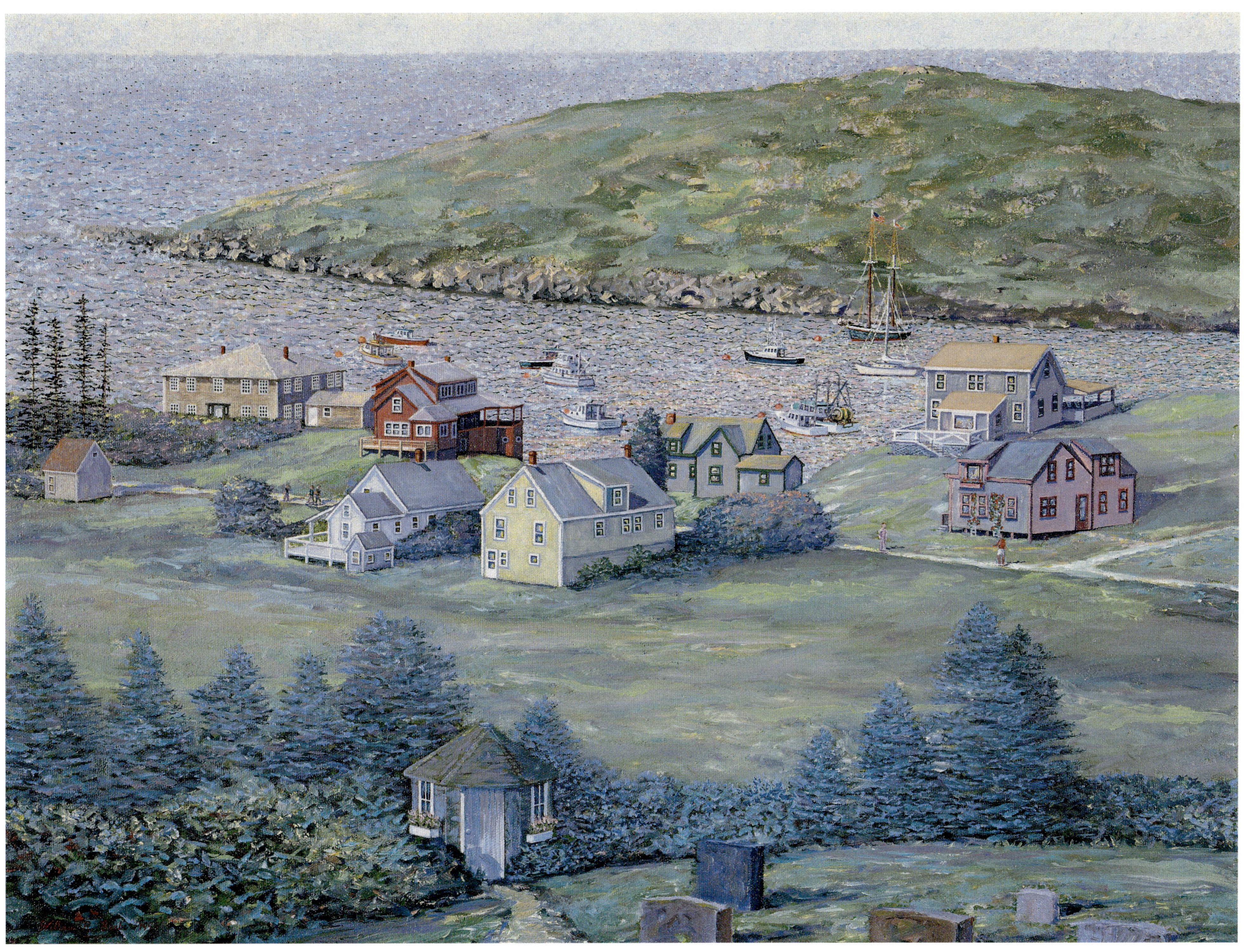

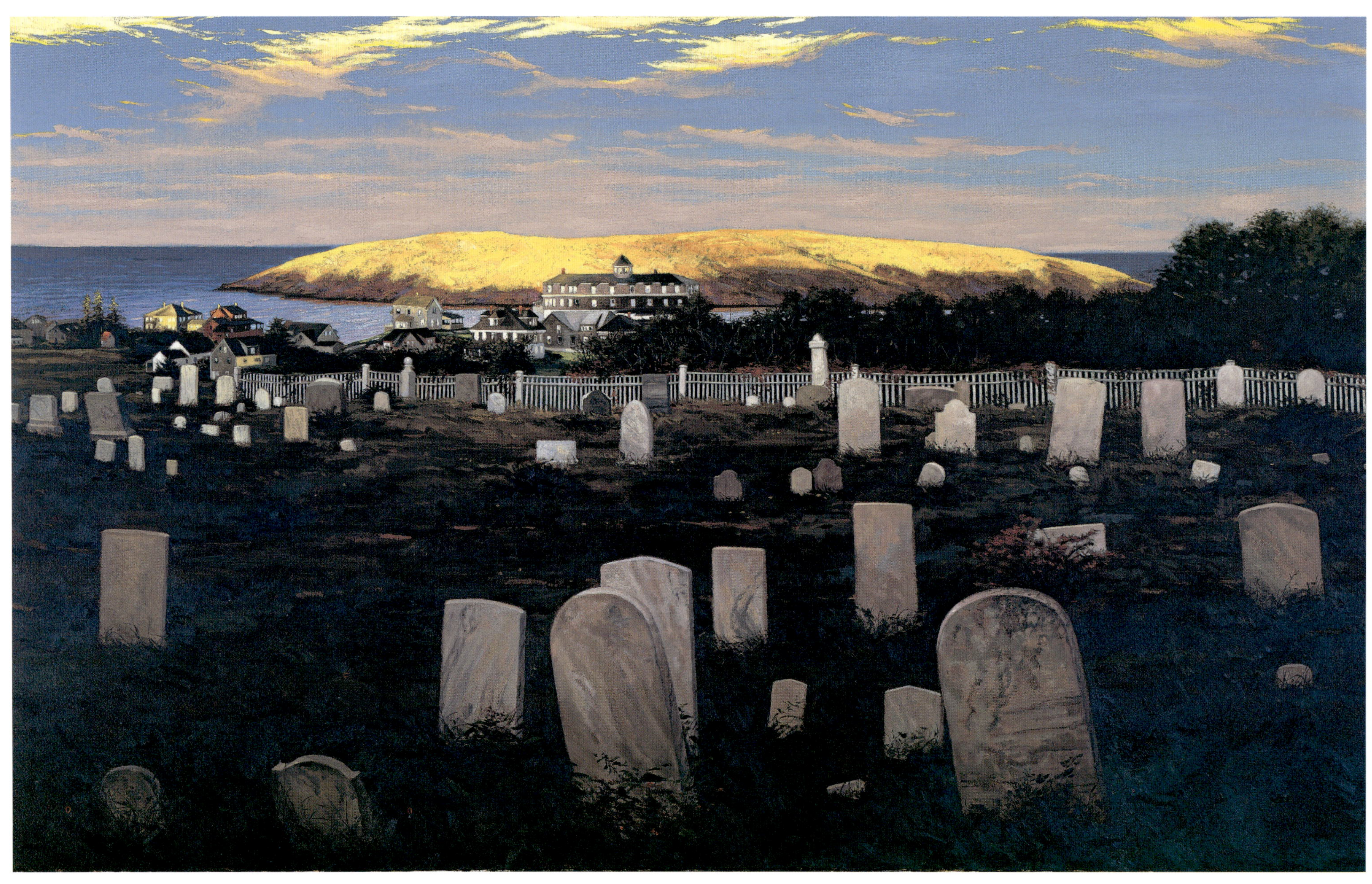

Island Cemetery

Worn stones,
inscriptions licked by rain, salt air.
From this distance
our sorrow is tempered by the cycle,
the wheel shoved against God's shoulder.

We do not think of little Lizzie in Dante's limbo.
She is just asleep beneath the ground's arm,
a blanket of rosa rugosa.

—MARILYN RINGER

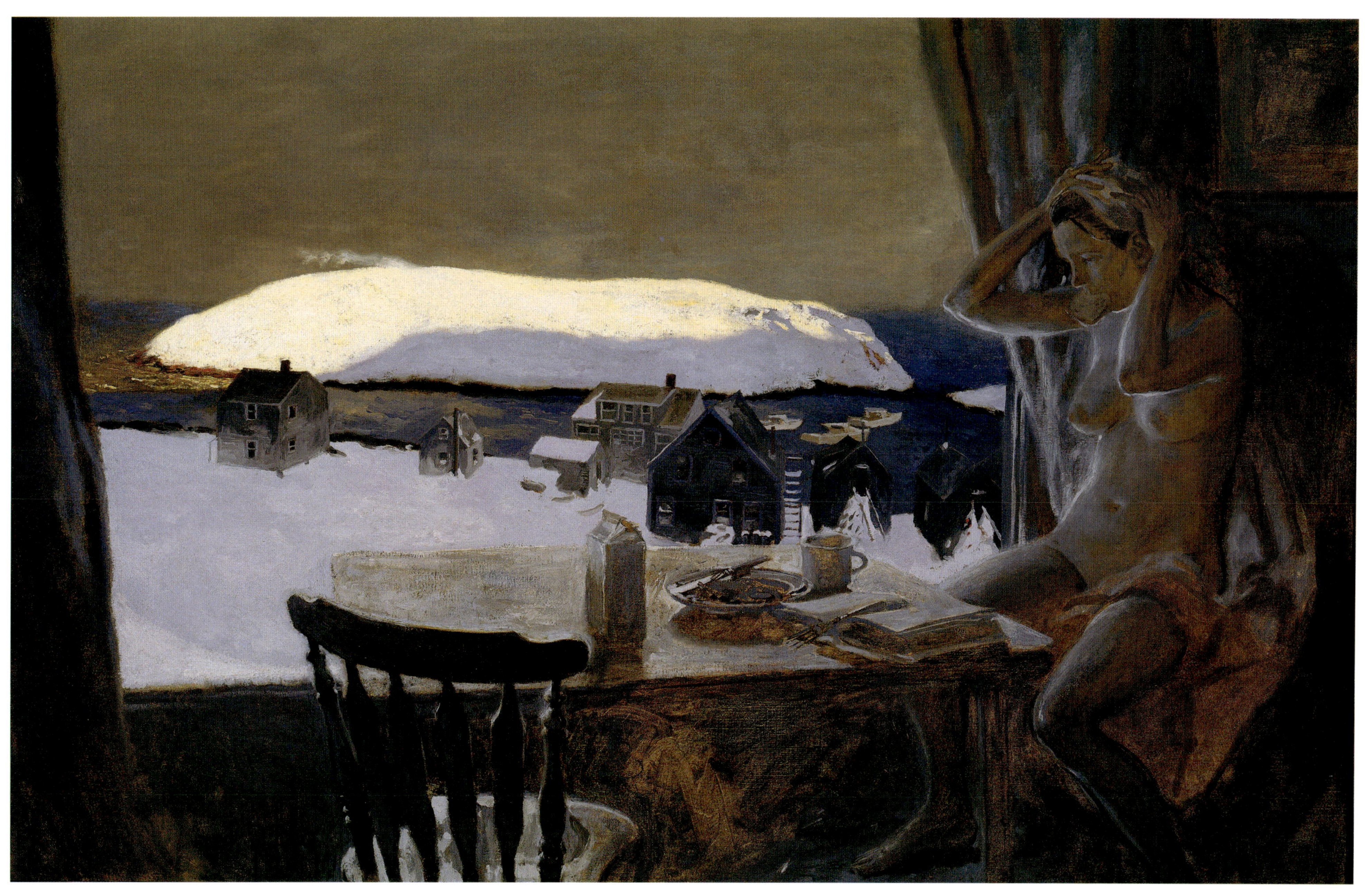

(OPPOSITE) RONALD FRONTIN, *FIRST LIGHT*, 2001, OIL ON CANVAS, 45 X 72 IN., PRIVATE COLLECTION

(ABOVE) JAMIE WYETH, *THE ISLAND SCHOOLTEACHER*, 2000, OIL ON CANVAS, 40 X 60 IN., COLLECTION OF BEBE AND CROSBY KEMPER

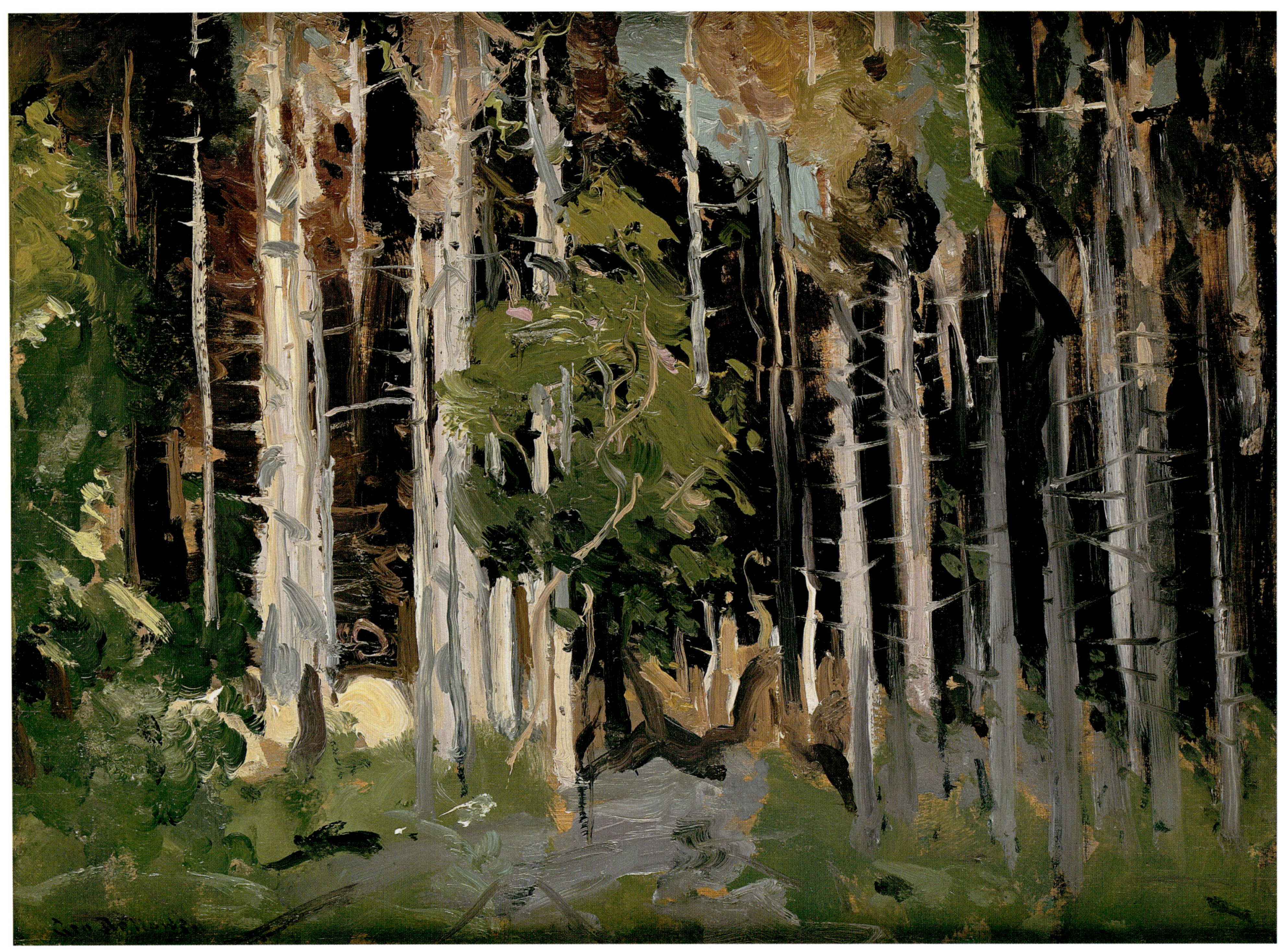

 GEORGE WESLEY BELLOWS, *THROUGH THE TREES*, 1913, OIL ON BOARD, 15 X 19 ¹/₂ IN., SCHWARTZ FAMILY COLLECTION

Cathedral Woods

Cathedral Woods are the gentlest, quietest part of this wonderful island. High, quiet as a church, the trees gentle the sound of wind and sea. Birds sing, hidden in the branches, and the air is aromatic with a heady mixture of balsam and sea. In here you feel remote and safe from storm, but even as you stand deep in the woods, you can feel the rote of the pull and the booming strength of the ocean, out of view; and you can begin to feel that special bond which links you closely to all those who stood centuries ago on this same island.

—BILL CALDWELL, "MONHEGAN, SHAPED LIKE A WHALE"

In 1954 Theodore Edison, son of the great inventor and a longtime visitor to Monhegan, helped to form the Monhegan Associates, a group devoted to keeping "the 'wild-lands' side of the Island in as natural a state as practical," as its original mission stated. Today, about seventeen miles of trails crisscross the island and follow its extremities. Many of these paths lead into Cathedral Woods, the forested interior of Monhegan.

When Robert Henri (1865–1929) visited Monhegan in 1918, he executed a number of studies of these thick woods, where residents and visitors alike seek refuge from the constant turmoil of the sea. Leader of "the Eight"—later called the Ashcan school—and a remarkable art teacher, Henri encouraged many of his students to go to Monhegan after he discovered the island in 1903. After the sooty existence of the city, these New York painters were entranced by the pristine air, dramatic headlands, sturdy fisherfolk and their simple shacks, Cathedral Woods and, above all else, the rocks and seas.

Henri's student George Bellows also was drawn to the woods, painting them with the same panache he treated other island motifs. The richness of the paint, the masterful effects of light, the dashing brushstrokes—hallmarks of Bellows' style—endow Cathedral Woods with a sense of life. The air moves and the trees breathe. The artist seems to have taken to heart something Henri said in his art classes: "Paint like a fiend when the idea possesses you."[31]

Contemporary painters Carol Sloane (b. 1945) and Joanne Scott (b. 1928) have responded to the magical quality of Cathedral Woods.

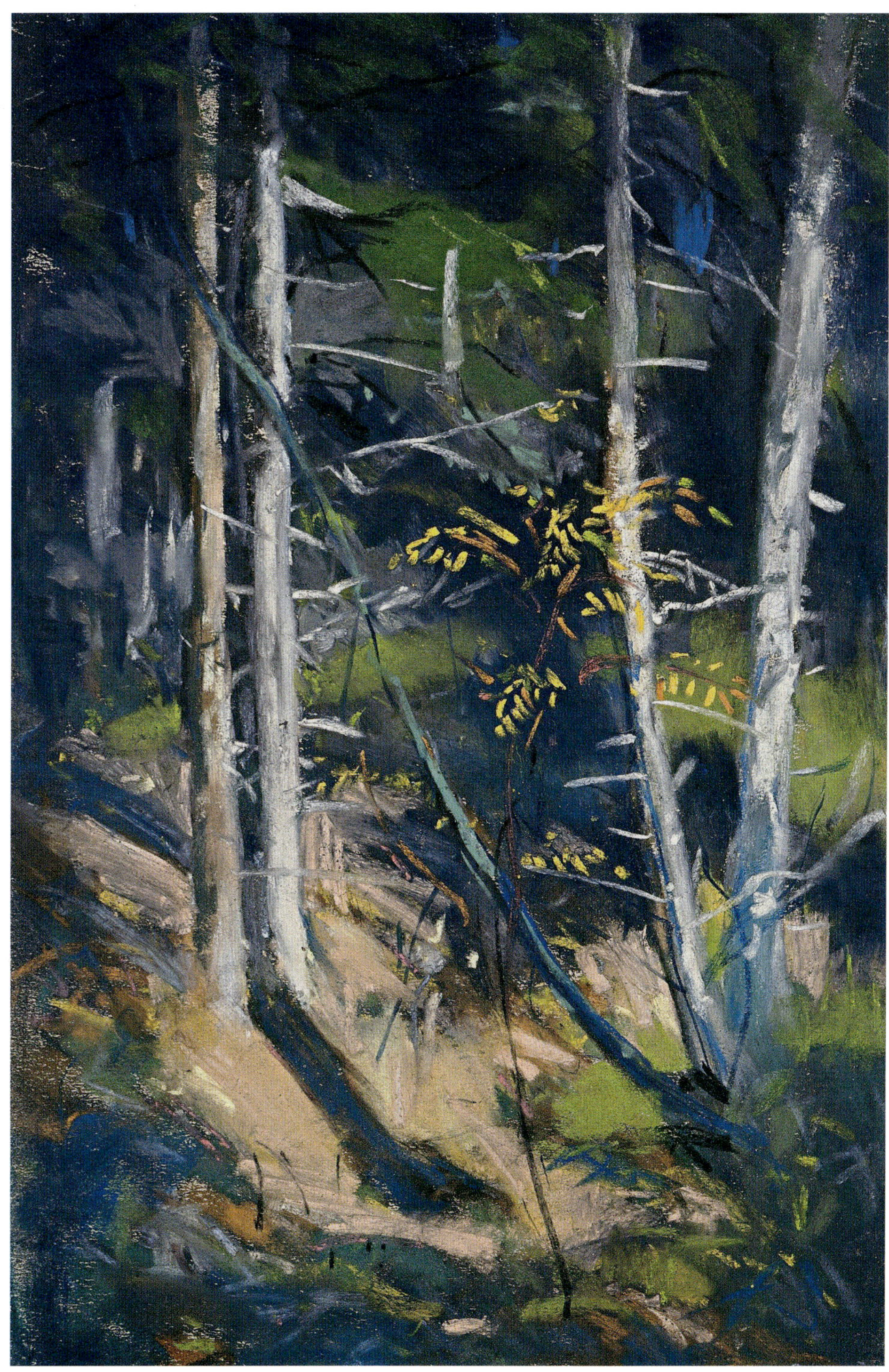

ROBERT HENRI, *CATHEDRAL WOODS*, 1918, PASTEL ON PAPER, 20 x 12 IN.
SCHWARTZ FAMILY COLLECTION

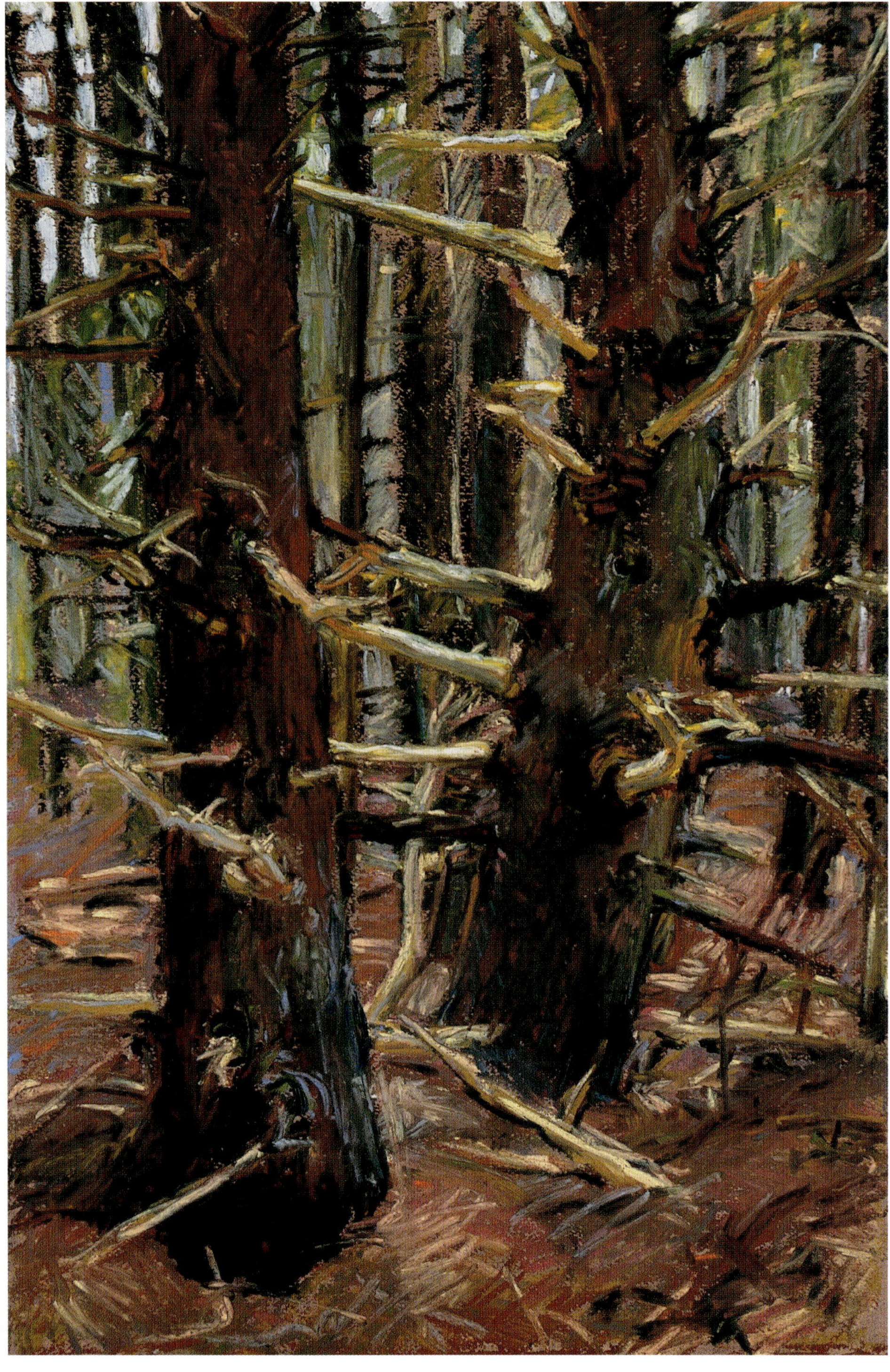

CAROL SLOANE, *DAY 28, CATHEDRAL WOODS, OFF TRAIL 10,* 2002
R & F OILBAR ON 140 LB COLD PRESS WATERCOLOR PAPER, 27 1/2 X 18 IN.
COLLECTION OF THE ARTIST

Cathedral Woods: giving thanks

For the strands of web that wet
my cheek, the autumn ash, its blast
of crimson berry; for the red
belted polypore, the spotted
collybia, the old man's beard
like wooly wire; for the hunch-
backed boulders bearing upon their
shoulders small sprigs of yew;
for slag water sprinkled with leaf,
its funky perfume; for roots
gnarled into knees and roots
bowed into questions I trip over
as I scan the tall spruce, a hopeless
fool for crows; for the braided
rope of felled trunk, a leviathan
laid out along a meadow frail
with weed and brown fern;
for all the wounded trees
that succor lichen, the spit
and snarl of broken branches;
for November sky, low, low
and layered grey; for the rain
pools, their time-warped reflections;
for the dull sparrow, the junco,
the cardinal in her dusty coat
and cap, the female jay;
for the half-blown carcass
of a gull wedged between two
rocks, its tiny nave of ribs
picked clean; for the maze
of blue mussels, fodder for ducks,
the coins of mottled lichen
along the ridges of the rocks;
for the dispassionate, the dying,
the unbecoming; and for my longing
to be unraveled, unnerved, undone
until I am grey air, sea, stone.

—JAN BAILEY

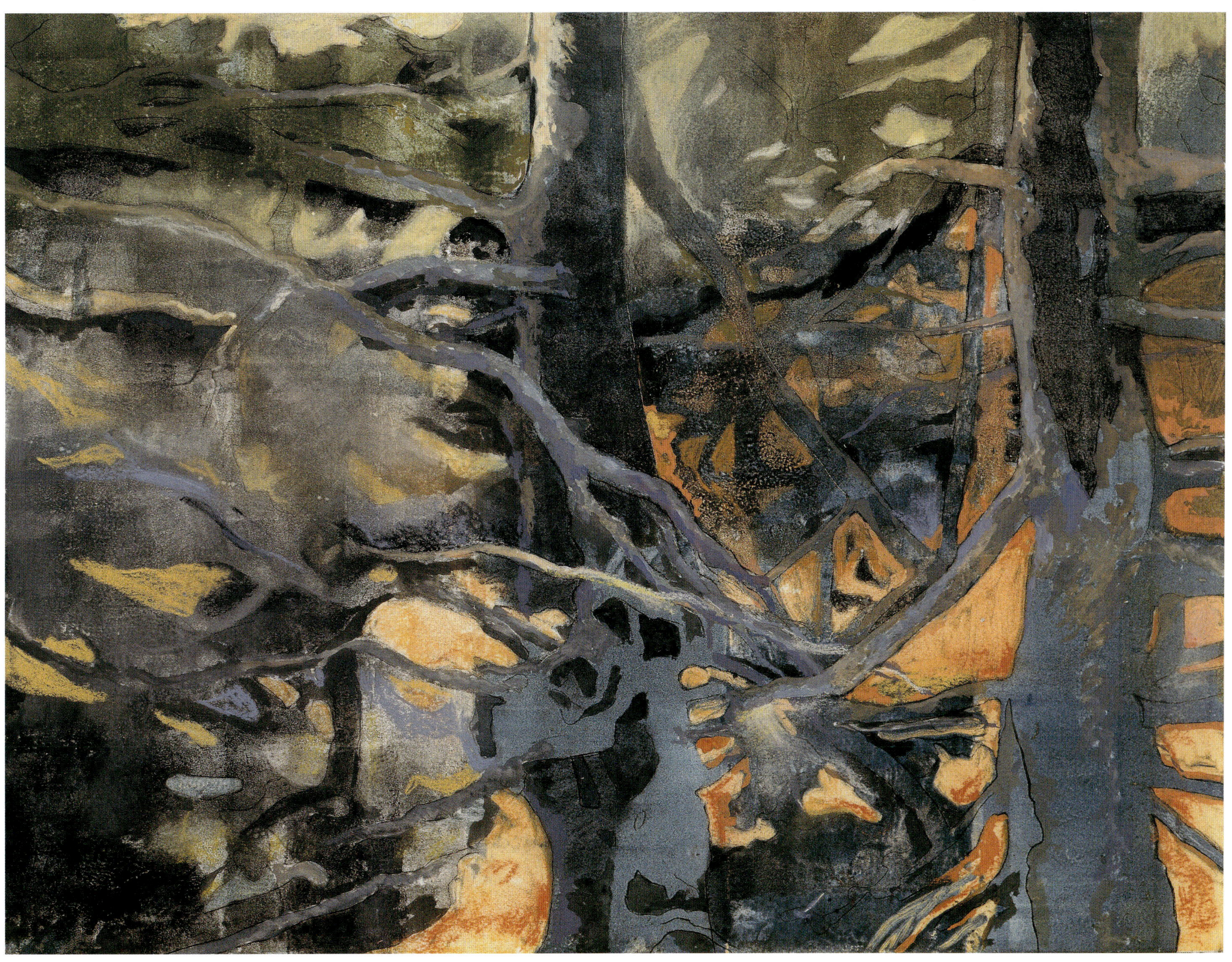

JOANNE SCOTT, *FIRE STORM (INSPIRED BY CATHEDRAL WOODS)*, 1995, MONOPRINT ON PAPER, 15 5/8 X 19 3/4 IN., COLLECTION OF REMAK RAMSAY

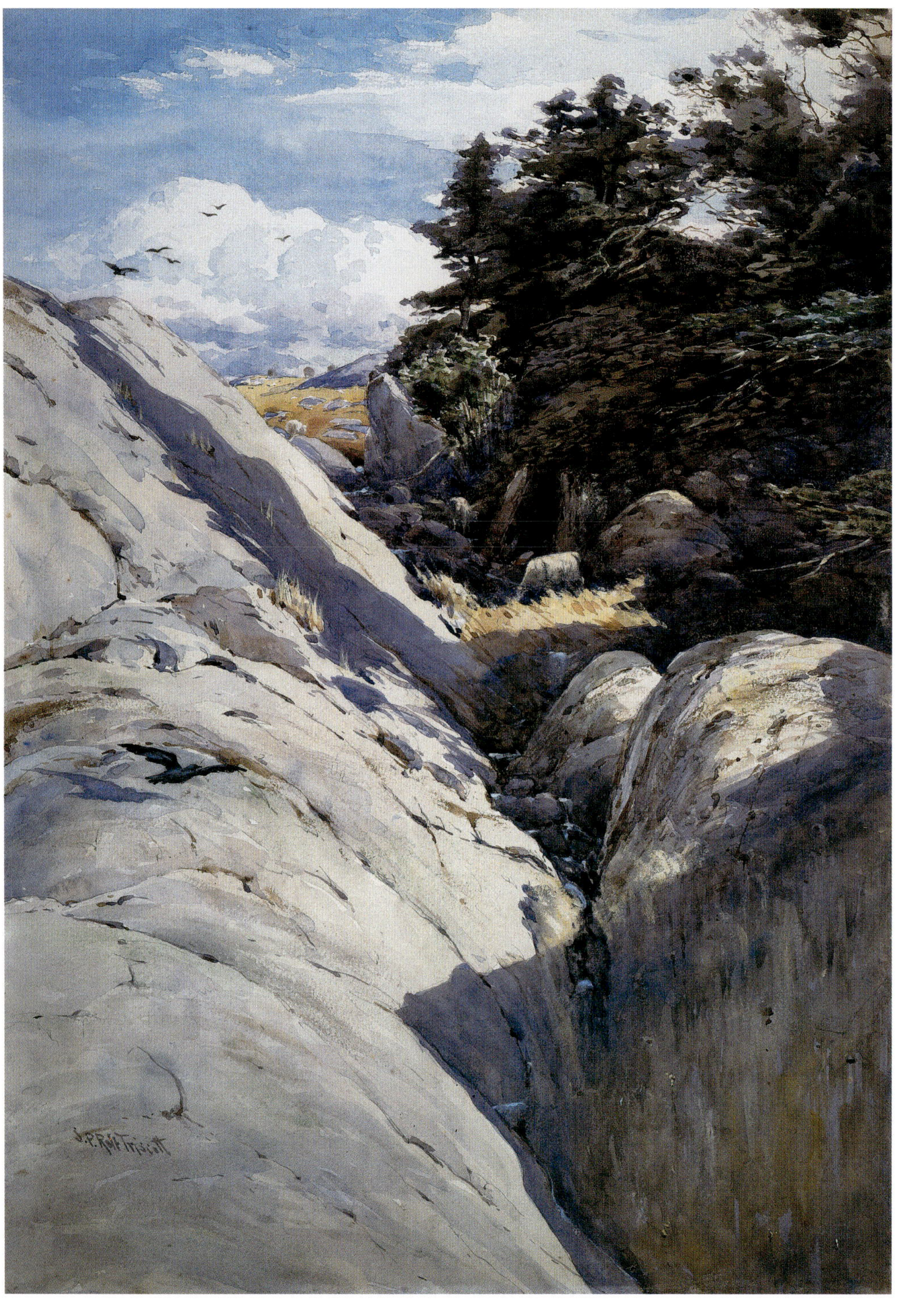

S. P. ROLT TRISCOTT, *A GULLY, MONHEGAN*, N.D.
68   WATERCOLOR ON PAPER, 24 x 16 ¹/₂ IN., COLLECTION OF DOROTHY MALONE

Sloane, who was a Carina House resident in 2001, has painted numerous studies of trees *(p. 66)*, many of them in a state of decay, their limbs broken off—signs of a forest in decline. Scott opened a studio on the island in 1981. A printmaker, painter, and poet, she has sought "the mystical essence of nature" on Monhegan. In the oil monoprint *Fire Storm*, she expresses this special essence by simplifying her trees to patterns of interlocking branches *(p. 67)*.

The Monhegan terrain is not for the faint of heart. Accessibility is sometimes an issue for artists coming to the island. Not every motif is easy to reach. The pathways are often rugged, the perches precarious. As the handy guide to the island recommends, "One should avoid plastic soled shoes, sling-backs, sandals, and, above all, platform shoes and high heels."

In his watercolor *A Gully, Monhegan*, British-born painter S. P. Rolt Triscott (1846–1925) depicts one of those treacherous places where one would do well to watch one's footing. This painting is based on a photograph of the spot taken by the painter. Triscott first came to the island in 1892, boarding at the Albee House, and later became the first artist to live year-round on Monhegan. He produced an exceptional body of work, almost all watercolors, depicting many elements of the island landscape in all seasons, his technique ranging from precise and elaborate to loose and atmospheric.

James Perry Wilson (1889–1976), who painted North American landscapes for the dioramas in natural history museums in New York, Boston, and elsewhere, spent summers on Monhegan from 1919 to 1940. A plein air painter, he appears to have been fearless in selecting his painting sites—if the precipitous angle found in an oil from 1929 is any indication. Wilson's Monhegan work has a freshness and clarity that testify to his passion for the island.

Maine is, in Sarah Orne Jewett's famous image, "the country of the pointed fir." One is reminded of this when wandering the landscape of Monhegan, where evergreens accent the horizon. Such is the case in Hans Moller's lovely view from the window of his island home, with clusters of hardy spruce standing out against the sky and distant sea *(p. 70)*.

David Vickery (b. 1966) painted a similar prospect at Lobster Cove. A resident of Cushing, Maine, Vickery first visited Monhegan as a Carina House artist in residents in 1993 and has returned every year since. "I enjoyed the tremendous freedom to roam the

Monhegan Villanelle

When day descends the stair of sky
And ribs of clouds exhale the light,
The sea breathes deep as colors die.

West bellows blow the ember high
And dark-winged terns stitch flames in flight.
When day descends the stair of sky,

She walks the stone where wild tongues lie,
And, lambent, searches cloud's delight.
The sea breathes deep as colors die,

And sieves the gold, the rose, the rye
Like coins through colanders of light.
When day descends the stair of sky,

Bright water cups, then darkly sighs
And laps the petal edge of night.
The sea breathes deep as colors die,

Makes grief in phosphorescence fly,
And spills it on horizon's height,
When day descends the stair of sky,
The sea breathes deep as colors die.

— Kate Cheney Chappell

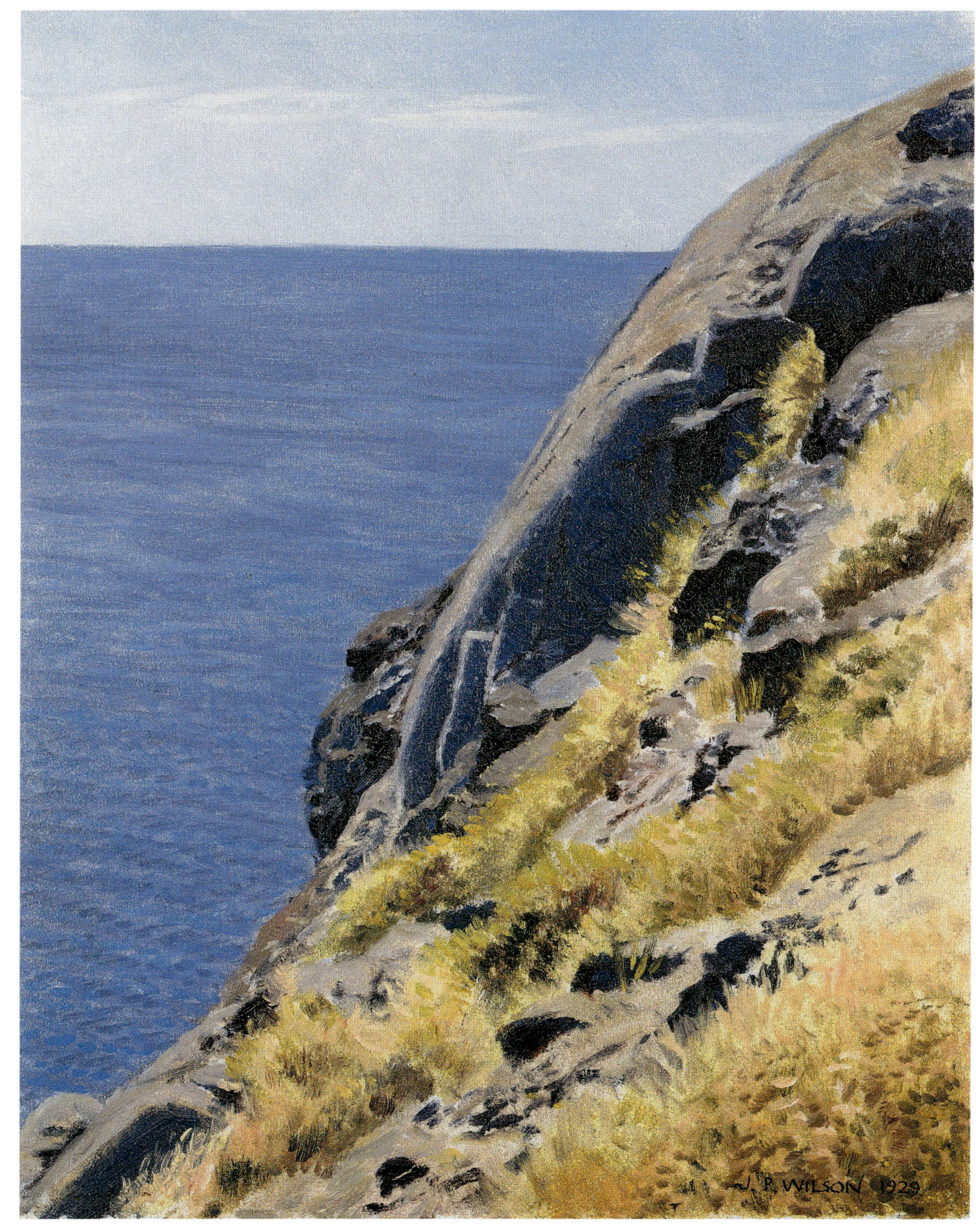

James Perry Wilson, *Whitehead*, 1929, oil on wood panel, 10 x 8 in.
collection of Remak Ramsay

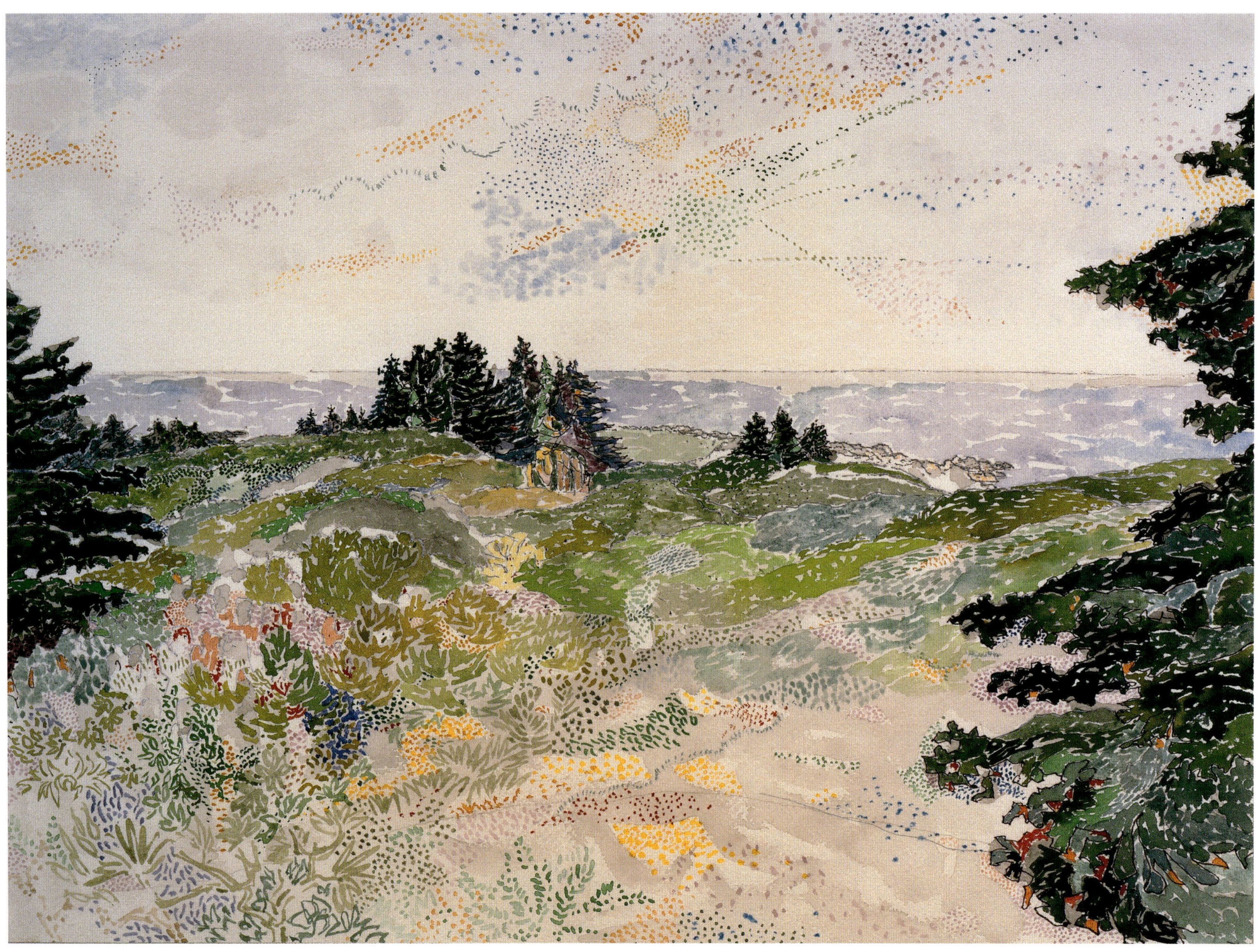

Hans Moller, *View from Our Window*, 1981, watercolor on paper, 18 x 24 in., collection of Edward L. Deci

island and open myself to whatever artistic ideas presented themselves," he wrote of his first stay.[32] It is this sense of freedom that has hooked generations of artists.

The vastness of the sky impressed Leni Mancuso (b. 1966), as well as "the moods of the sea, the incredible intimacy within the island along its trails and lanes, through Cathedral Woods or from Burnt Head to the harbor." Her experience of Monhegan, she has written, "has more to do with insight than with site alone." A casein painting, *Approaching Gull Cove*, exemplifies the abstract means by which Mancuso responds to the island.

There is plentiful wildlife on Monhegan, especially of the avian sort. In a lively pastel from around 1960, Morris Shulman (1912–1978) depicts several birds perched among tall grasses. Shulman was one of a distinguished group of New York–based abstract painters who discovered the island after World War II.

One of the most recent island devotees is painter Michael Schweigart (b. 1956). "Monhegan's history of being a haven for

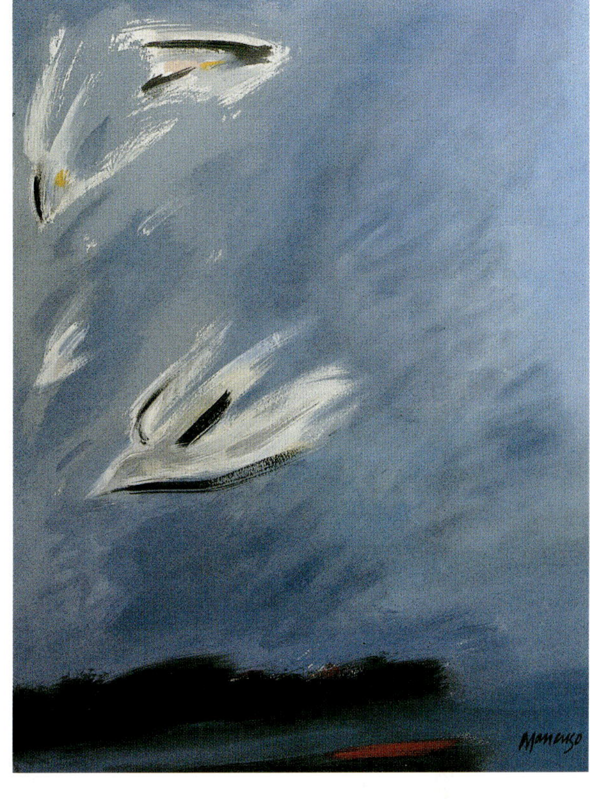

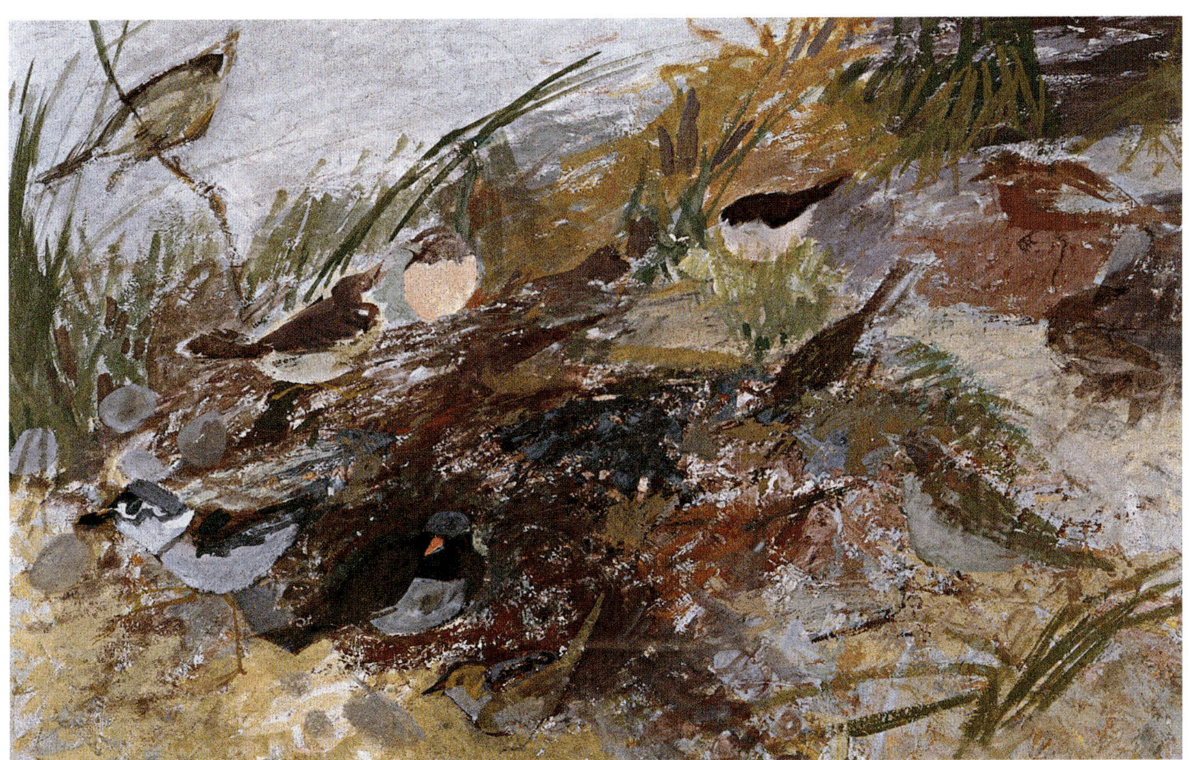

(ABOVE RIGHT) LENI MANCUSO, *APPROACHING GULL COVE*, 1977, CASEIN ON PAPER, 30 x 22 IN., COLLECTION OF THE ARTIST

(ABOVE) MORRIS SHULMAN, *MONHEGAN BEACH*, N.D., PASTEL ON PAPER, 30 x 40 IN., COLLECTION OF JOHN M. DAY

Monhegan

Looking beyond my island
of sun-filled spruce and ash,
time ripples off a bending light—
a world of fish and birds within a seamless sea.

At the island's black and brilliant edge,
thoughts float on feathered light.

—GEORGE V. VAN DEVENTER

artists was what lured me to its shores," he states. On his first visit, the fog obscured much of the island, putting a damper on the keen anticipation of exploring a new place. After exploring the island, Schweigart accepted his fate and chose to work with the fog. No sooner had he begun painting than the sun broke through. "Slowly (as if a veil was being lifted), I could distinguish objects—cliffs, trees and water—from sky," he relates. "The light, purer color, contrasting shapes and textures were being revealed." He realized at that point that he was going to experience "as much in one day as one could in a week."

Such epiphanies are the stuff of Monhegan art.

Notes

31. Robert Henri, *The Art Spirit* (Philadelphia: J.P. Lippincott Company, 1923), 166.
32. *Carina House: The First Decade, 1989–1999*, 22.

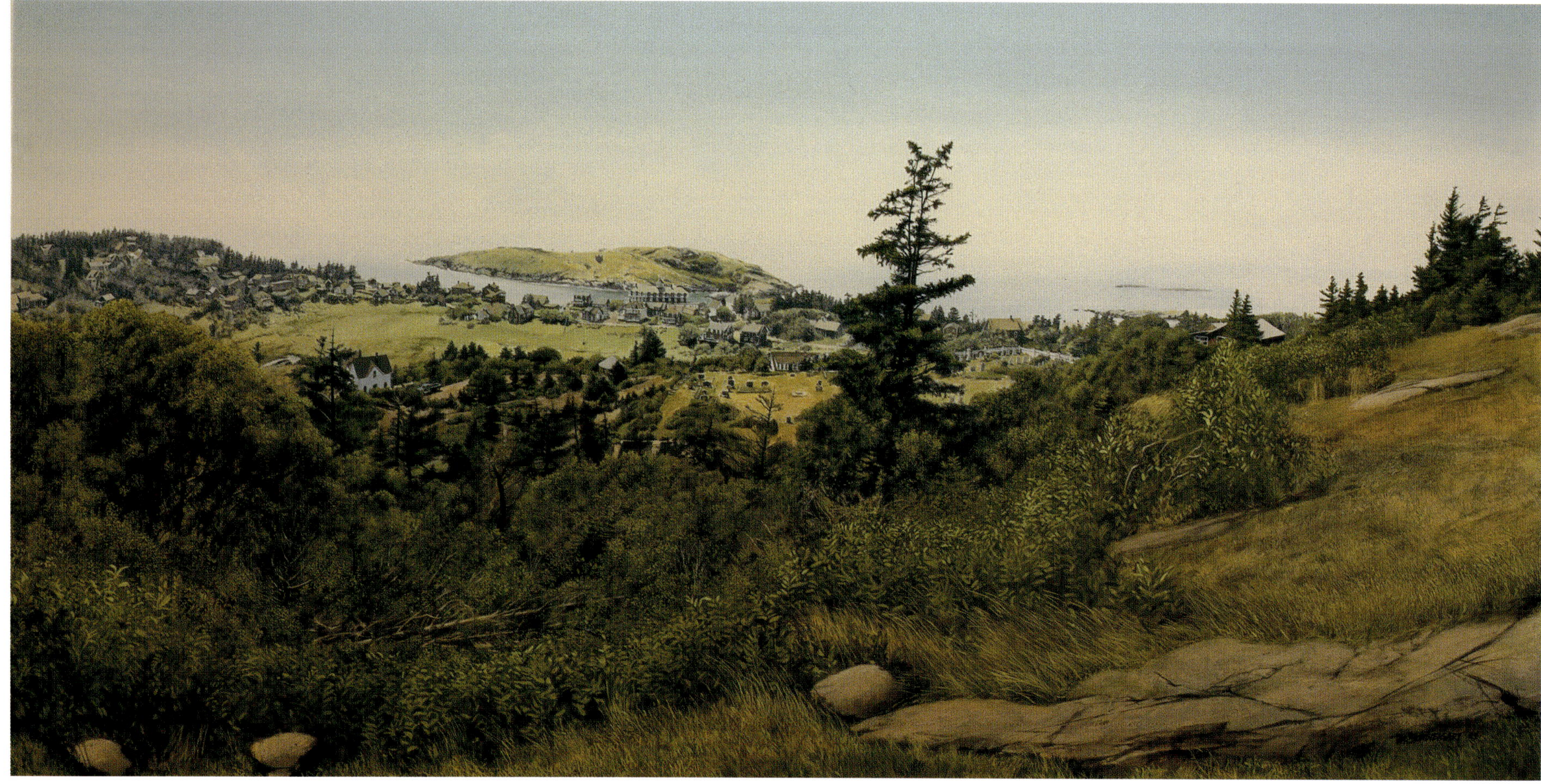

 MICHAEL SCHWEIGART, *MONHEGAN CLEARING*, 2004, ACRYLIC ON PAPER, 25 x 49 IN., COURTESY OF SHERRY FRENCH GALLERY, NEW YORK

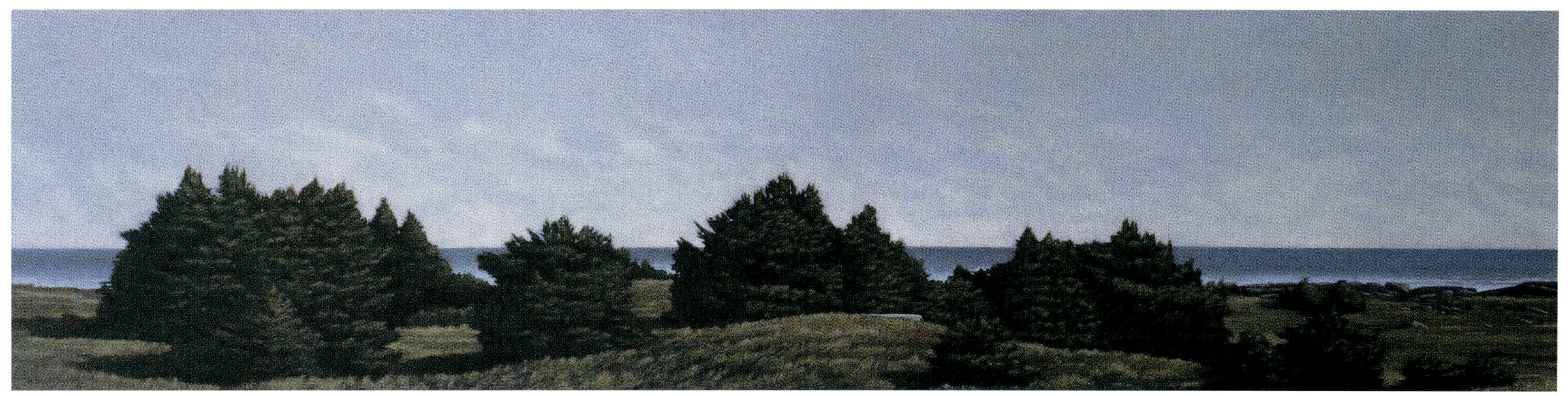

Approaching these great cliffs we experienced a peculiar terror which others have doubtless felt: not that we would slip and fall off, but that we would be drawn helplessly to the edge to throw ourselves off in a last swan-dive into the deep, to leap out of this small life into the eternal meeting of land, sea, water and rock. At least one person did that, and others were swept away during a birthday picnic on the rocks. Others have been hopelessly lost in the small woods. Time folds into eternity here, and it is terrifying. That is what makes the Eastern side of the island so cleansing and exhilarating: utter wildness within a half-mile of the peaceful village. Like the little fairy houses in the Cathedral Woods, the whole island is a miniature. Heaven and Hell, life and death, all in a space of three-quarters of a square mile.

—Reverend Rob McCall, *Awanadjo Almanack*, May 17–24, 2001

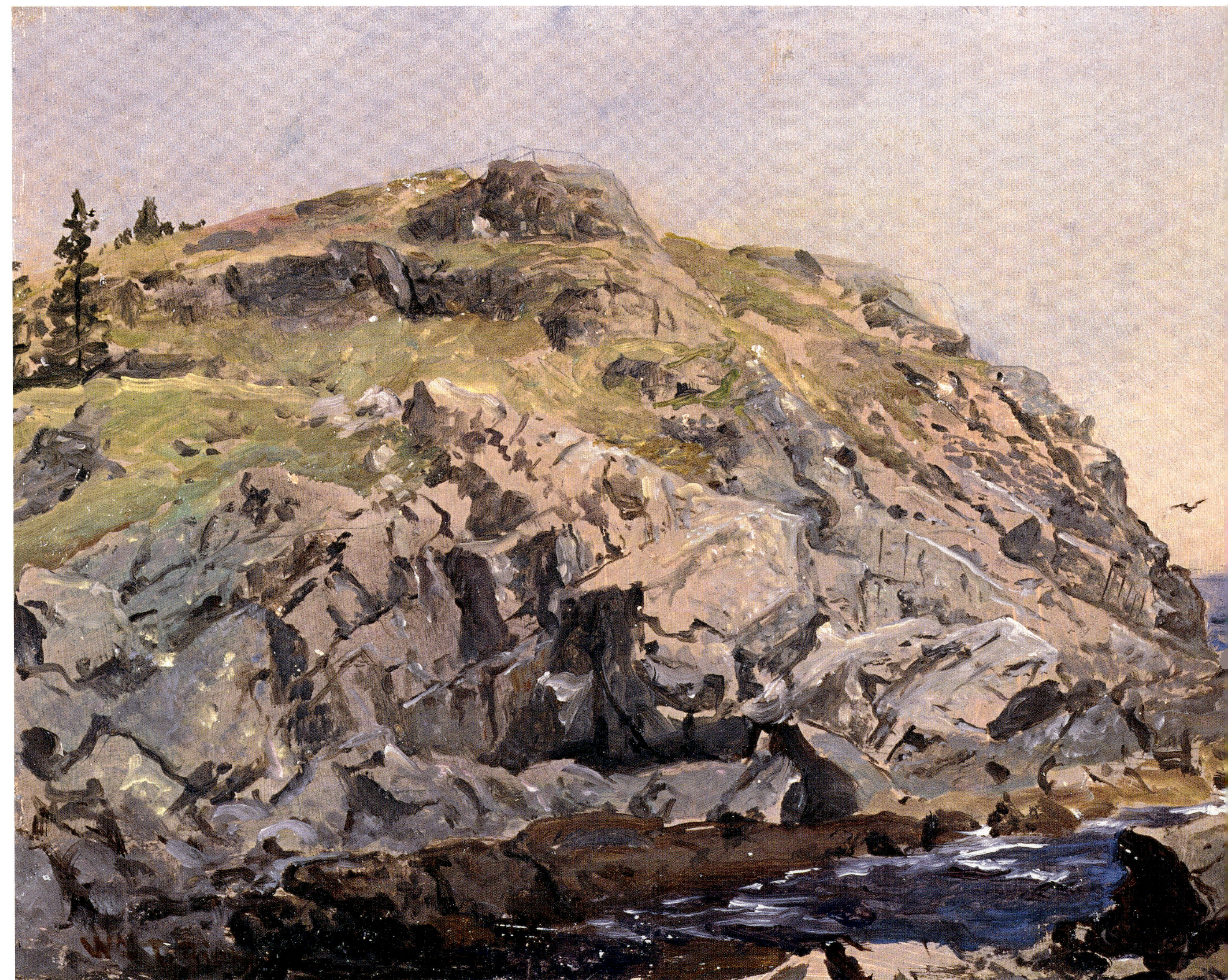

Headlands

Over paths that paths have crossed,
over gnarled root,
sphagnum and bog, out to hump-backed
boulders and cliffs
that stagger and drop into seas.
    —LENI MANCUSO, "ISLAND LIKE A WHALE"

North America boasts some formidable headlands, from the cliffs at Big Sur to the bluffs at Montauk and Martha's Vineyard. Yet no place of like characteristics has been painted as much or as often as the headlands of Monhegan: White, Black and Burnt, by name. Over the 150-plus years that artists have been traveling to the island, these mighty cliffs on the eastern shore have acted like a lodestone.[33] Finding paint marks on the rocks in the vicinity is common.

For members of the Hudson River school who visited the island in the late 1800s, the headlands represented an ideal sub-ject—remote, dramatic and transcendent. In one of his island stud-ies, William Trost Richards (1833–1905) turned a scrupulous eye on White Head, delineating the nooks and crannies of its rocky demeanor. He often worked outdoors; "I and my umbrelly and a weather beaten nose," he once wrote with humor to a patron, "go up and down the shore together and take the sunshine and pictures."[34]

The luminist painter Alfred Thompson Bricher (1837–1908) chose a perspective of the headlands that emphasizes their grandeur and bold imposition on the Atlantic, which sends endless rows of combers to beat against the island's shores *(p. 77)*. Working from pen-and-ink and watercolor sketches, Bricher created full-fledged landscapes replete with light and scenic qualities that heighten the experience of a particular view.

The headlands cast an equally powerful spell on the impres-sionist painters who spent time on the island in the early decades of the twentieth century. Two members of the famous Old Lyme, Connecticut, contingent of American impressionists, Charles Ebert and the English-born William Chadwick (1879–1962), deployed

WILLIAM TROST RICHARDS, *WHITE HEAD, MONHEGAN,* C. 1895
OIL ON PAPER LAID DOWN ON BOARD, 8 3/4 X 16 IN.
COLLECTION OF EDWARD L. DECI

75

warm palettes, transforming brooding cliffs into shimmering vistas *(pp. 78–79)*. The seas are relatively calm in their canvases, with irregular lines of foam following the coastline—the residuum of crashing waves.

Part of the allure—and challenge—of painting the headlands lies in the way their forms change according to weather and light conditions. In the beneficence of the sun, they appear warm and inviting—to picnickers and painters—but under the influence of a storm, the headlands show their dark and dangerous side. S. P. Rolt Triscott painted the cliffs on numerous occasions, but no two views are alike.

"This is the real thing, I have never seen anything so fine," wrote Robert Henri upon arriving on Monhegan in 1903. He went on to describe the painting possibilities: ". . . from the great cliffs you look down on a mighty surf battering away at the rocks—or you can descend and get a side view of the cliffs from lower rocks."[35] An advocate of the lively brush, Henri practiced what he preached in his island marines, matching a painterly esprit with the dash and turmoil of his subject matter *(p. 89)*. Monhegan inspired a prolific output: during his first visit, Henri painted 26 canvases and 131 paintings on panel (the latter measuring 8 by 10 inches, ideal for transport over rough terrain).

George Bellows also sought to capture the monumental quality of the headlands, sometimes including a vessel to heighten the scale and drama of the scene. In *Beating Out to Sea*, one senses the urgency of the fishing boat to sail beyond the rocky embrace of the dark island *(p. 81)*. Bellows, too, was highly productive during his stays on Monhegan. Reporting to Henri toward the end of his 1913 visit, he counted "one hundred and twenty five [panels and canvases] all covered with paint."[36]

Where Henri and Bellows sought to represent the primal encounter of sea and rocks, Rockwell Kent preferred calmer prospects *(p. 80)*. "The fairest, clearest, sharpest days I loved the most," he wrote in his autobiography; "the northwest days when the wind-blown ocean plain stretched dark as indigo to a horizon knife-sharp against the golden lower sky."[37] Against this backdrop of sea and sky, Kent's headlands are a mighty sight, bold and imposing.

"When I was still in school in Hawaii," the painter Reuben Tam (1916–1991) once recalled, "I saw two reproductions of paintings by Rockwell Kent of Monhegan—one was of Black Head—and I knew I had to come here, and as soon as I could, I did."[38] Tam first visited the island in the mid-1940s and ended up spending parts of thirty summers at his studio cottage, accompanied by his wife, Geraldine, who painted studies of island flora.

Monhegan offered an elemental landscape perfectly in synch with Tam's abstract leanings. A poet as well as a painter, he preferred evocation to detail. "I paint to embody the spirit of place," he once stated, "and thus make objective those poetic conditions, portents and possibilities of nature that move me deeply and hauntingly."[39] While we recognize the headlands in an oil from 1968 *(p. 82)*, Tam blends rock, sea and sky into a single flowing entity.

Although not officially a headland, Gull Rock near Burnt Head presents a dramatic subject for painters, its bold contours imposing on the sea and sky. In Andrew Winter's painting of the rock, snow lies upon its flanks *(p. 87)*, brightening the chilly vista. A similar perspective by Donald Demers (b. 1956) reveals the fissures and folds of the rounded promontory, with hikers visible on its crown *(p. 86)*. Demers, who moved to Maine in 1984, refers to himself as a conduit between natural phenomena and their manifestation on the painted canvas.

Today the headlands continue to hold in thrall artists who encounter them on island trips, inspiring inventive visions. In one of his island studies, Donald Holden (b. 1931) creates a visual tone poem that brings to mind the atmospheric landscapes of Whistler *(half-title)*. When painting, Holden says he seeks "the spirit of the thing, rather than the details," an approach that places him in Tam's school of lyric invention.[40]

Working from sketches and photographs, Philip Frey (b. 1967) also seeks to interpret the landscape in his acrylic paintings. His

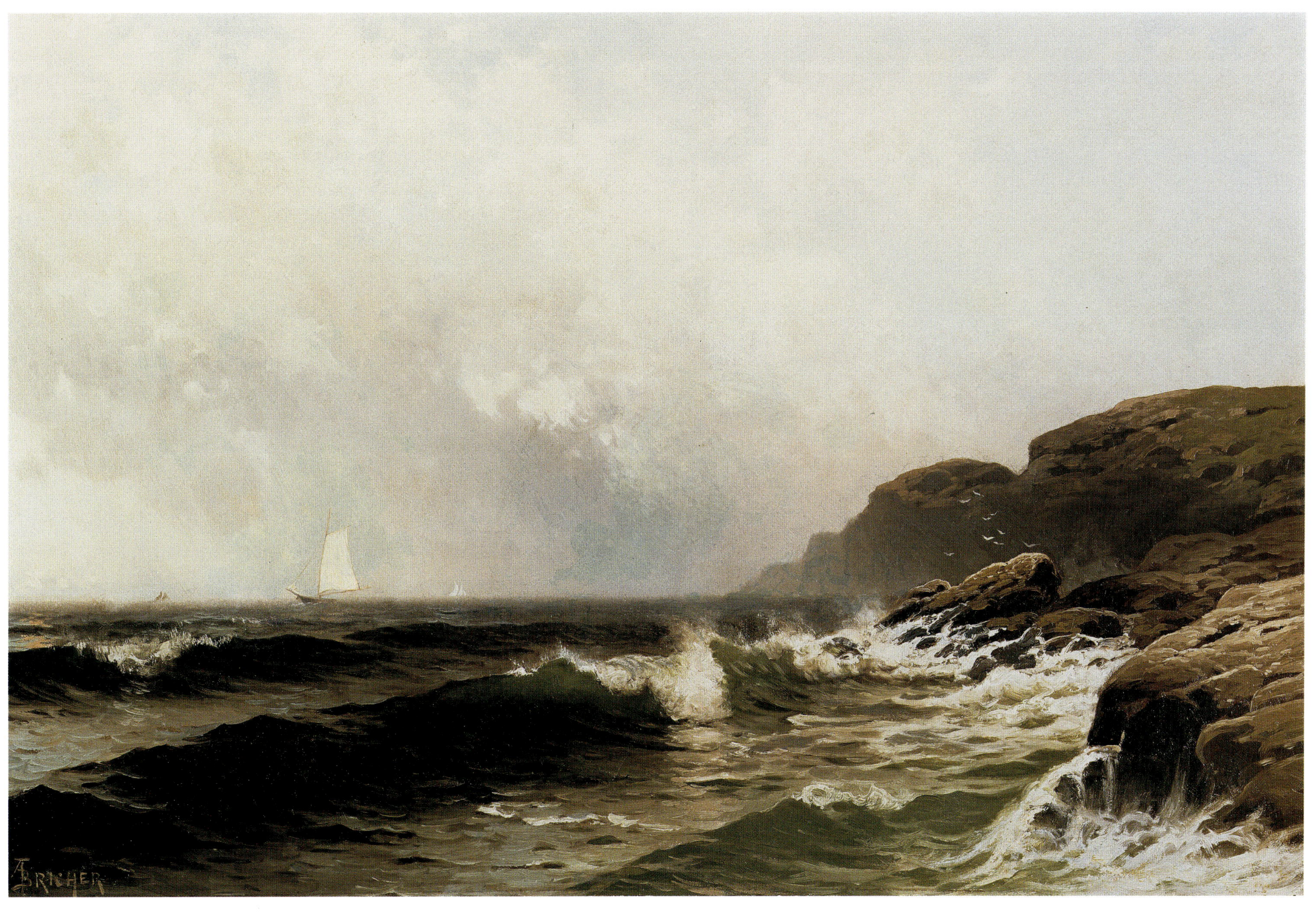

Alfred T. Bricher, *Marine*, 1895, oil on canvas, 21 x 31 in., collection of Monhegan Museum, gift of Jacqueline Hudson   *77*

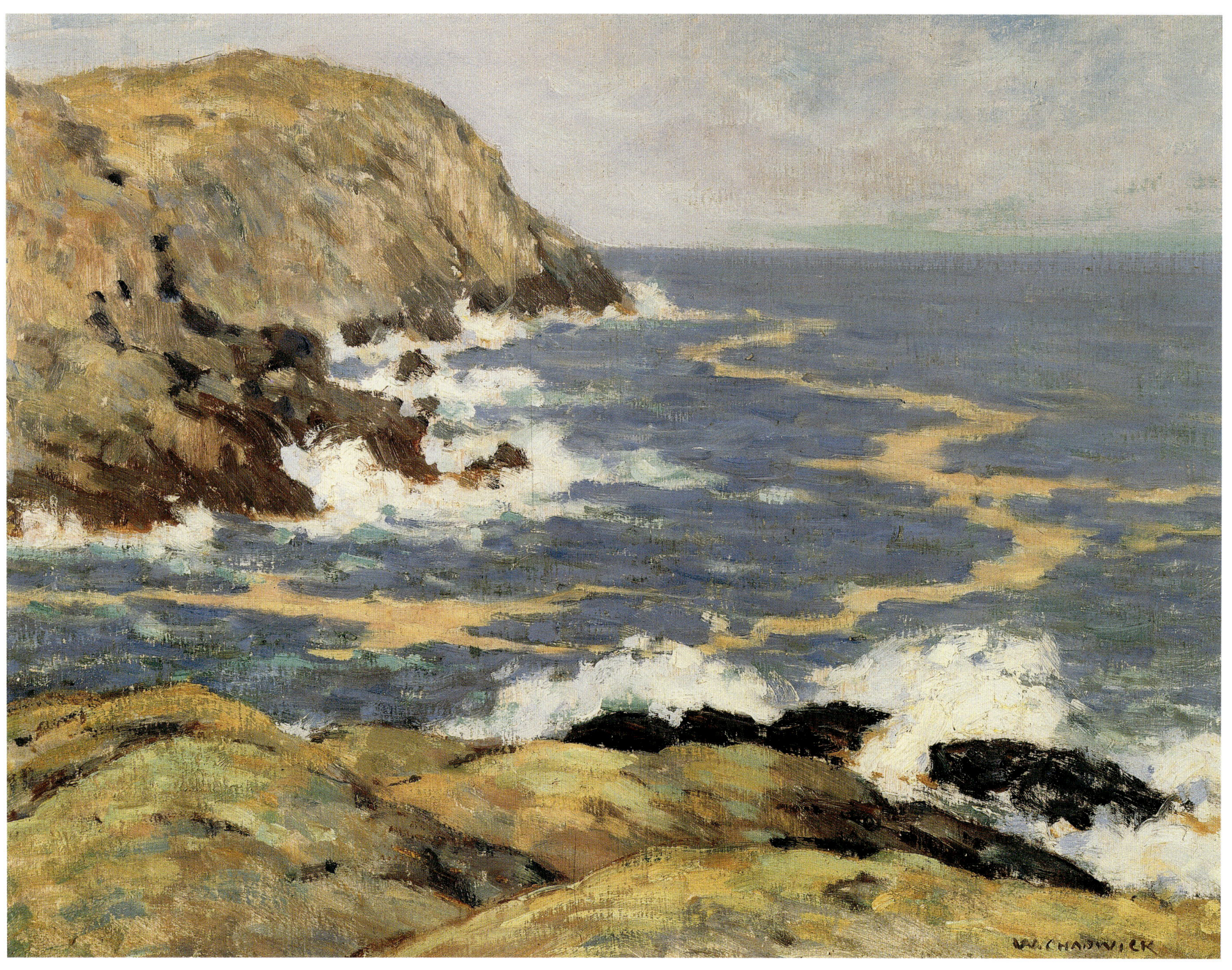

William Chadwick, *After a Storm*, c. 1918, oil on canvas panel, 14 x 18 in., collection of Edward L. Deci

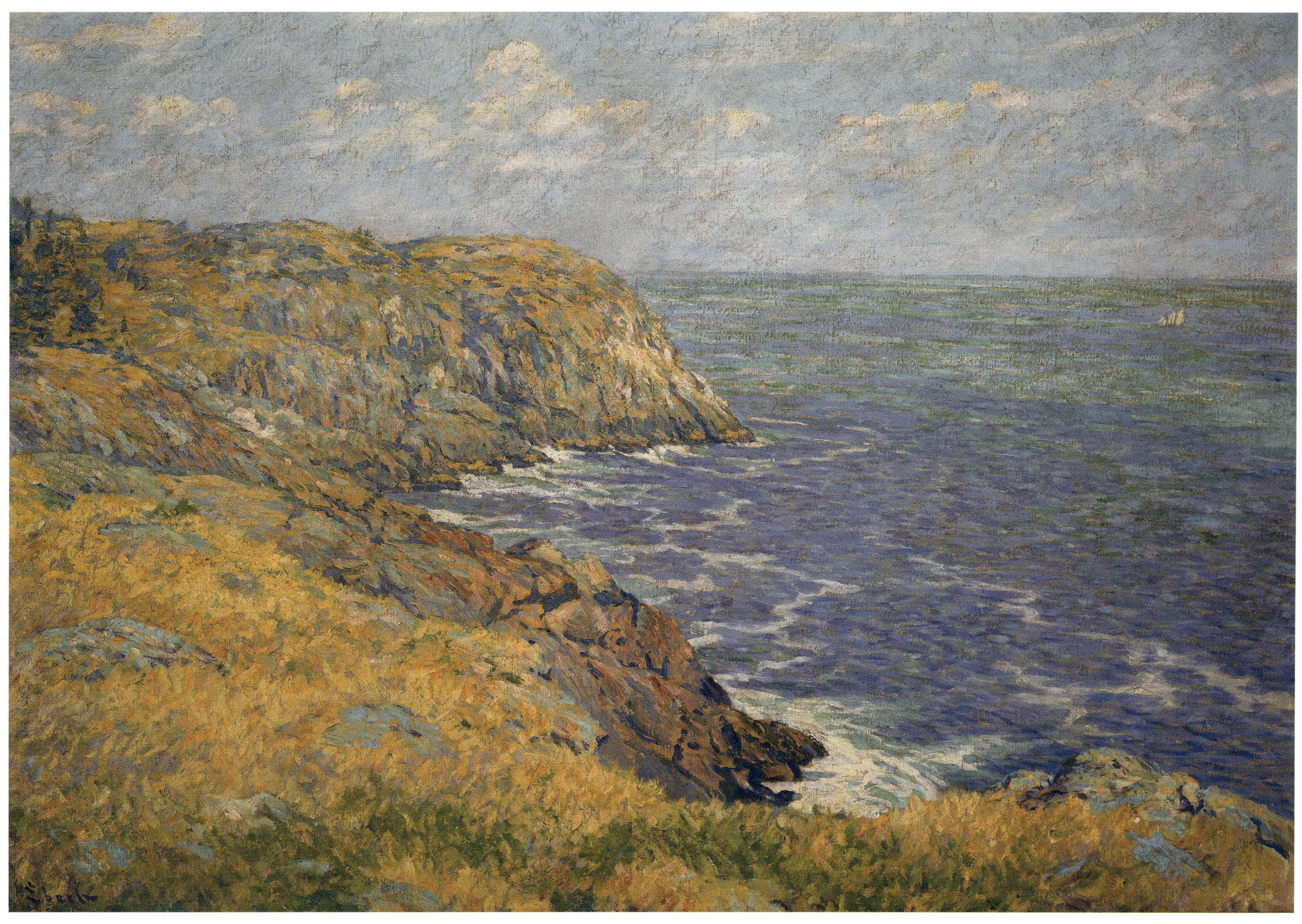

Charles Ebert, *Monhegan Headlands,* 1909, oil on canvas, 30 x 42 in., Florence Griswold Museum, gift of Miss Elizabeth Ebert. 1977.18.1

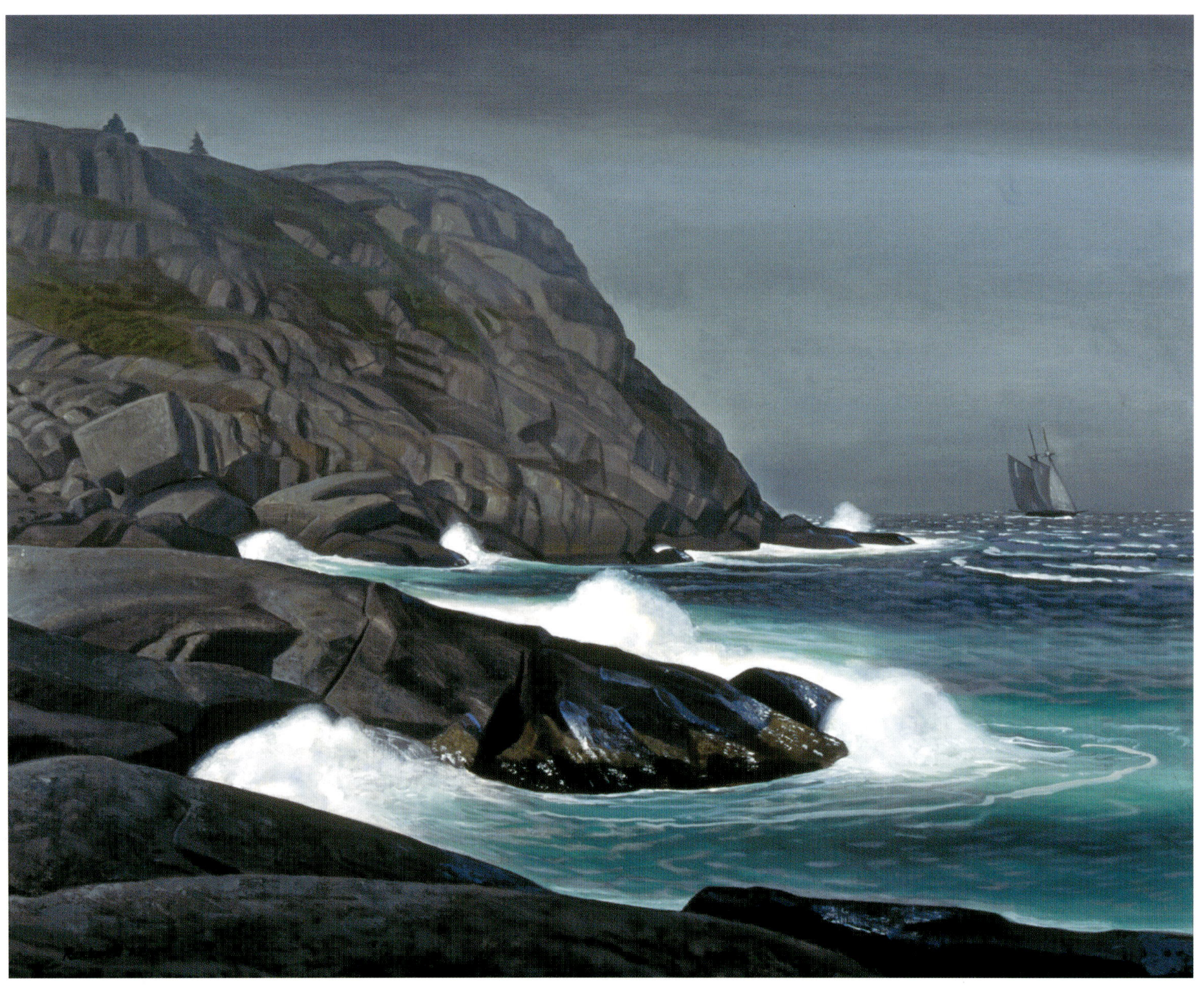

Well anyhow, I painted. Up onto the headlands, down off the headlands, down into gulleys and out of them again, close to the thunderous surf or in the stillness of the island's woods—Cathedral Woods they're called, so dark and silent are their columned aisles—from one end of the island to the other I walked or climbed, carrying my cumbersome canvases and heavy paints; in acceptance of whatever discomfort was forced upon me; I'd spend my hours struggling to transmute paint on canvas into some semblance of the lovely, sunlit, three dimensional world of land and sea and heaven that confronted me. I'd try—as the expression goes—to capture it; undaunted by Mohammed's failure, we artists try to bring our mountains home.

—ROCKWELL KENT, *IT'S ME OLORD,* 1955

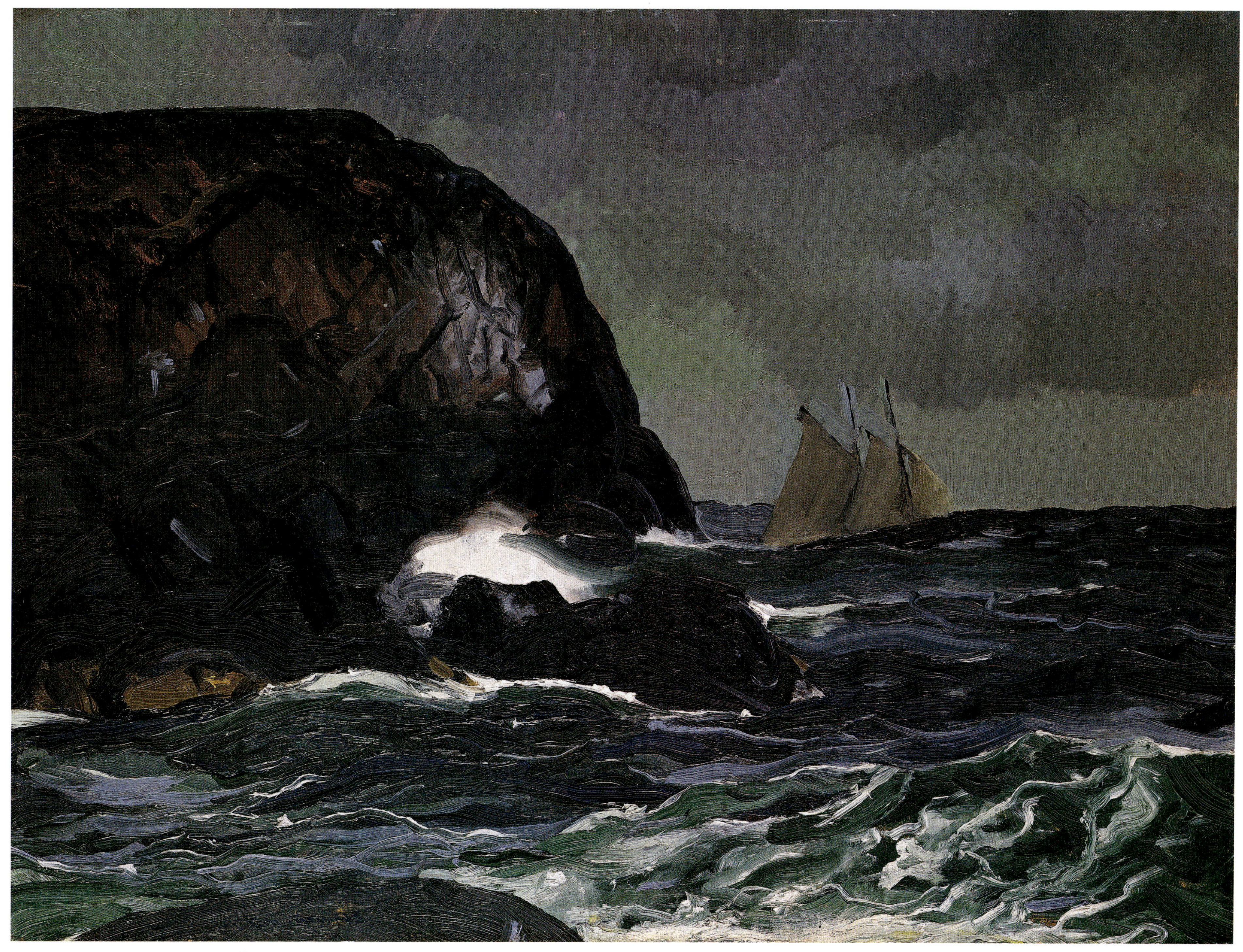

(OPPOSITE) ROCKWELL KENT, *BLACKHEAD*, 1950, OIL ON CANVAS, 28 $^1/_4$ X 34 IN., COURTESY OF PLATTSBURGH STATE ART MUSEUM, PLATTSBURGH COLLEGE FOUNDATION, ROCKWELL GALLERY AND COLLECTION, GIFT OF SALLY KENT GORDON

(ABOVE) GEORGE WESLEY BELLOWS, *BEATING OUT TO SEA*, 1913, OIL ON PANEL, 14 $^5/_8$ X 18 $^7/_8$ IN. COLLECTION OF THE FARNSWORTH ART MUSEUM, MUSEUM PURCHASE, 1945

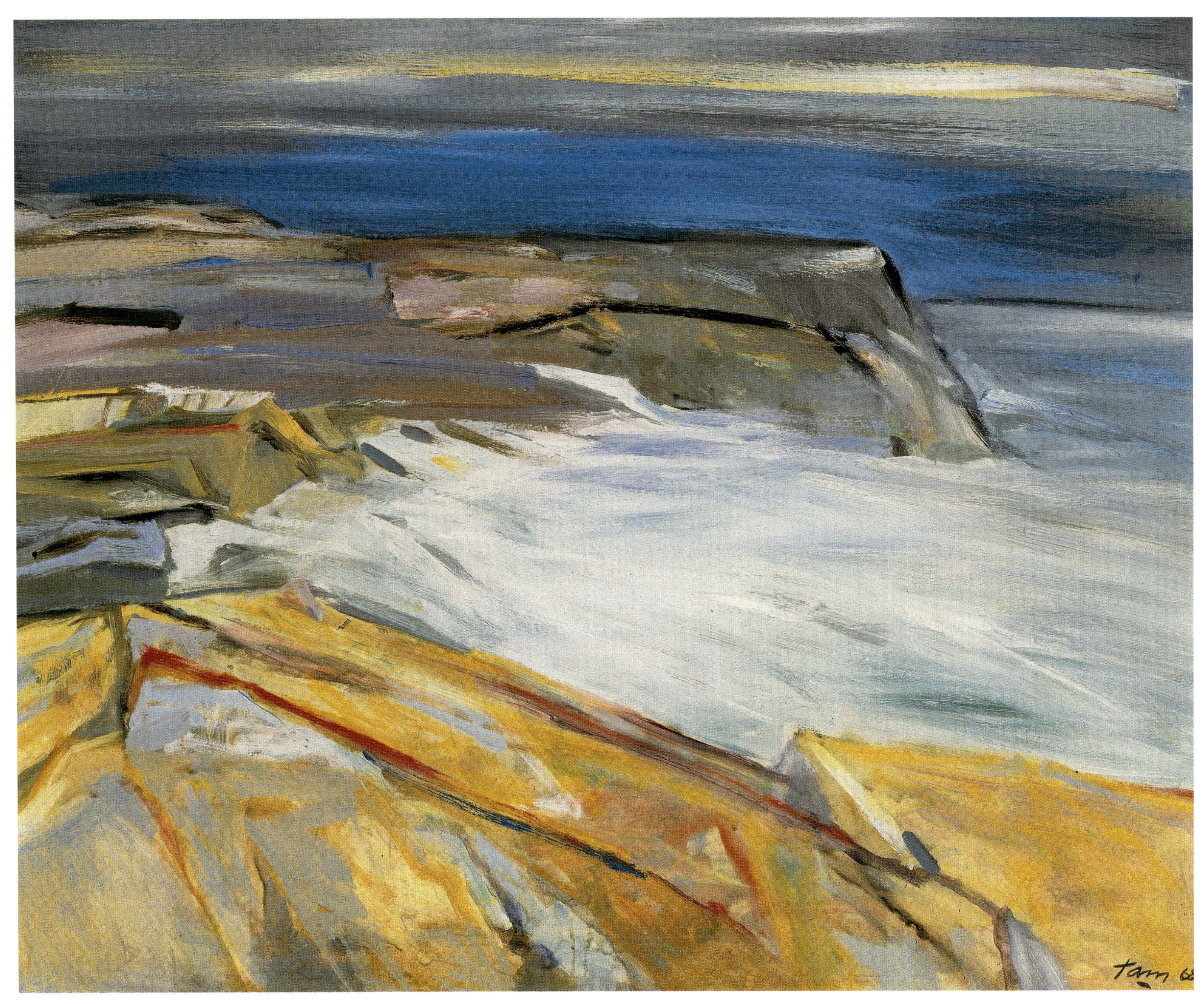

Reuben Tam, *Monhegan Headland*, 1968, oil on academy board, 20 1/8 x 24 in.
collection of the Farnsworth Art Museum, gift of Mr. James T. Wallis, 1972

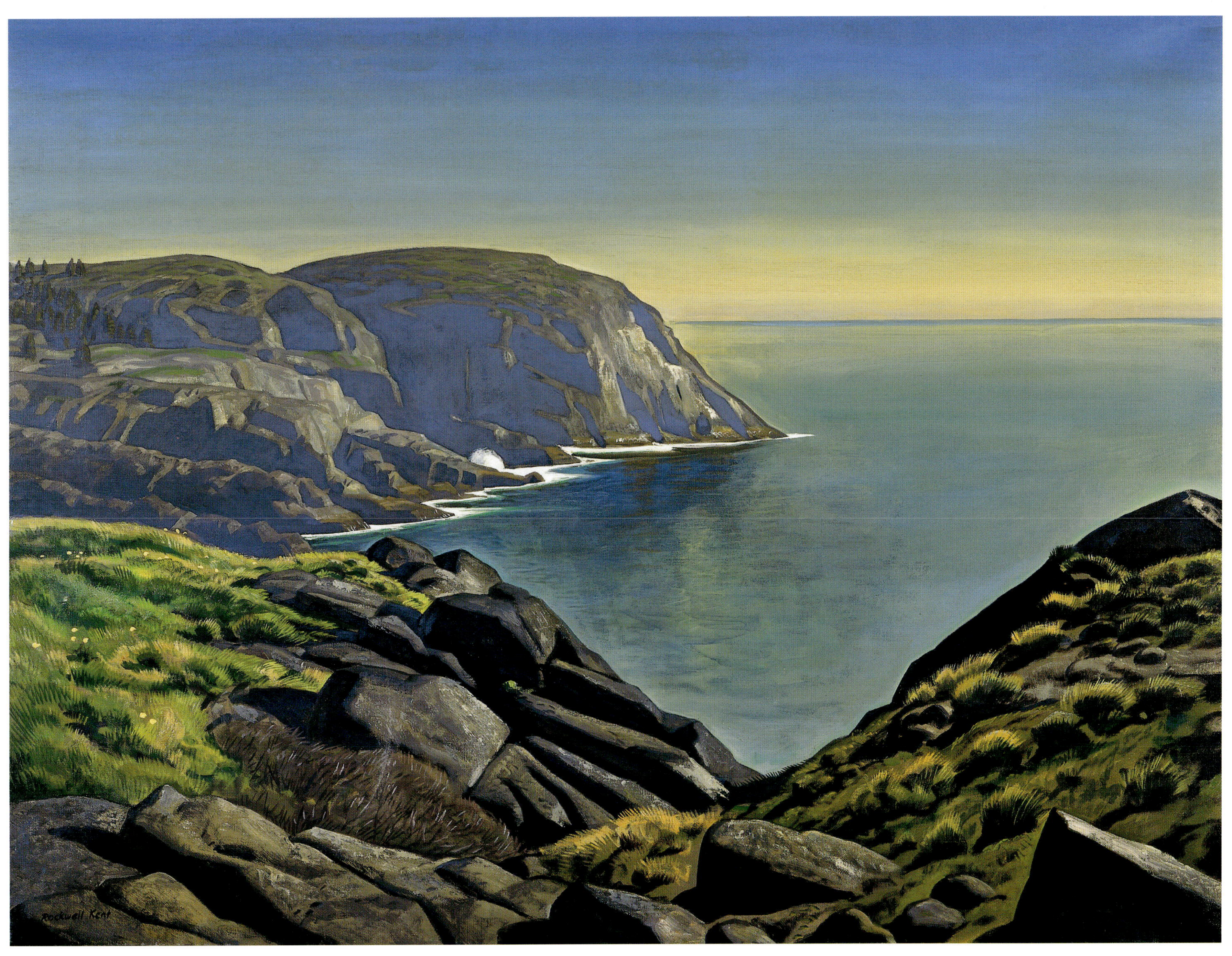

Rockwell Kent, *Maine Headland: Morning*, 1955, oil on canvas, 34 x 44 in., Armenia Museum, Yerevan, Armenia
by permission of Plattsburg State Art Museum, Plattsburg College Foundation, Rockwell Kent Gallery and Collection, Bequest of Sally Kent Gordon

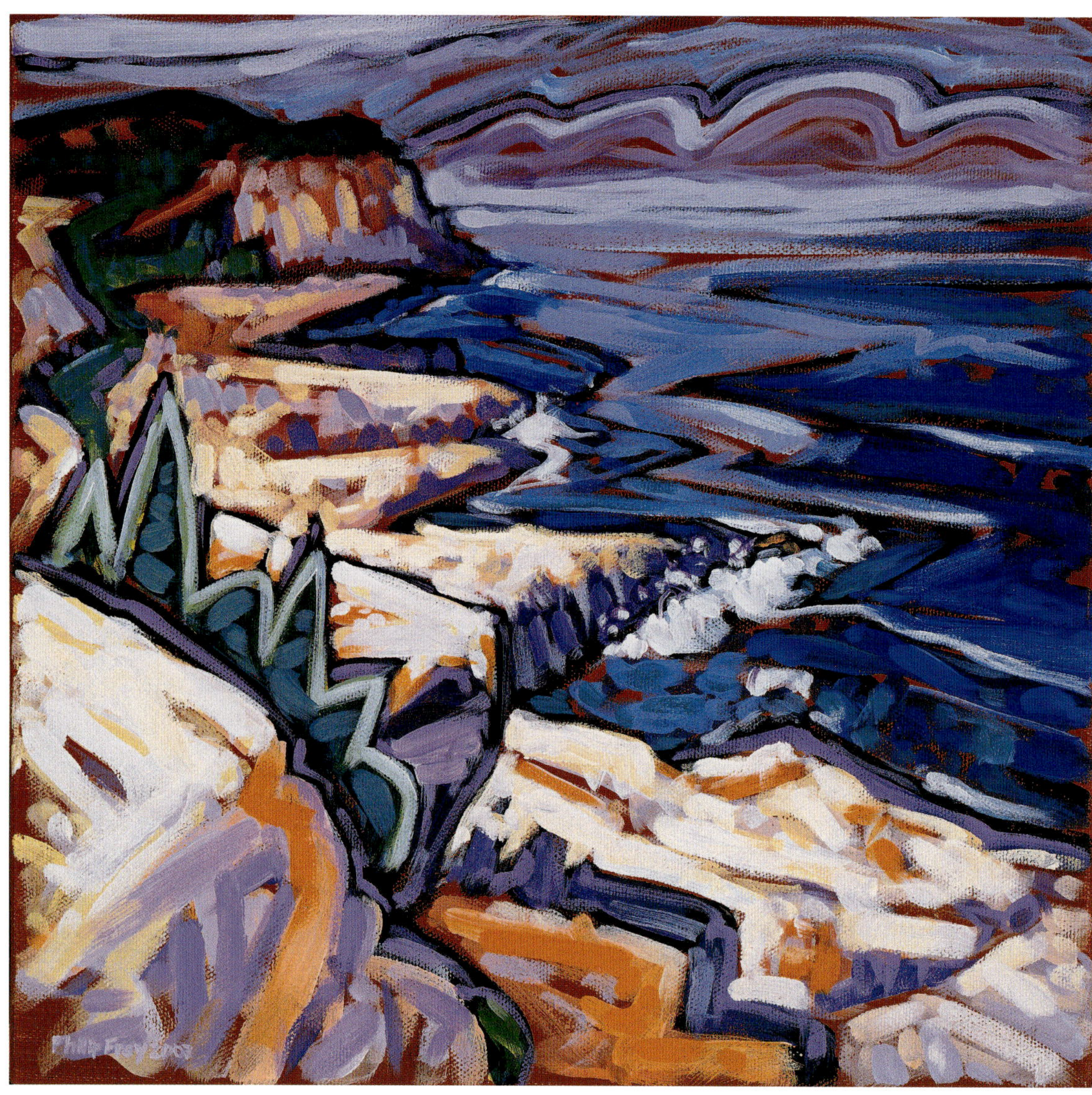

dynamic style and high-pitched palette derive from a keen admiration for the fauvists, those revolutionary French painters who liberated representation in the early years of the twentieth century. Careening brushstrokes turn the island cliffs and their surroundings into a frenzied landscape.

John LeBlanc (b. 1955) first visited Monhegan in 1999, staying at the Eider Duck House with a group of fellow Bangor-area artists. LeBlanc discovered a community and a context for his art that led him to become a full-time painter. His island canvases, developed from pastel sketches, offer a vision of an enchanted Maine isle. LeBlanc returns to Monhegan every year, each time finding something new on which to focus his attention.

   PHILIP FREY, *THE HEADLANDS—MONHEGAN*, 2003, ACRYLIC ON CANVAS, 12 X 12 IN., COLLECTION OF BELINDA AND PETER AICHER. PHOTO BY JAY YORK

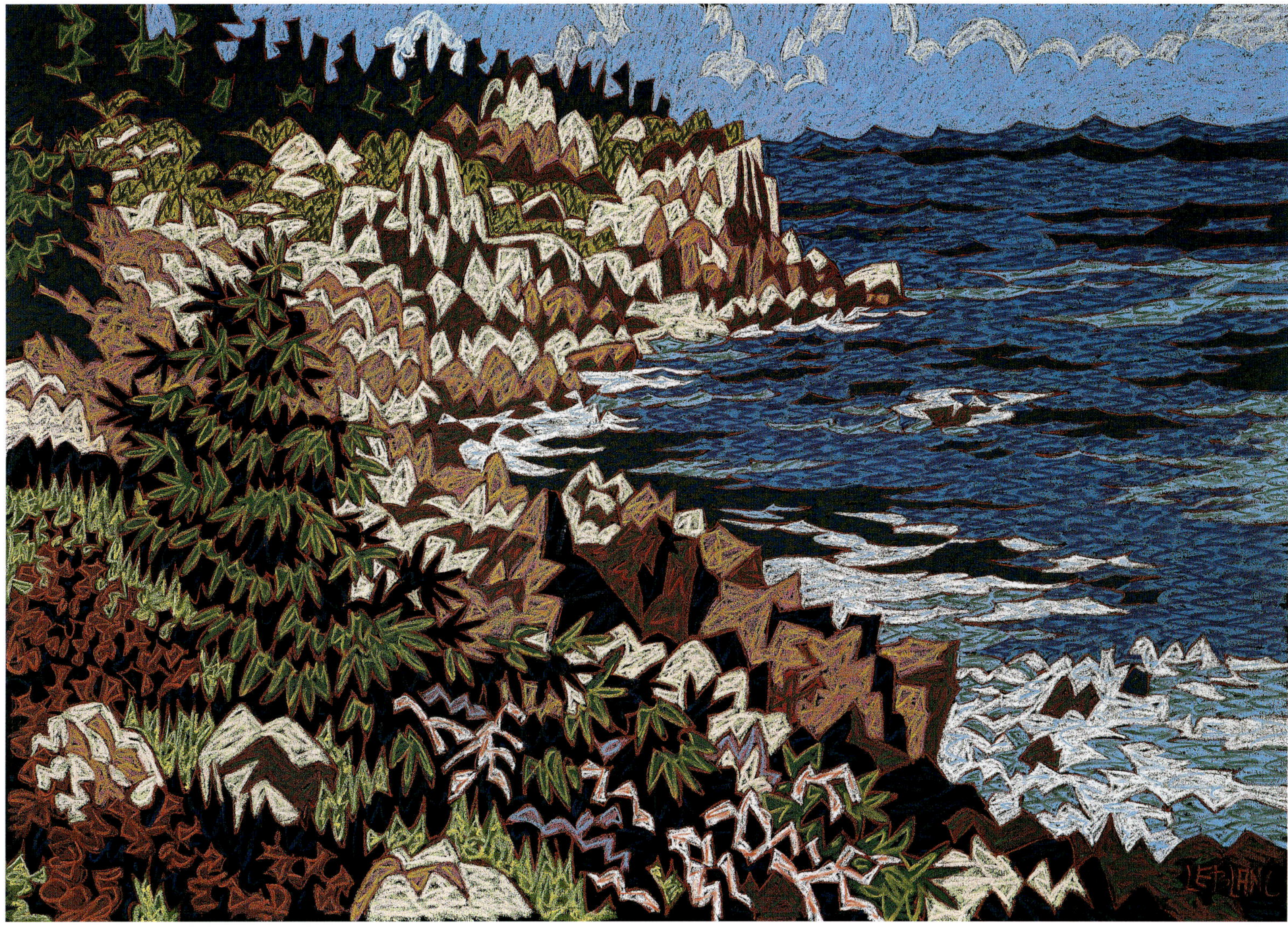

Notes

33. "Millions of years in the making, the headlands are made up of gabbro, a dark rock similar to granite that is commonly found deep in the earth rather than on the surface. These headlands are testament to the scraping glaciers and lashing ocean that molded Monhegan Island, lopping off the top and beating down its sides." Amy Sutherland, "Maine's Mecca," *Maine Sunday Telegram*, 30 August 1998.

34. Cited in Carol M. Osborne, "William Trost Richards Drawings from Stanford," *Drawing*, March–April 1993, 123.

35. Jessica Nicoll, *The Allure of the Maine Coast: Robert Henri and His Circle, 1905–1918*, exhibition catalogue, Portland Museum of Art, 1995, 8.

36. Ibid., 22.

37. Kent, *It's Me O Lord*, 191.

38. Martica Sawin, "Reuben Tam: Island Paintings." *Arts Magazine*, December 1975, 93.

39. Lee Nordness, ed., *Art USA Now*, vol. 2 (New York: Viking Press, 1963), 309. "If it weren't for the statement of a horizon in most of Tam's paintings," art historian James Carpenter once observed, "one would have difficulty in sensing surface and solids at all, so embracing is the feeling of light." *Landscape in Maine 1820–1970: A Sesquicentennial Exhibition*, exhibition catalogue, Colby College Museum of Art, 1970, 118.

40. Roberta Hershenson, "Working with Brush Strokes of Light," *New York Times*, 6 April 2003.

JOHN LEBLANC, *VIEW OF WHITEHEAD, MONHEGAN*, 2003, PASTEL, 21 X 29 IN., COURTESY OF CLARK HOUSE GALLERY, BANGOR, MAINE

To him who loves the rocks, and the sea-weed, and the bits of ocean life among them, and the breaking waves with their rushing foam and tossing spray, the shore line of this outpost of the main is a continual marvel. In the whole circuit of the coast there are scarcely two places that are similar. The minerals range from the fine sand at the landing, up through wonderfully varied pebbles and gigantic boulders, to the great shapeless masses of rock forming the headlands at the north.

—A. T. Pettingill, "Monhegan, Historical and Picturesque," 1898

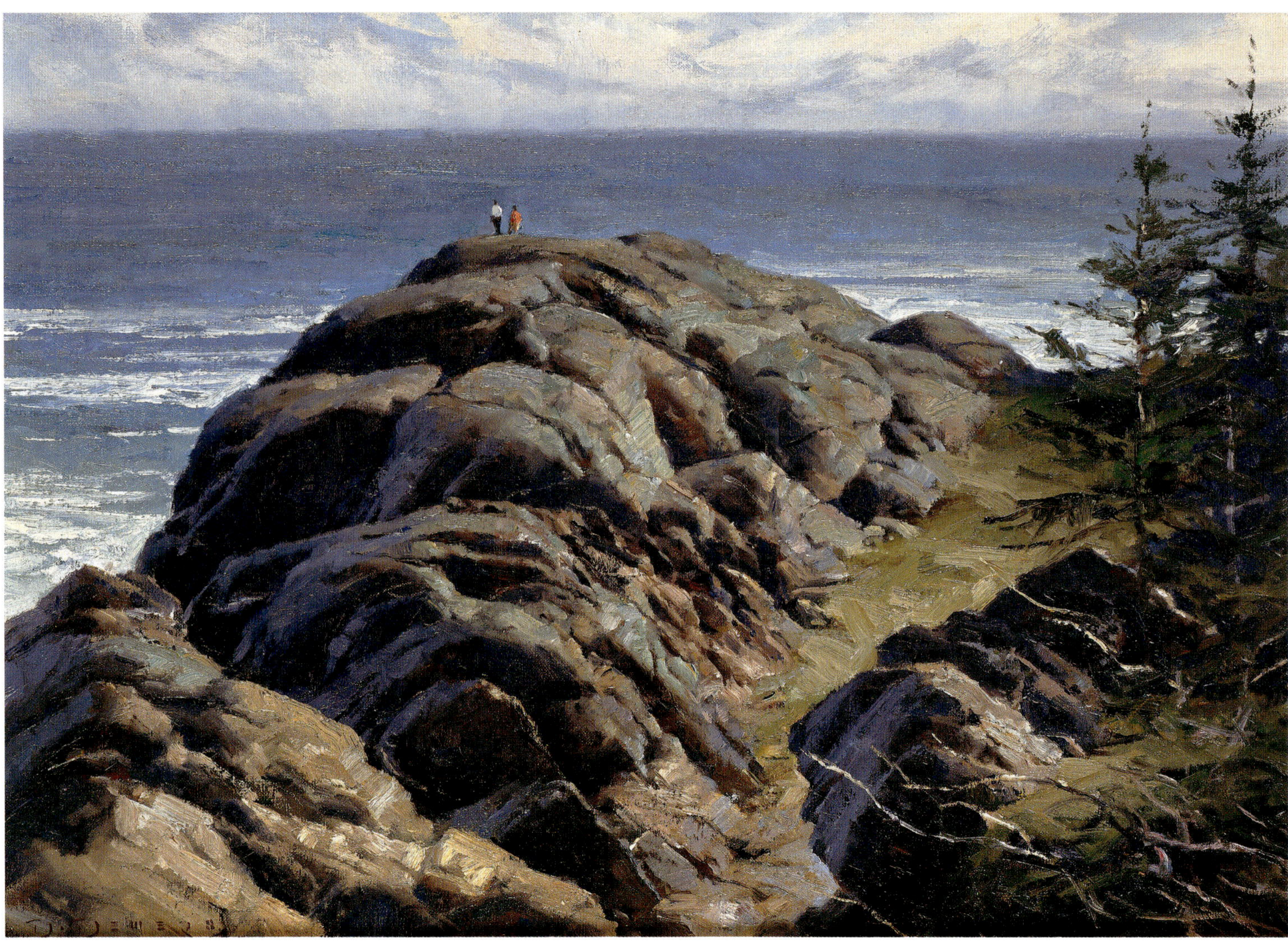

 Donald Demers, *Gull Rock*, 2001, oil on canvas, 12 x 16 in., collection of Remak Ramsay

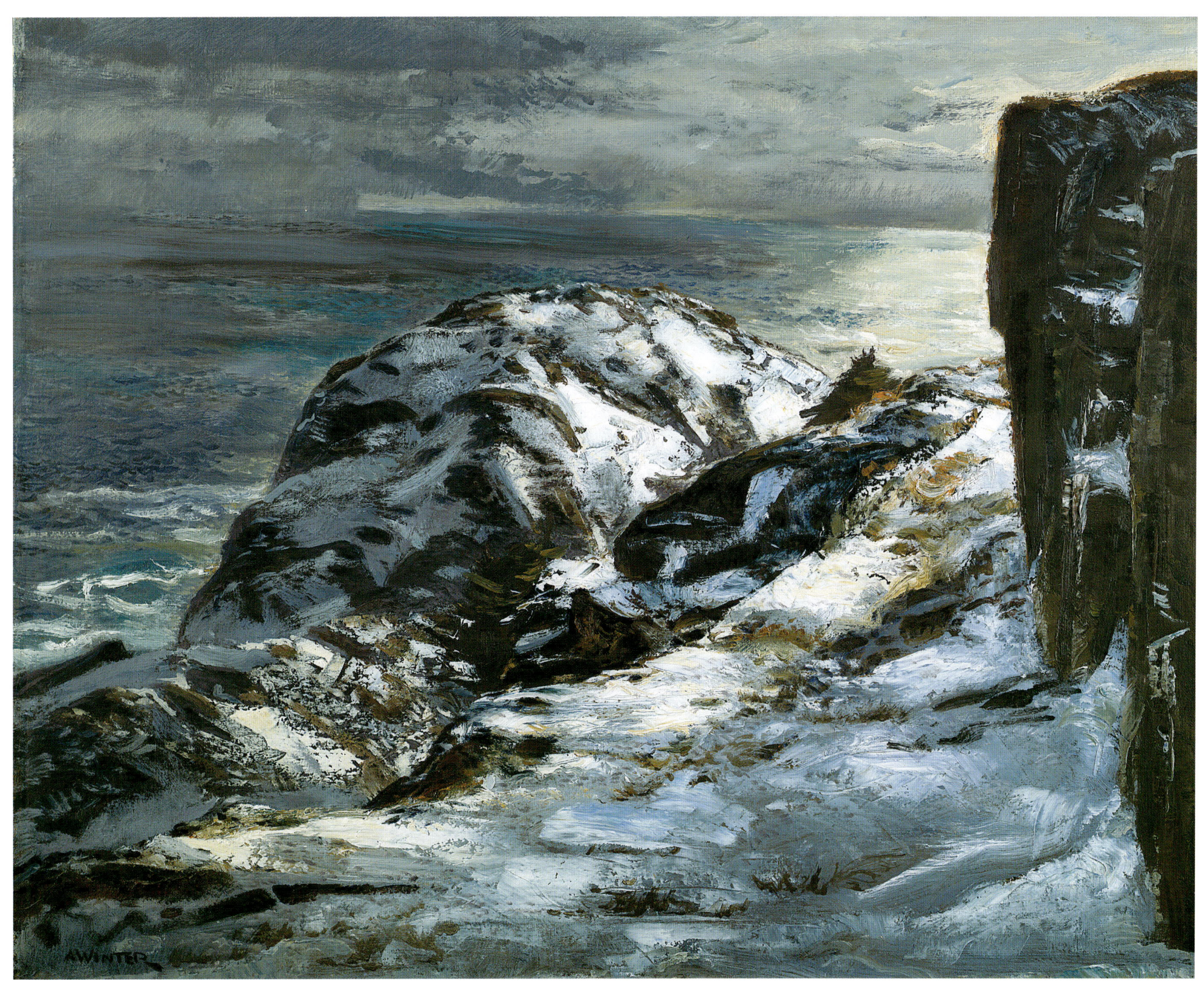

Andrew Winter, *Gull Rock, Blackhead in Winter, Monhegan Island, Maine*, n.d., oil on canvas, 25 x 30 in. courtesy of Spanierman Gallery, LLC, New York

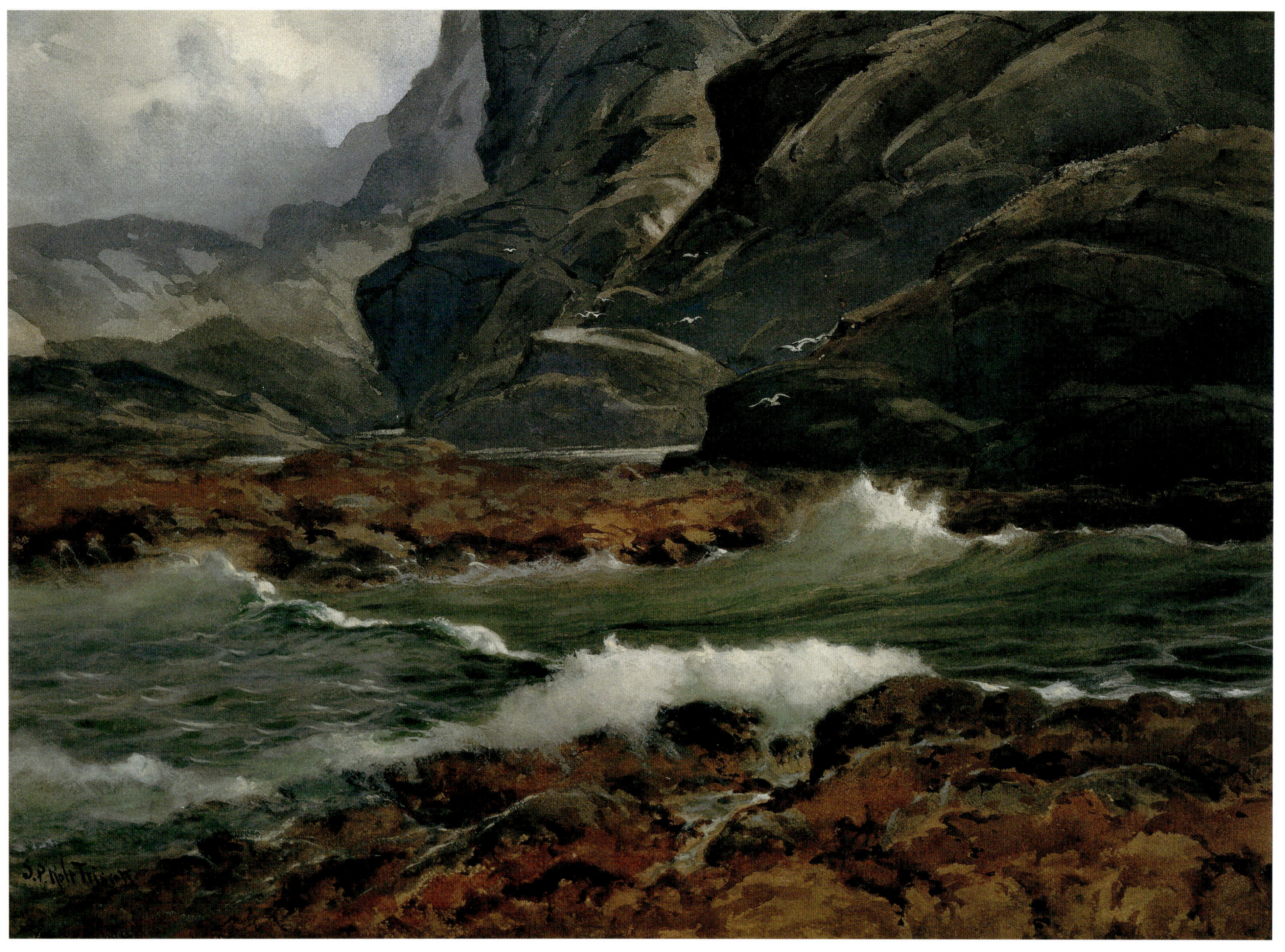

 S. P. ROLT TRISCOTT, *MAINE COAST*, N.D., WATERCOLOR ON PAPER, 19 X 25 1/2 IN., COLLECTION OF DOROTHY MALONE

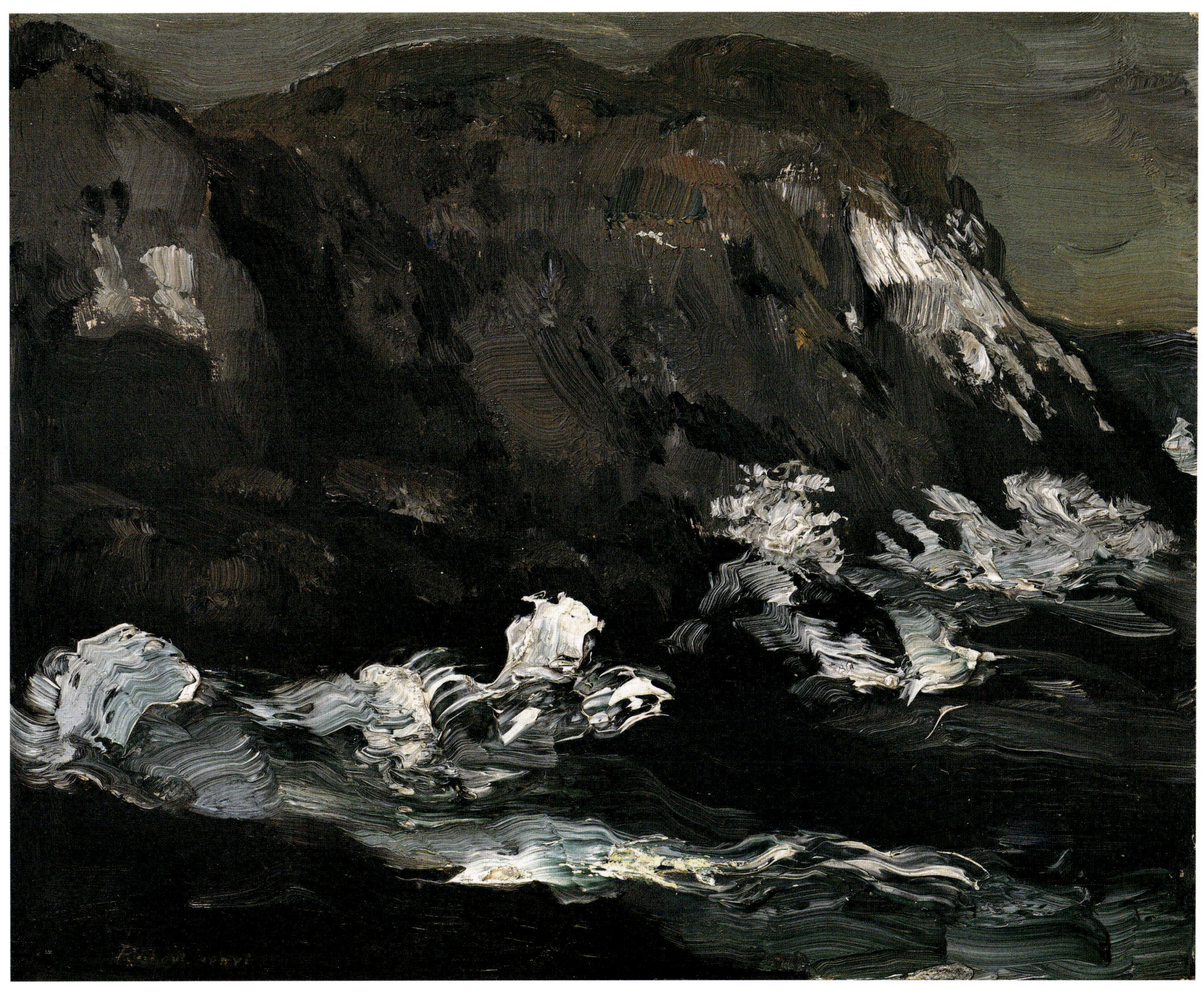

Robert Henri, *Monhegan Island*, 1903, oil on panel, 8 x 10 in., collection of the Farnsworth Art Museum, Museum purchase, 1991

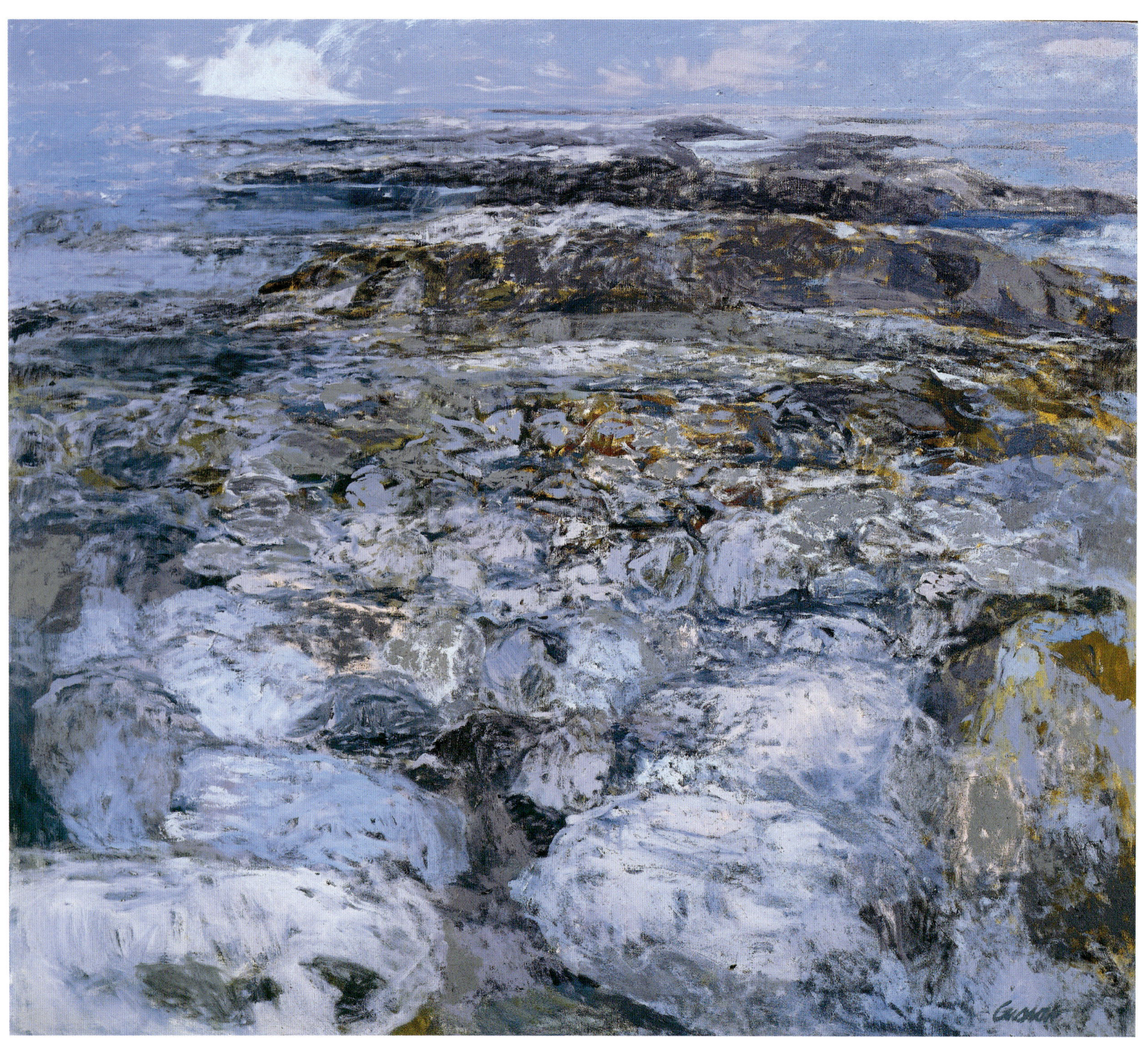

ALAN GUSSOW, *BEACH BOULDERS AND SEAL LEDGES*, 1969, OIL ON CANVAS, 55 X 60 IN.,
PORTLAND MUSEUM OF ART, MAINE, MUSEUM PURCHASE 1970.49

Island Edges

*I am attracted to the island's edges, defined by those great
expanses of changing sea and sky and light. I love the aftermath
of storms with great masses of green and white water piling up
layer upon layer onto rocky shores, the edges of ocean and island
meeting and overlapping in continuous dialogue.*

—Elena Jahn, "50 Years: Growing Up an Artist on Monhegan"

Monhegan is defined by its edges, its rugged periphery of
rocks, its tidal and surf zones (often one and the same),
its crevices, coves and outcroppings. Situated in the very trough of
the sea, the island lies largely unprotected, its circumference never
completely free of the ocean's influence. Waves wash against its
sides, swell and swirl over and around boulders, pound and lash
the steadfast littoral. Thanks to its setting, the island holds a place
of prominence in the history of American marine painting.

At any given moment, the island and the ocean are confronting
each other, creating that "continuous dialogue" described by Elena
Jahn (b. 1938). Jahn began her life as a painter on Monhegan at
age eleven, so she has been privy to that conversation between
sea and stone for more than fifty years. She studied with Sarah
MacPherson, and Reuben Taman was an important artistic men-
tor. Like the latter, she has been attracted to the commingling of
elements that lends itself to semi-abstract canvases *(p. 94)*.

When Alan Gussow (1931–1997) arrived on Monhegan in 1949,
he was enamored of "picturesque" island motifs: "lobster pots, fishermen's houses smelling of herring bait in big, brine-filled barrels,
and activities of the harbor." Eventually, his interests turned to
more elemental subject matter. "Now the place the tides own fascinates me," he wrote in the prologue to *A Sense of Place: The Artist
and the American Landscape*.[41] Sea wrack offered a rich and complex
tapestry to which the artist could respond in different mediums.

Weed-covered rocks fill in the foreground of a sunset view by
Peter K. Nelson (b. 1958), painted on a July afternoon *(p. 93)*. "One
can return to this same spot below the Gussow cottage and experience an infinite number of atmospheric and lighting conditions,"
Nelson states with wonder. The Arizona-based painter first stepped
foot on Monhegan in 1994 and has returned every year, extending

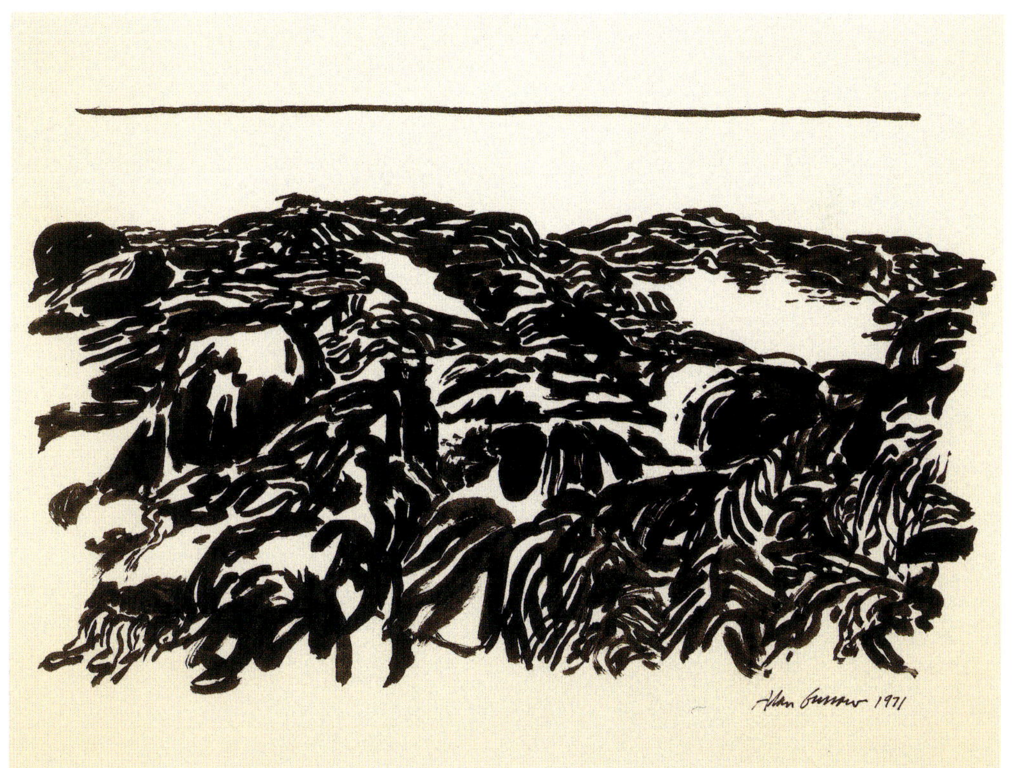

Alan Gussow, *Tidal Pool, High Tide*, 1971
ink on paper, 16 x 20 1/5 in., collection of John M. Day

An Island in the Sea

I want to go away—some place where sea
and land embrace, the sky a hundred miles
wide, horizons blue with hills, where no
one from this flat and corn-fed state can find
us. For a week, or two—or three—enough
to recreate, rejuvenate, to breathe

the salted air, and walk the beach—if we
could go there, love, for just a little while,
an island in the sea, if we could go
and find a tiny cottage, buy some wine
and cheese and bread, pretend we own the rough
and tumbled shore, imagine never leaving.

Come away! This year I need it more
than ever I have needed it before.

—LAWRENCE E. WILSON

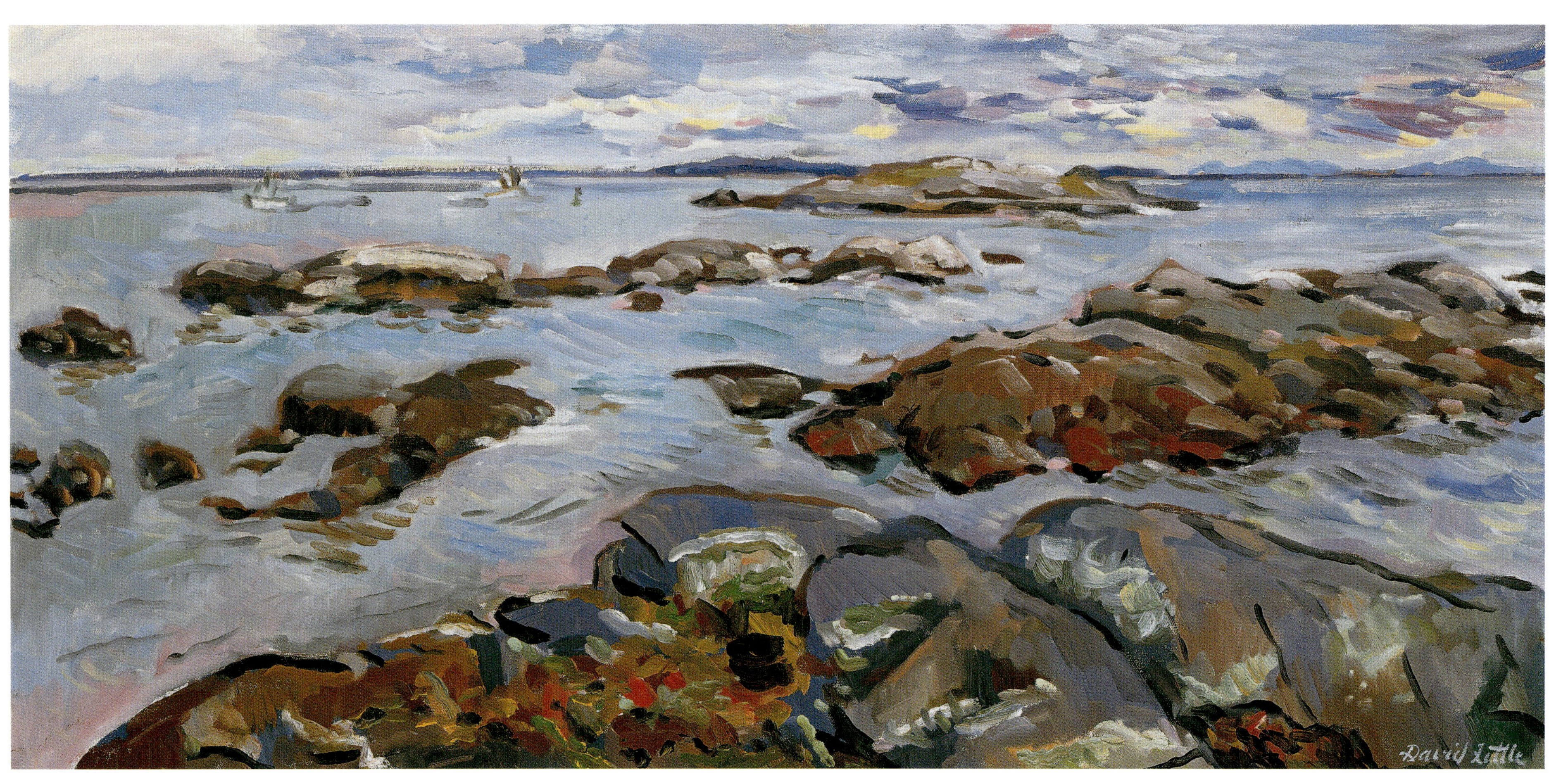

   DAVID LITTLE, *SEAL LEDGES (MONHEGAN ISLAND)*, 1998, OIL ON CANVAS, 18 x 36 IN., COLLECTION OF THE ARTIST

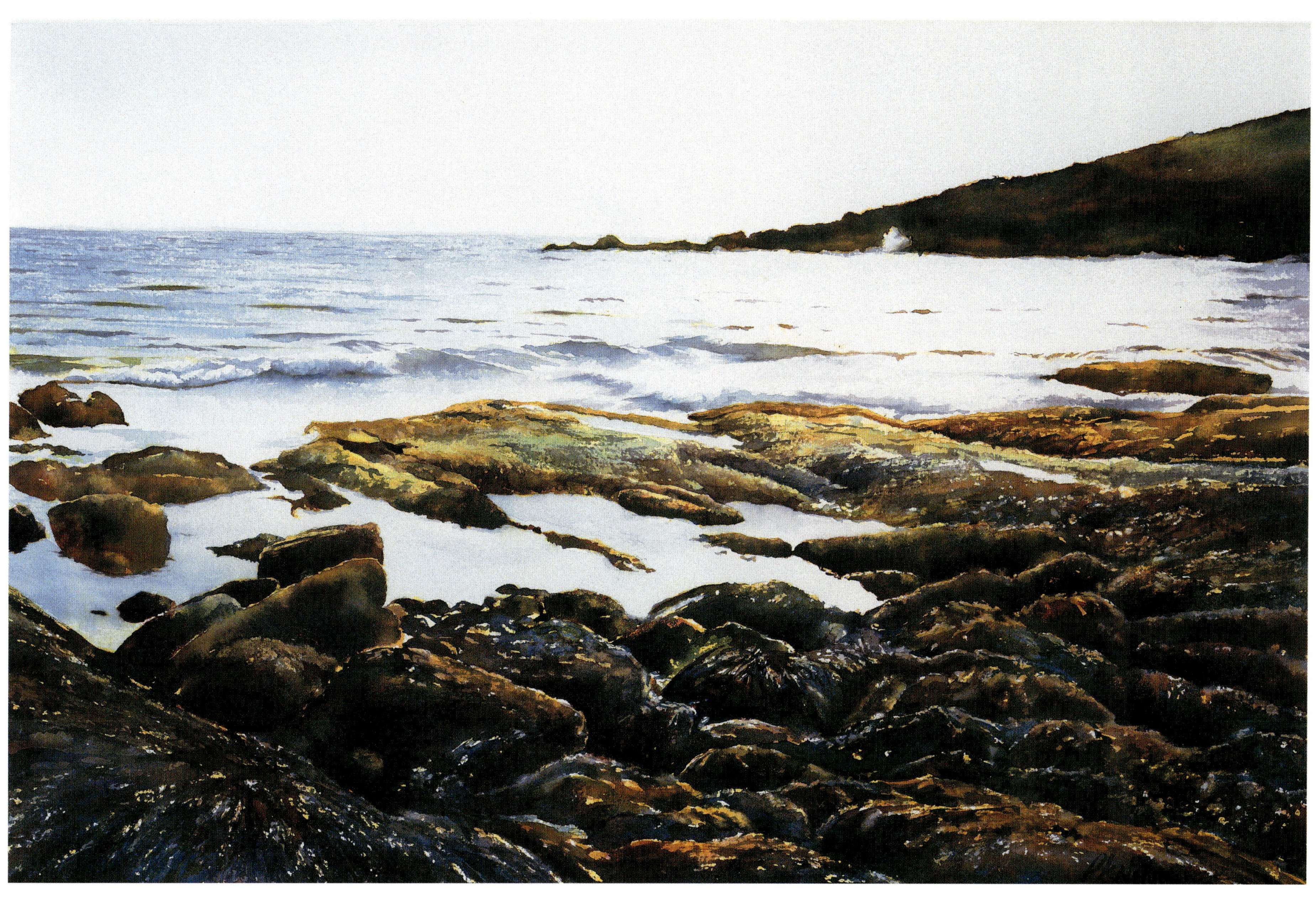

Peter K. Nelson, *Low Tide, Sunset, Monhegan Harbor*, 2002, watercolor on paper, 14 1/2 x 22 1/2 in., collection of Remak Ramsay

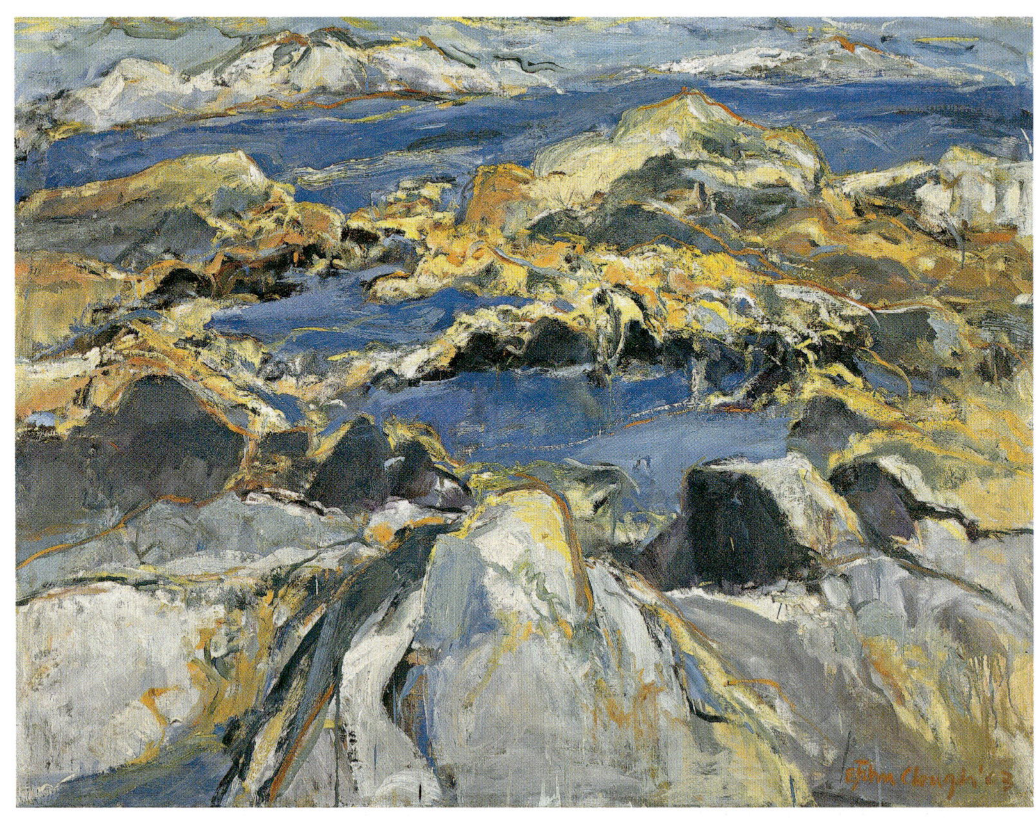

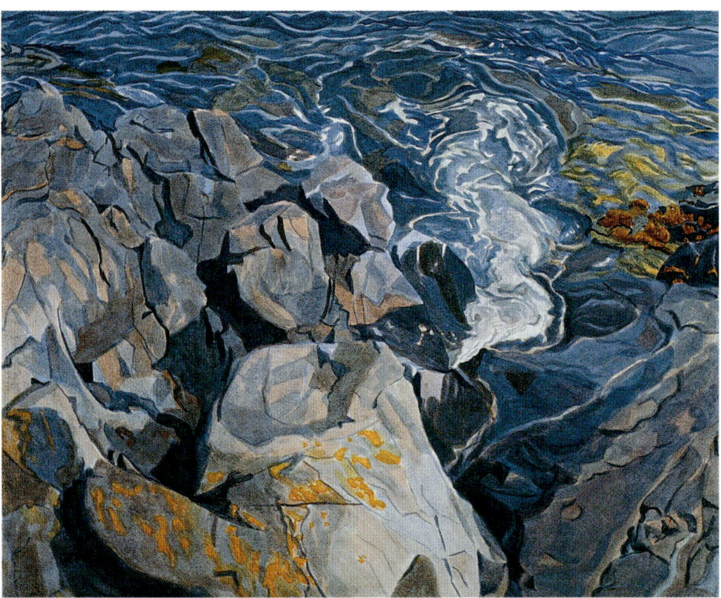

(ABOVE) ELENA JAHN, *TIDAL POOLS*, 1963, OIL ON CANVAS, 46 X 59 IN.
COLLECTION OF JOHN M. DAY
COURTESY OF THE BATES COLLEGE MUSEUM OF ART. PHOTO BY MELVILLE MCLEAN

(RIGHT) SUSAN SHATTER, *SWIRLING WATER*, 1982, WATERCOLOR ON PAPER, 44 X 54 IN.
COLLECTION OF THE FMC CORPORATION

his stay each time. "I doubt I will ever tire of Monhegan's beauty," he says.

David Little (b. 1952) would second that statement. Since spending five weeks on the island as a Carina House artist in residence in 1999, he has traveled back to Monhegan from his home in Portland, Maine, on numerous occasions, unable and unwilling to shake its hold on his eye and heart. Little relishes the freedom he has discovered "to find a new voice" on the island. In his painting *Seal Ledges (Monhegan Island)*, named for the pinnipeds that come there to sun themselves, he captures the half-submerged rocks on a blustery fall day *(p. 92)*.

Abraham J. Bogdanove recognized the special attraction artists feel toward Monhegan's craggy formations. "I have painted the Gaspe, the cliffs of Cornwall, the Riviera," he once stated, "but there's a magnetic force in these rocks here *(p. 101)*, I believe, which brings us back again and again."[42] He was a master at limning those shadowy crevices and gullies that form much of the island's fringe.

"This island is endless in its wonderful variety," George Bellows wrote to his wife, Emma, in 1911. "It's possessed of enough beauty to supply a continent." The artist was especially drawn to Monhegan's extremities, the tide pools and the rocky nooks and basins *(pp. 98–99)* where the sea surged and shattered. "I tramped all over the ocean rocks today," he wrote in another letter to his wife, "& my outfit is easily portable and the basket ball shoes clutch the cliffs like a fly's feet."[43]

A member of Robert Henri's circle and a friend of Bellows, Leon Kroll (1884–1974) visited Monhegan in the 1910s. To paint his *Sunlit Sea*, he appears to have situated himself at the water's edge *(p. 100)*. The backwash of waves spreads white foam among the dark rocks. Kroll's island paintings display less of the classicism found in much of his work—as if Monhegan's primal milieu freed him from a more orderly compositional manner.

In an interview in 1918, Edward Hopper (1882–1967) told a reporter, "Maine is so beautiful and the weather is so fine in the summer—that's why I come up here to rest and to paint a little too."[44] In the years 1916–1919, Hopper visited Monhegan on several occasions, another of Henri's pupils encouraged by the master to make the trip. Working on site, he created oil sketches, many of them studies of the rocky shoreline *(pp. 96–97)*. He favored wood panels rarely larger than 12 by 16 inches.

In his biography of Frederick Judd Waugh (1861–1940), George Havens described the routine of a plein air painter on Monhegan. "He has to go on foot, laden down with easel, paintbox, canvases, an extra coat perhaps for additional warmth, and certainly a sustaining lunch for a long day's work outdoors." Waugh specialized in paintings of surf, preferring a close-up viewpoint *(p. 104)*. "To paint [the sea] convincingly," the painter once wrote, "means long, careful observation of its many phases and anatomy, for the sea has anatomy."[45]

A visitor to Maine since the late forties, Frank Mason (b. 1921) has studied the sea and the shape of waves, his technique and vision influenced by a long-standing passion for the old masters. In *Monhegan Harbor*, he focuses on a sentinel rock besieged by storm-tossed waves.

In her book *The Edge of the Sea*, Rachel Carson reported with wonder how spray from breaking waves in a violent storm can be thrown "over the crest of White Head, about 100 feet above the sea."[46] In a brush-and-ink study *(p. 102)* made on a trip to Monhegan in 2001, Arnold Skolnick (b. 1937) deftly renders seawater flung onto the rocks along the shore by Lobster Cove.

Lamar Dodd (1909–1996) first traveled to Monhegan in 1950 under a Carnegie Grant-in-Aid for research in painting and subsequently returned on numerous occasions. "Standing on the rock-bound cliffs of Monhegan Island, off the coast of Maine," he once recounted, "I watched the pounding surf and the sprays of water, and as I listened to the roar of the mighty ocean, certain musical themes were produced."[47] For his painting of the raging battle between sea and shore, *Heaven, Hell and Wagner (p. 103)*, Dodd invoked the dramatic music of German composer Richard Wagner.

Quieter music comes to mind when viewing a stunning watercolor study of water and rock by Susan Shatter (b. 1943). Devoid of horizon, her cliff-side perspective seems to draw us down past rugged outcroppings to mesmerizing eddies below *(p. 94)*. By contrast, a watercolor rendering of Boar's Head by Carol Raybin (b. 1941) directs the eye skyward, the "snout" of the jagged prominence pointed toward the clouds *(p. 106)*.

The Boar's Head is one of a number of distinctive rock formations found on the island. Another is the aptly named Pulpit Rock,

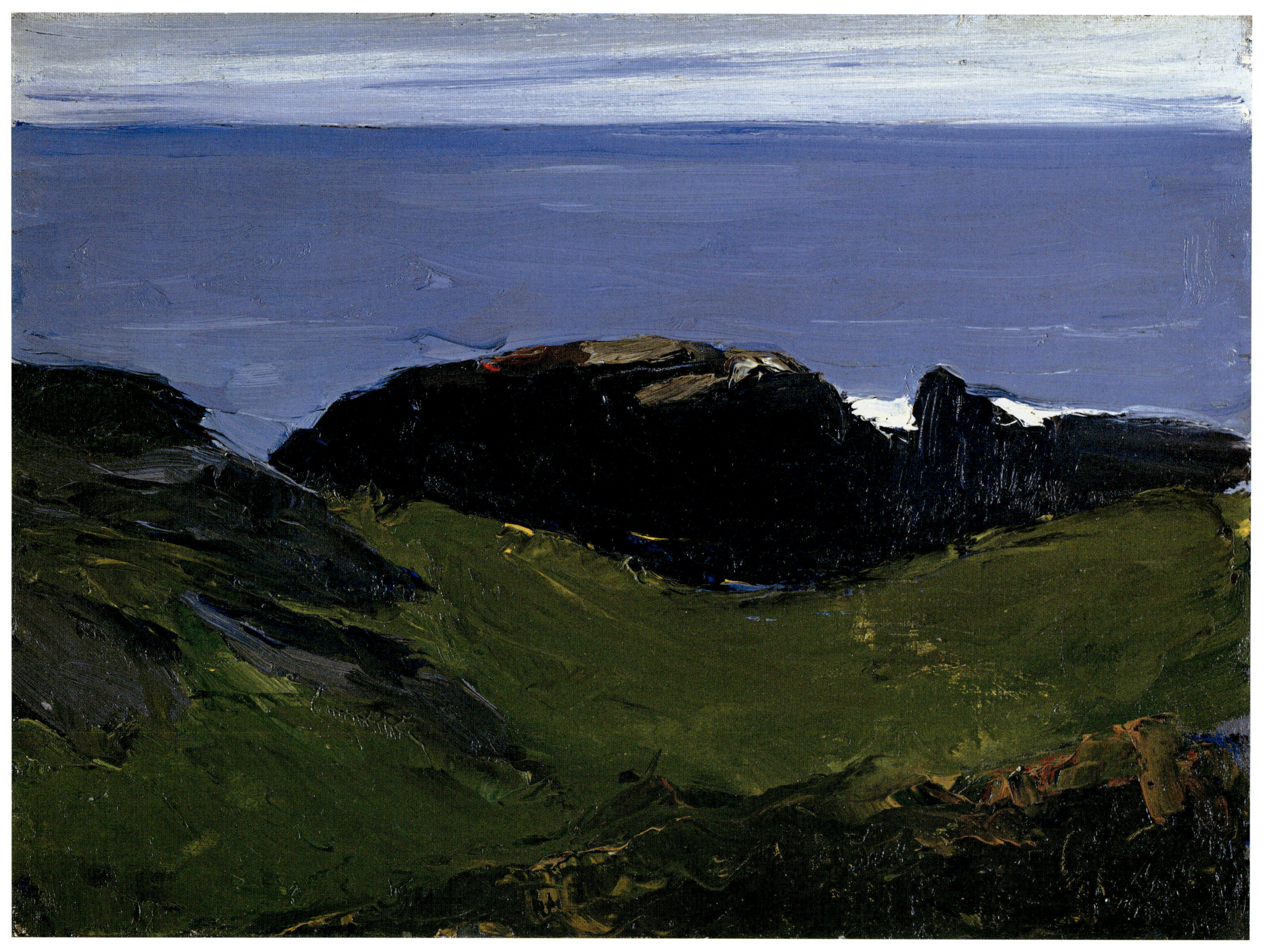

EDWARD HOPPER, *SEA AND SHORE*, 1916–1919, OIL ON BOARD ON CANVAS, 9 9/16 X 12 7/8 IN.
WHITNEY MUSEUM OF AMERICAN ART, NEW YORK, JOSEPHINE N. HOPPER BEQUEST. 70.1673

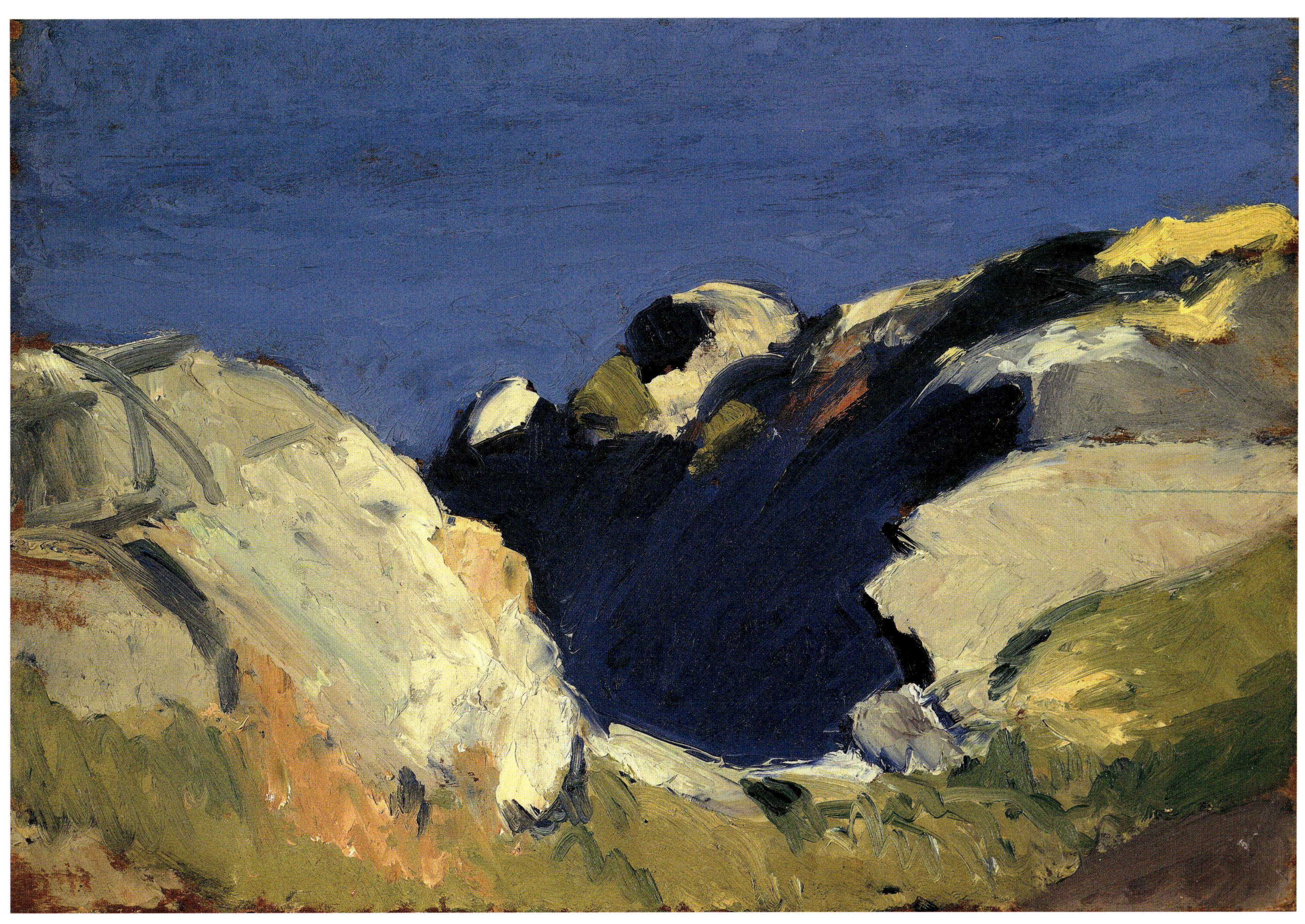

Edward Hopper, *Rocks and Sea,* 1916–1919, oil on wood, 10 11/16 x 15 in.
Whitney Museum of American Art, New York, Josephine N. Hopper, bequest. 70.1292

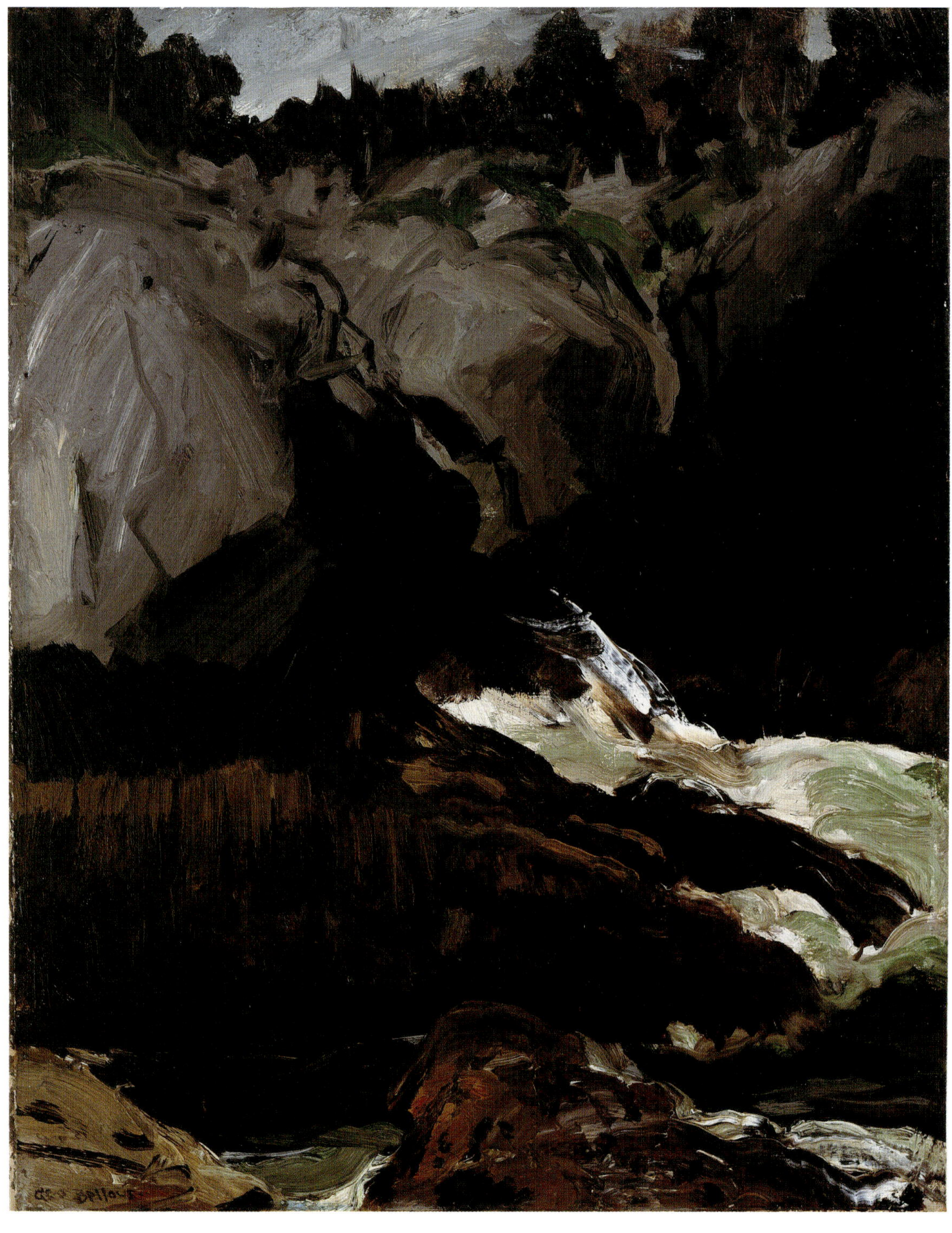
George Wesley Bellows, *Gorge and Sea*, 1911, oil on canvas, 34 x 26 in.
The Mint Museums, Charlotte, North Carolina
Gift of the Mint Museum Auxiliary. 1983.35

Like the sea itself, the shore fascinates us who return to it, the place of our dim ancestral beginnings. In the recurrent rhythms of tides and surf and in the varied life of the tide lines there is the obvious attraction of movement and change and beauty. There is also, I am convinced, a deeper fascination born of inner meanings and significance.

—Rachel Carson, *The Edge of the Sea*

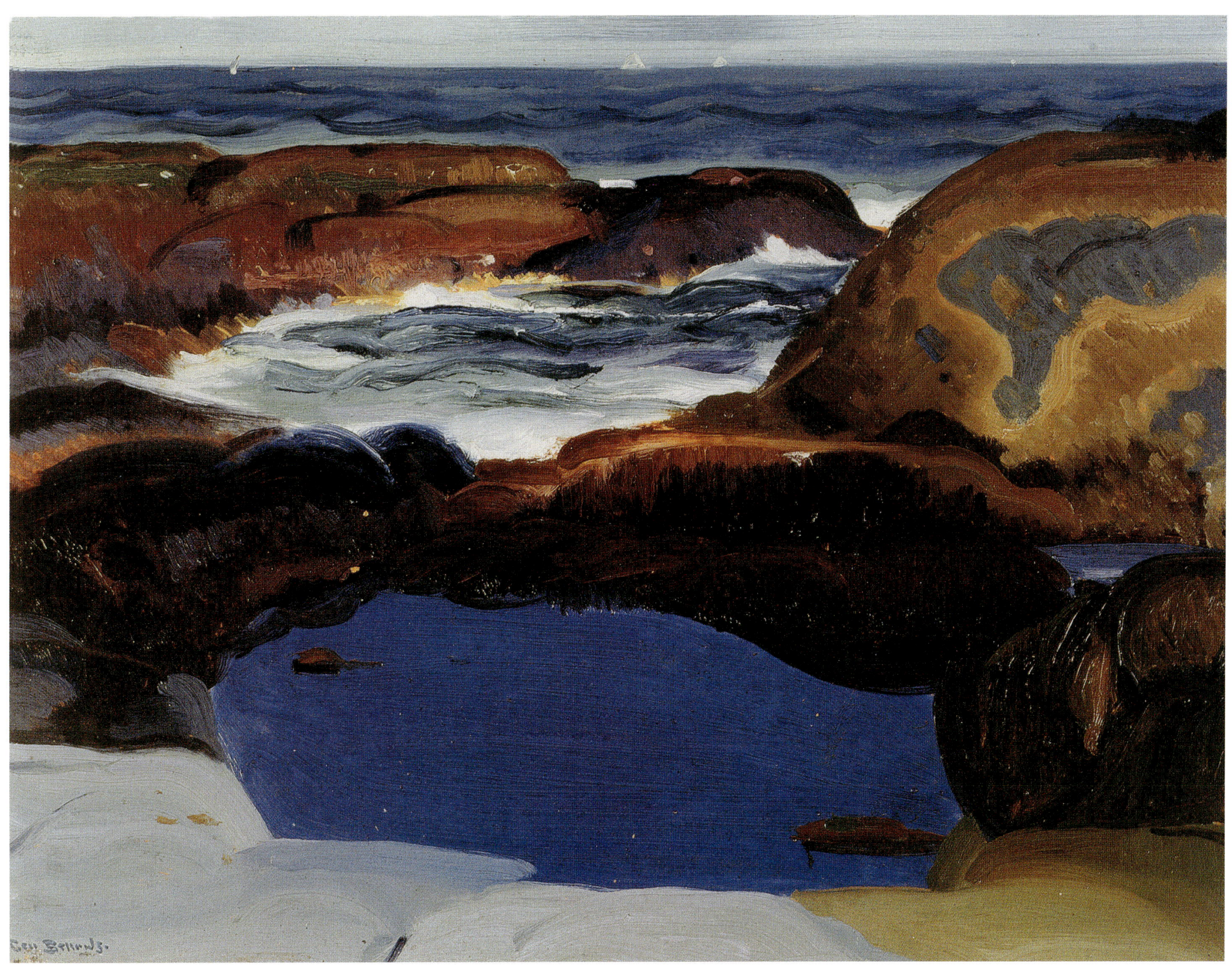

GEORGE WESLEY BELLOWS, *THE BLUE POOL*, 1913, OIL ON PANEL, 15 x 19 1/2 IN.
PRIVATE COLLECTION. PHOTO COURTESY OF OWEN GALLERY, NEW YORK

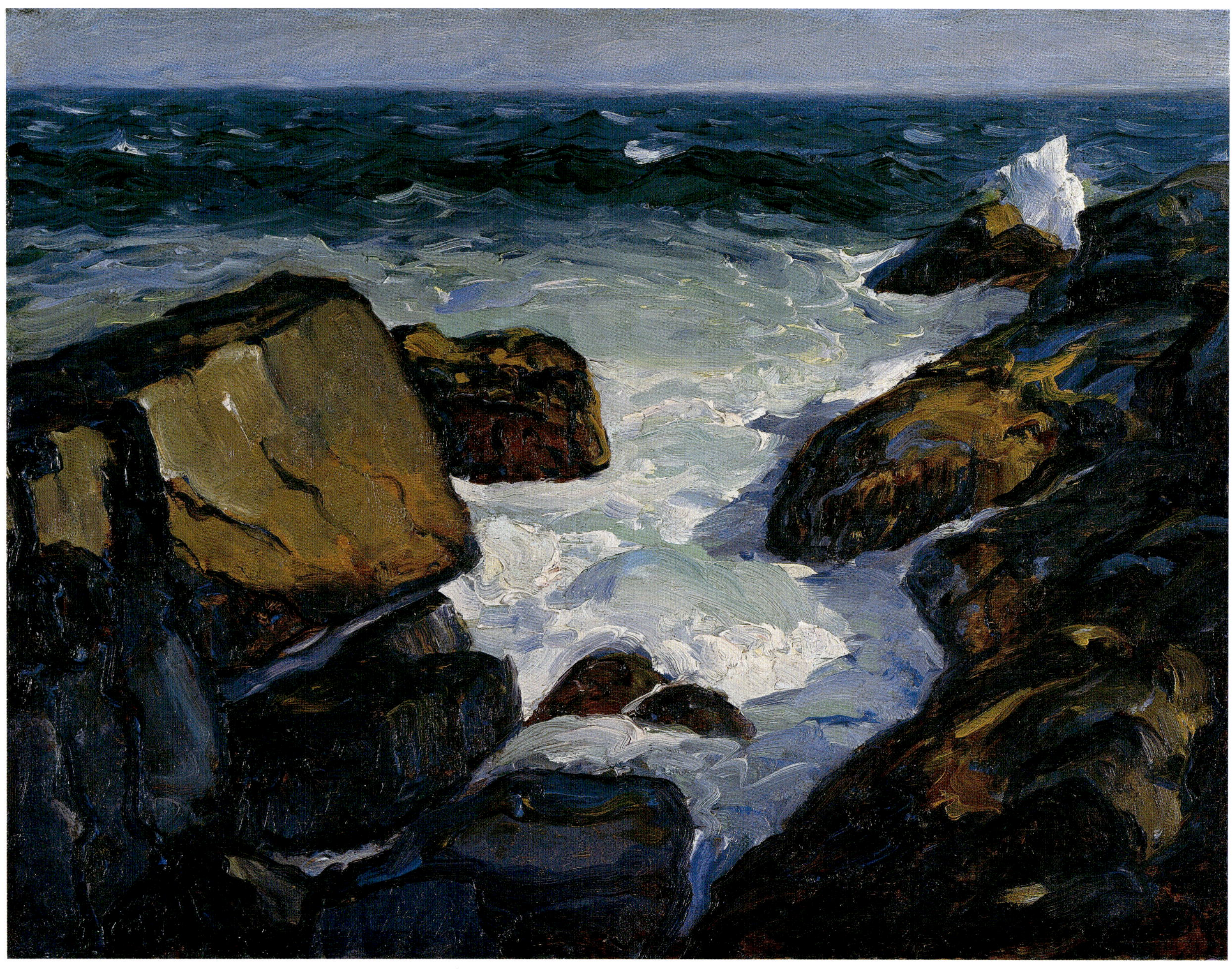

    LEON KROLL, *SUNLIT SEA*, 1913, OIL ON PANEL, 15 X 19 IN., COLLECTION OF MONHEGAN MUSEUM, GIFT OF REMAK RAMSAY

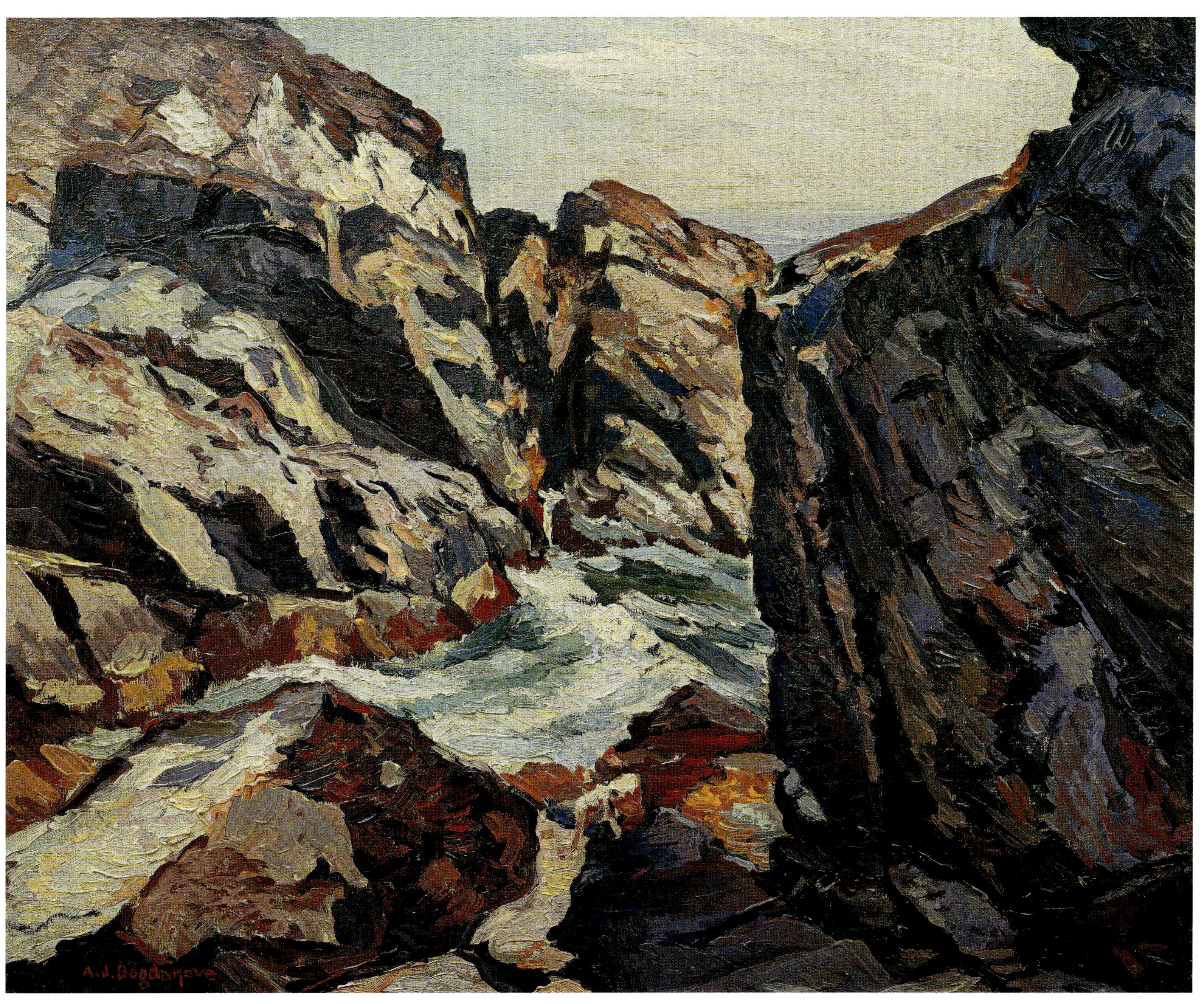

Abraham J. Bogdanove, *The Gully, Monhegan Island, Maine*, c. 1930–1940, oil on canvas, 25 x 30 in. courtesy Spanierman Gallery, LLC, New York

a natural platform by the sea from which one might imagine some mad preacher haranguing the elements. Joseph McGurl (b. 1958) and David Vickery painted this glacier-carved lectern from different angles *(pp. 108, 109)*, attracted to its sculpted shape and dramatic setting.

A resident of Cape Cod, McGurl paints along the New England coast, going from place to place aboard his floating studio, a cruiser aptly named *Atelier*. This approach by sea harks back to the arrival of the first artist known to have paid a visit to the island, Aaron Draper Shattuck (1832–1928), sailing aboard the U.S. schooner *Vigilant*. "Monhegan Island has some wonderful things about it, lots of beautiful coves and grand cliffs rising high out of the sea," Shattuck wrote in a letter dated June 13, 1858.[48] He made sketches, some of which he developed into canvases, which are remarkable for their faithfulness to the subject.

The landscape has changed substantially since Shattuck's day, although the rocks remain much the same. The once bare headlands now bear spruce and other vegetation. Islanders are currently battling an invasion of a non-native plant known as Japanese barberry, of serious concern as it can create thickets that block out other growth.

The island community has also experienced change, but it perseveres. Harry Odom—one of Monhegan's oldest and most stalwart residents, who, with his brother Doug, ran the island store for nearly half a century—offered his personal prediction in 2001. "Fifty years from now," he said, "I don't think it will have changed too much. It's nice to have it that way."[49]

Many of the lobster traps may be wire where they once were wood, but they are still stacked around houses and along the dock.

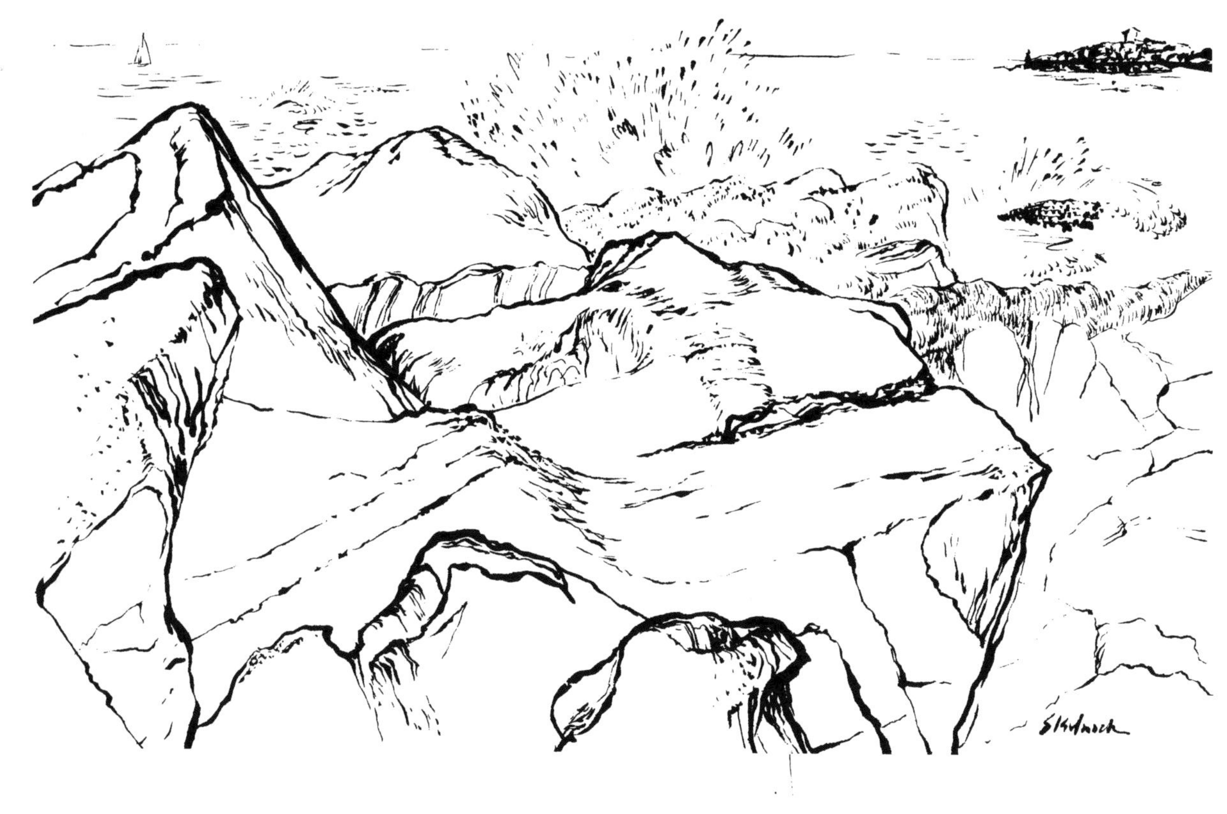

  ARNOLD SKOLNICK, *LOBSTER COVE*, BRUSH-AND-INK ON PAPER, 5 1/2 x 8 1/2 IN., PRIVATE COLLECTION

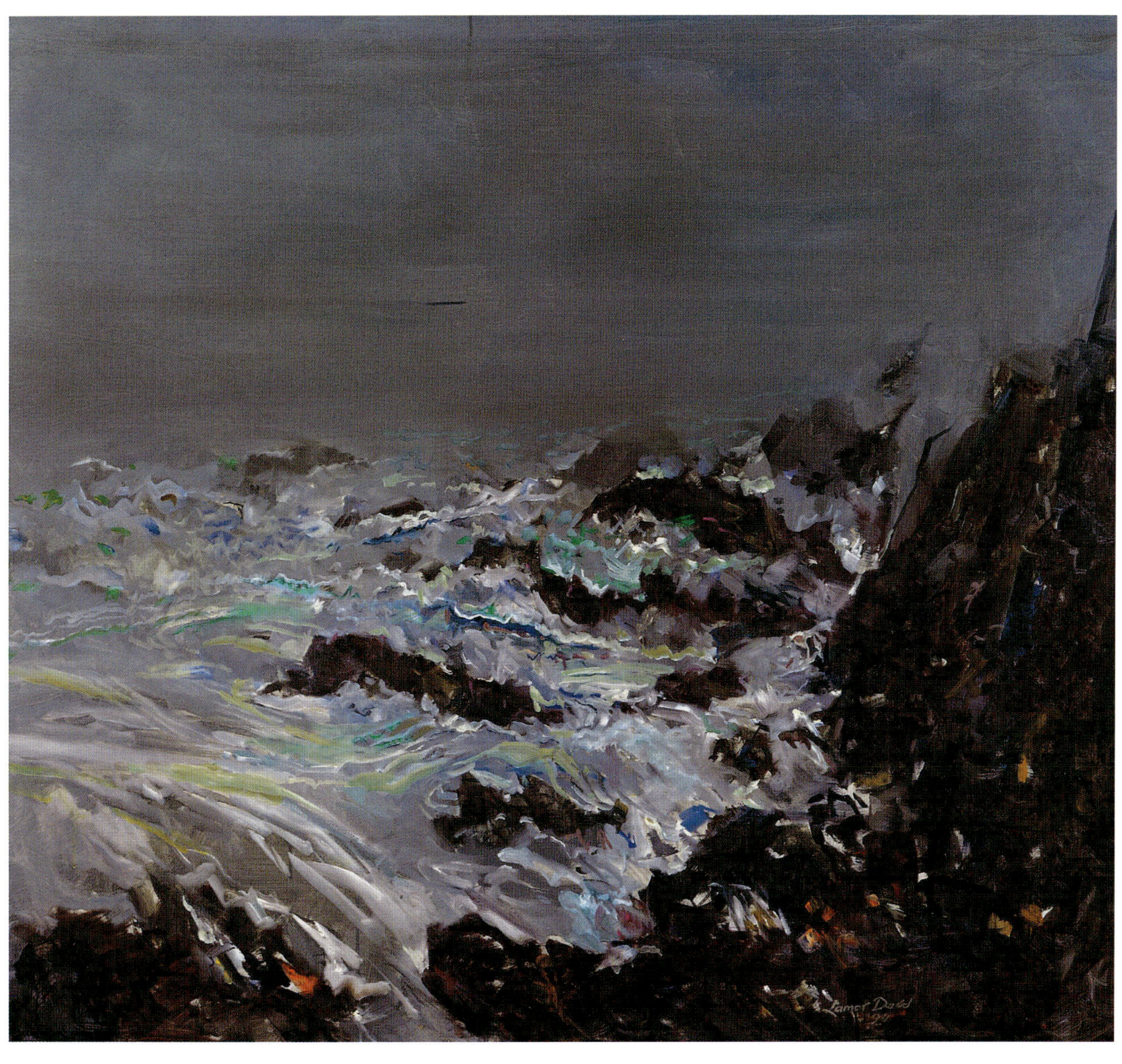

LAMAR DODD, *HEAVEN, HELL AND WAGNER*, 1990, OIL ON CANVAS, 46 x 50 IN., THE C. L. MOREHEAD COLLECTION

Visitors come and go throughout the summer and fall. As writer Anne Fuller has put it so eloquently, "The residents accept this influx as a recurrence as inevitable as the Biblical swarms of locusts, and those catering to the tourists appreciate them as a source of revenue."[50]

"Although a visitor myself," Jamie Wyeth has written, "I am selfish about Monhegan. I liken her to a great ship whose beauty and majesty will somehow be diminished by too many visitors, too many storms."[51] Over the years, Wyeth and other artists have voiced concern over the way the island has been developed, yet they return from year to year to partake of what the British writer John Fowles has referred to as Monhegan's "almost metaphysical sense of isolation."[52]

The island remains a place apart. What Rockwell Kent wrote in his autobiography still holds true for many artists who discover Monhegan. "Small, sea-girt island that it was, a seeming floating speck in the infinitude of sea and sky, one was as though driven to seek refuge from the impending cosmic immensity in a closer relationship to people and to every living thing."[53]

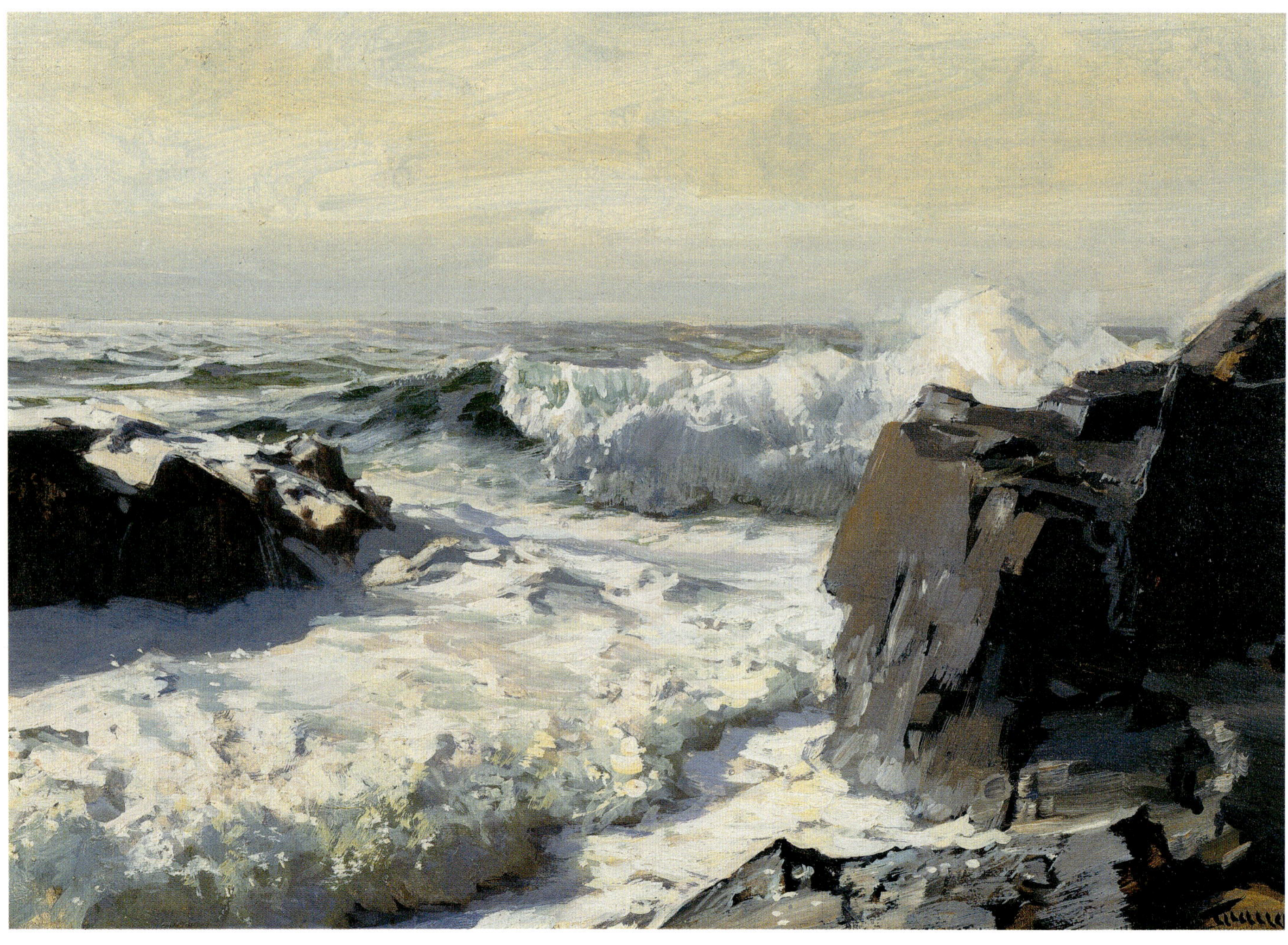

 FREDERICK JUDD WAUGH, *POUNDING SURF*, N.D., OIL ON MASONITE, 11 1/2 x 15 3/4 IN., COLLECTION OF REMAK RAMSAY

Notes

41. Alan Gussow, *A Sense of Place: The Artist and the American Landscape,* (San Francisco, CA: Friends of the Earth, 1971), 5.

42. Robert Creighton, "Meeting Monhegan Folks," *Rockland Courier Gazette*, 21 Sept. 1945.

43. Nicoll, *The Allure of the Maine Coast*, 17–18. "His athletic nature was much like the ocean itself, and his bold brush work, sense of design and ability to see simple forms and capture the moment, have never been surpassed in the history of American art." Christopher Huntington, *Maine: 100 Artists of the 20th Century* (Waterville, Maine: Colby College Museum of Art, 1964), 6.

44. Gail Levin, *Hopper's Places* (New York: Alfred A. Knopf, 1989), 49.

45. George Havens, *Frederick Judd Waugh, American Marine Painter* (Orono, Maine: University of Maine Press, 1969), 203.

45. Rachel Carson, *The Edge of the Sea* (New York: New American Library, 1955), 21.

47. Emily Ann Arthur, ed., *Lamar Dodd: The C. L. Morehead Jr. Collection* (Athens, Georgia: C. L. Morehead Jr., 1996), 113.

48. Will and Jane Curtis, *Monhegan: The Artists' Island* (Camden, Maine: Down East Books, 1995), 26.

49. Colin Woodard, "Brothers on the Rock," *Island Journal* 19 (May 2002): 37.

50. Anne Fuller, "Monhegan: The Fortunate Island," in *The Down East Reader: Selections from the Magazine of Maine,* ed. *Nancy C. Fuller* (Philadelphia & New York: J.B. Lippincott Company, 1962), 23.

51. Shettleworth and Bunting, *An Eye for the Coast*, ix.

52. Katherine Tarbox, "A Siren Call," *Island Journal* 16 (1999): 25. Fowles stated: "I loved the close-community feel of the island and then its croodling male eiders close offshore, to say nothing of so many much rarer creatures, both avian and human."

53. Kent, *It's Me O Lord*, 138.

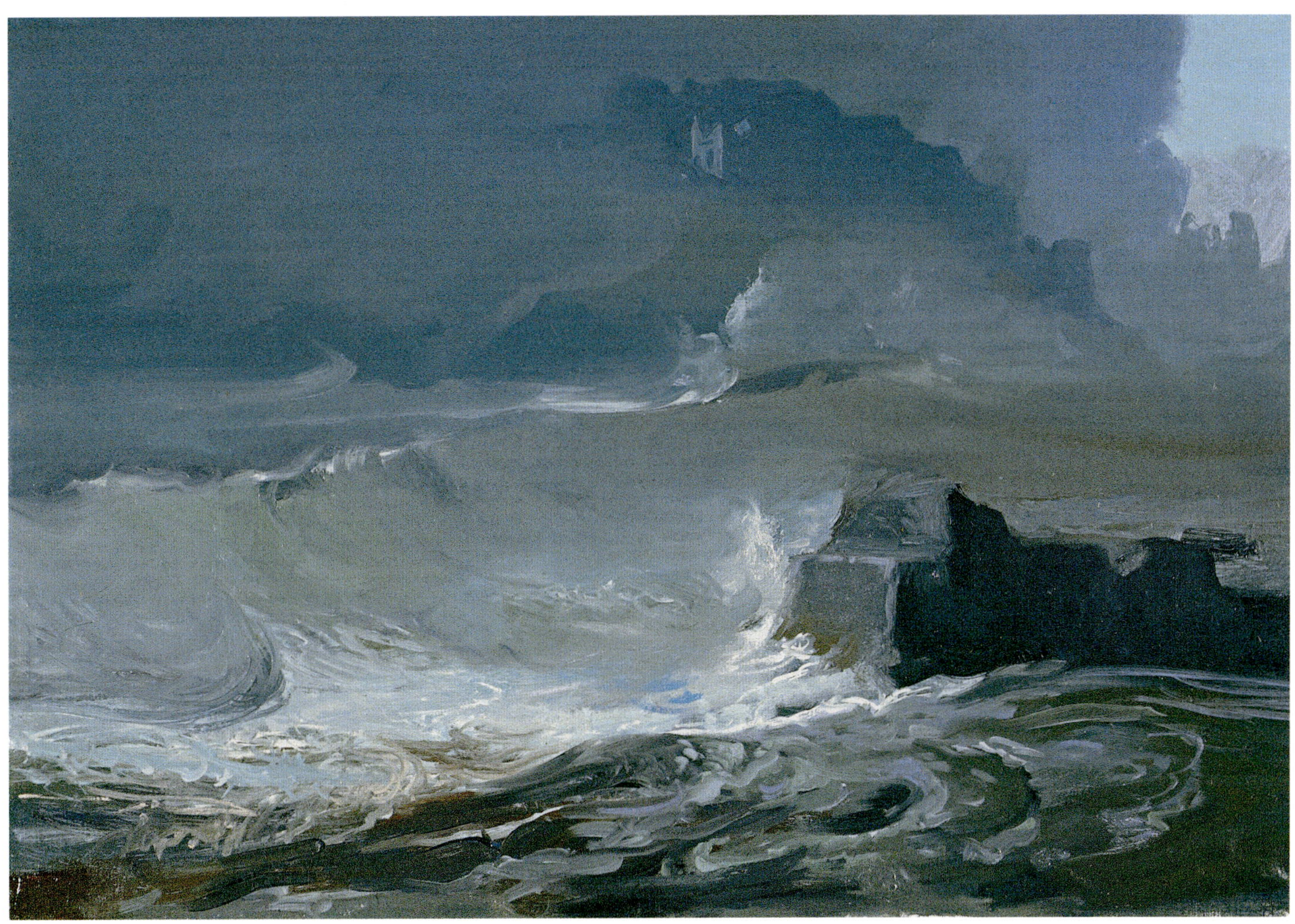

FRANK MASON, *MONHEGAN HARBOR*, 1997, OIL ON CANVAS, 18 X 25 IN., COLLECTION OF THE ARTIST

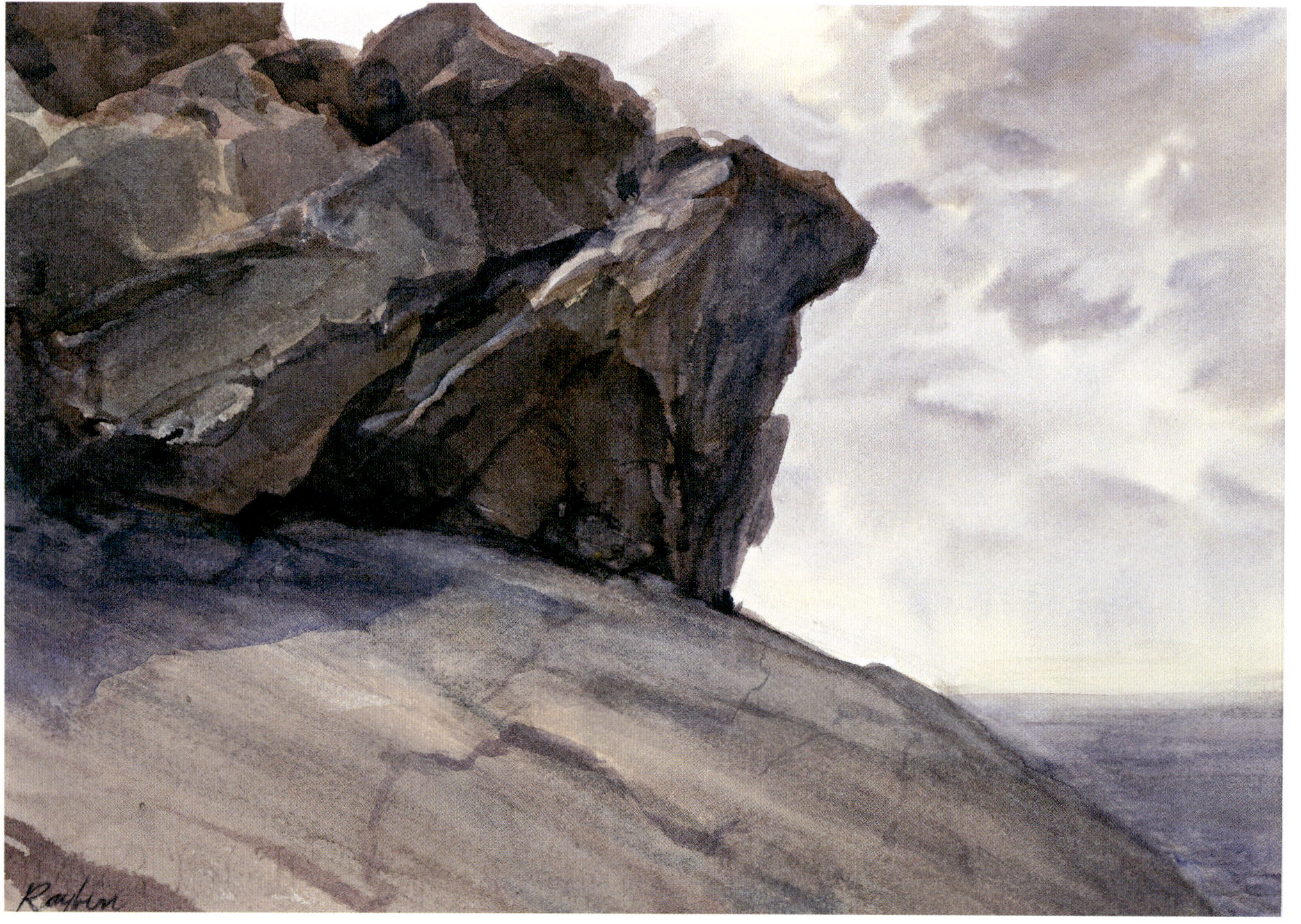

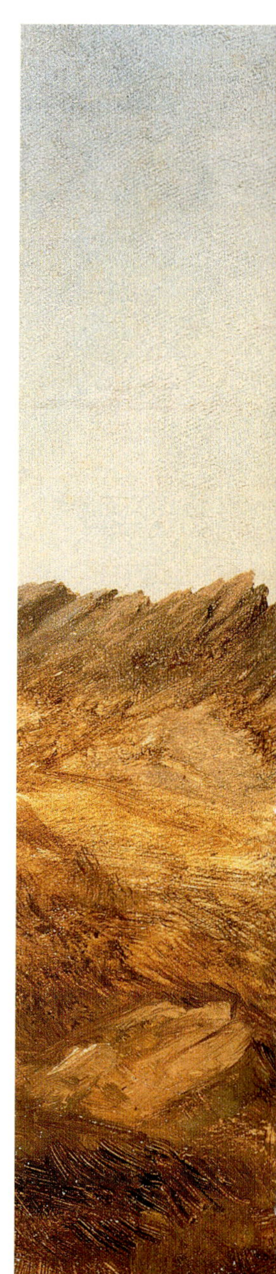

106   CAROL RAYBIN, *BOAR'S HEAD,* 2000, WATERCOLOR ON PAPER, 11 x 15 IN., COLLECTION OF REMAK RAMSAY

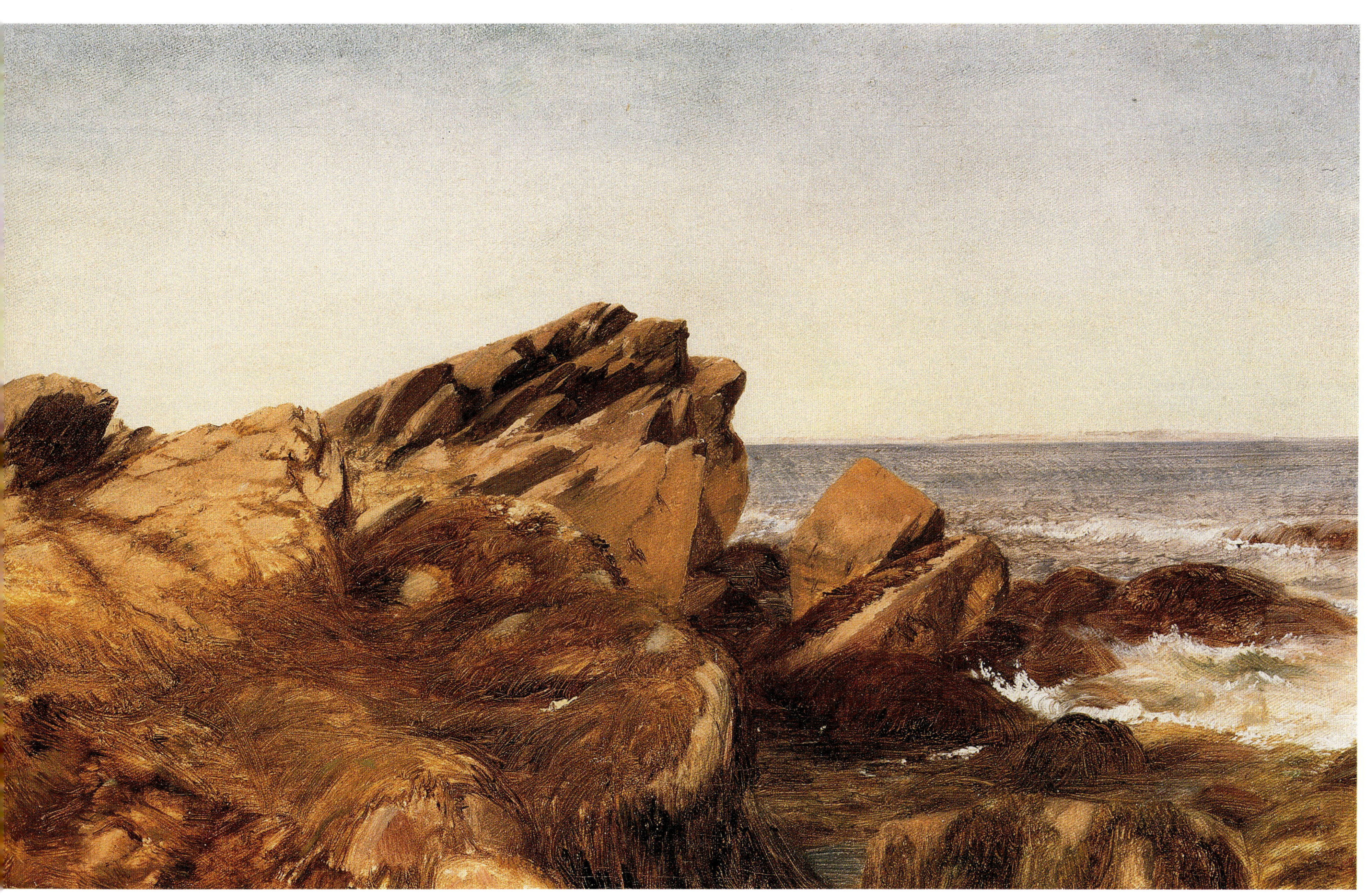

Aaron Draper Shattuck, *On the Maine Coast,* 1859, oil on canvas, 11 $^1/_8$ x 20 in.
collection of Monhegan Museum, permanent loan of Robert Snow

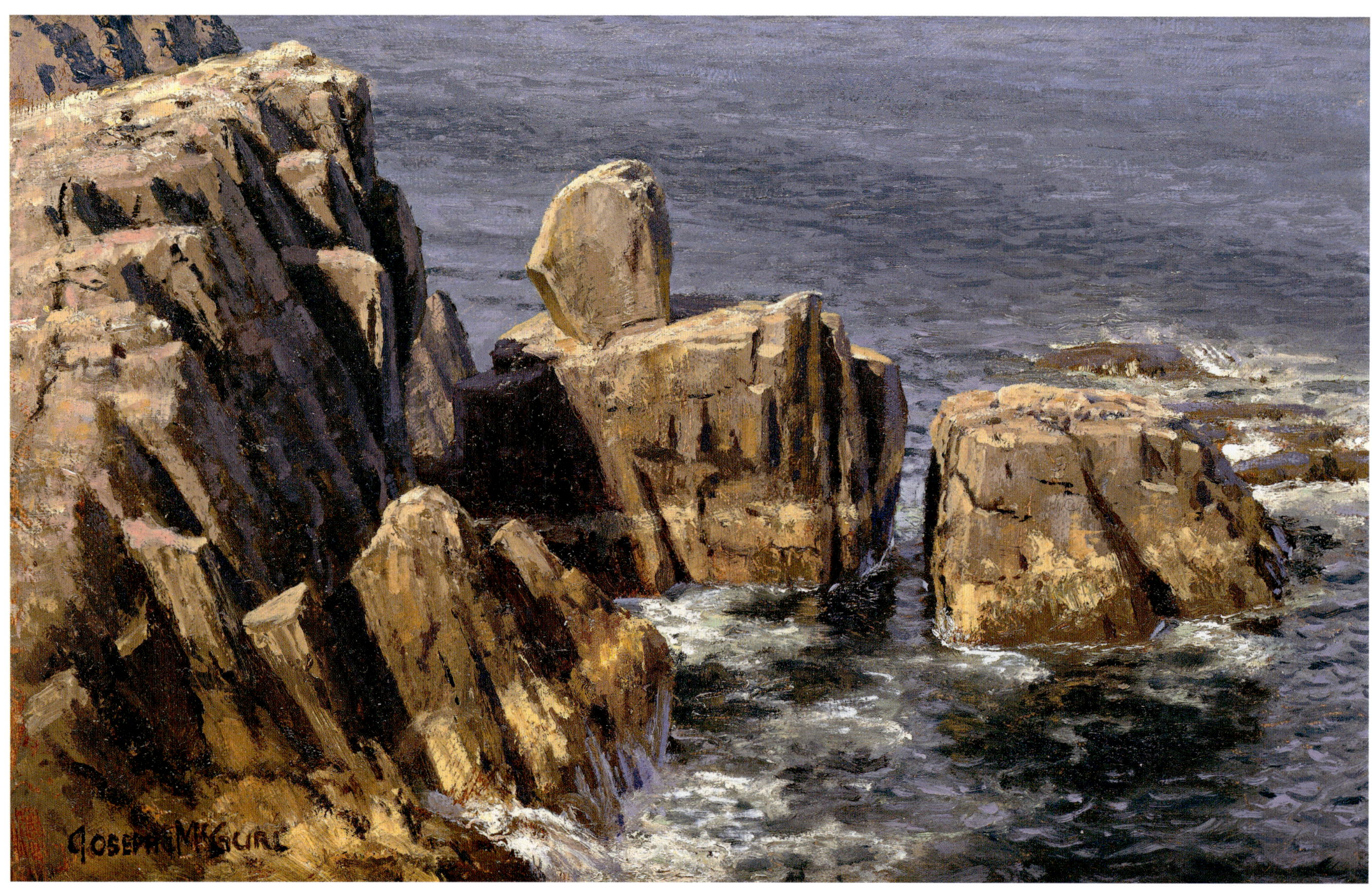

  JOSEPH McGURL, *PULPIT ROCK*, 2000, OIL ON BOARD, 8 x 12 IN., COLLECTION OF REMAK RAMSAY

For it seems to have the power—as the Irish say about some beauty spots in Ireland—of "casting a spell over you." You either like Monhegan or you don't like it. But if it "casts its spell" over you—then you are its lover for life.

—A. J. PHILPOTT, *BOSTON GLOBE*, 1939

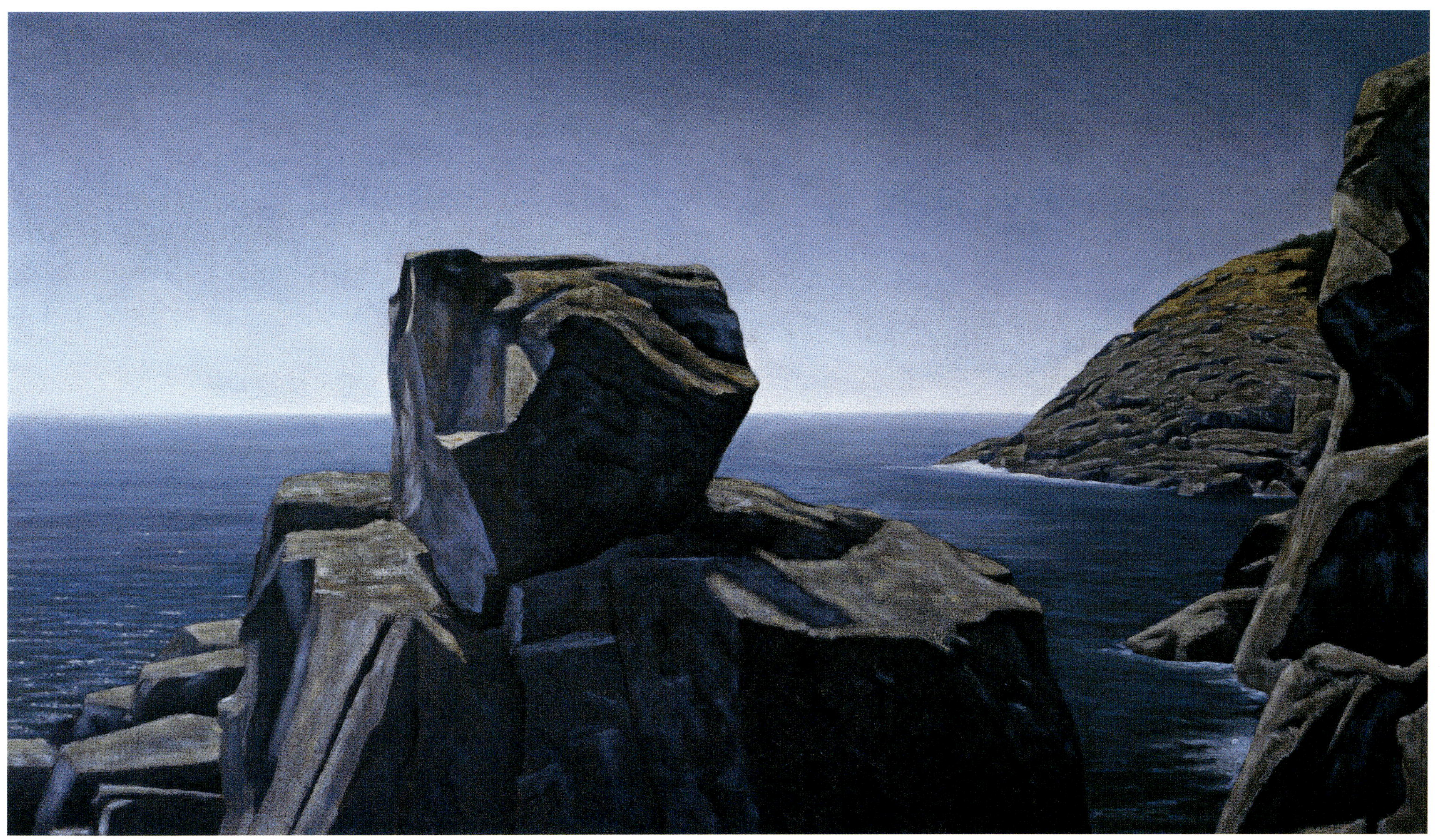

DAVID VICKERY, *PULPIT ROCK*, 1997, OIL ON PANEL, 18 x 30 IN., COURTESY OF SHERRY FRENCH GALLERY, NEW YORK

Artist List

Thomas R. Barrett, *Monhegan Lobsterman*, 35

William Beebe, *On Monhegan Island*, 61

Kevin Beers, *Orange Manana Panorama*, 24–25

George Wesley Bellows, *Beating Out to Sea*, 81; *Emma on Gull Rock*, 21; *Gorge and Sea*, 98; *Prayer Meeting*, 21; *The Blue Pool*, 99; *Through the Trees*, 64

Abraham J. Bogdanove, *On the Beach*, 33; *The Gully, Monhegan Island, Maine*, 101

Alfred T. Bricher, *Marine*, 77

Leo Brooks, *Coming Home II*, 34

Robert Casper, *Red House*, 48

William Chadwick, *After a Storm*, 78

James Floyd Clymer, *Lobstermen, Maine Coast*, 26

Jay Hall Connaway, *Monhegan Dock*, 13; *Snow on Black Head*, 30

Ted Davis, *Monhegan Harbor*, 38; *Monhegan Musicale*, 22

Joseph DeMartini, *Wreck in Squeaker Cove*, 29

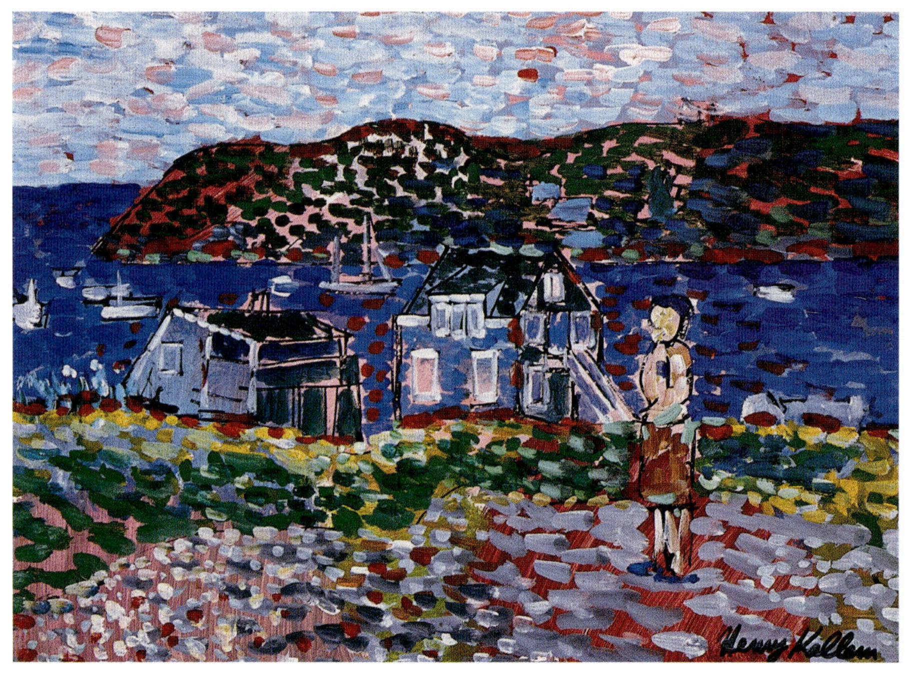

Donald Demers, *Gull Rock*, 86

Lamar Dodd, *Heaven, Hell and Wagner*, 103

Charles Ebert, *Gram Richards' House*, 43; *Monhegan Headlands*, 79

James Elliott, *Fire Fire Fire on Monhegan*, 28

Harry Fenn, *A Silvery Morning on the Coast of Maine*, 14

James Fitzgerald, *Fisherman*, 31; *Hauling the Nets*, 32; *Reflections of the Old Monhegan Beam*, 55

Dyan Fitzpatrick, *Island Winter*, 111

Richard Knapp Fletcher, *Monhegan Island*, 20

Linden Frederick, *Islander*, 53

Philip Frey, *The Headlands —Monhegan*, 84

Ronald Frontin, *First Light*, 62

Alan Gussow, *Beach Boulders and Seal Ledges*, 90 *Tidal Pool, High Tide*, 91

Connie Hayes, *Baldwin House, Monhegan*, 47

Robert Henri, *Cathedral Woods*, 65; *Monhegan Island*, 89

Donald Holden, *Monhegan Morning IV*, half-title

Emil Holzhauer, *Fishermen at Cribbage*, 23

Edward Hopper, *Rocks and Sea*, 97; *Sea and Shore*, 96

Margaret Morris Hoskins, *The Ferry Dock*, 12

Eric Hudson, *The End of the Day*, 36; *Maude Knowlton and Alice Swett Sketching*, 17;

Jacqueline Hudson, *Lobster Buoys*, 37

Elena Jahn, *Tidal Pools*, 94

Henry Kallem, *Catching the Ferry*, 110

Evelina Hollins Kats, *Monhegan*, 111

Scott Kelley, *Sally Dear Wish You Were Here*, 5

Rockwell Kent, *Blackhead*, 80; *Interior of a Cottage, Monhegan, Island*, 18; *Maine Fog: Monhegan*, 19; *Maine Headland: Morning*, 83; *Mother and Child at Monhegan*, 18

William Kienbusch, *Kerosene Lamp, Monhegan*, 4

Sarah Knock, *Monhegan and Manana Island—Fall*, 59; *Monhegan Rooftops*, 46

Leon Kroll, *Sunlit Sea*, 100

John LeBlanc, *View of Whitehead, Monhegan*, 85

Hayley Lever, *Monhegan*, 10

David Little, *Seal Ledges (Monhegan Island)*, 92

Leni Mancuso, *Approaching Gull Cove*, 91

Anne-Emmanuelle Marpeau and Bernard Lagny, *Monhegan—July 4, 1899*, 39

Frank Mason, *Monhegan Harbor*, 105

Mary T. Mason, *Sidney's Garden*, 42

Joseph McGurl, *Pulpit Rock*, 108

Sarah McPherson, *Sarah's Room, The Trailing Yew*, 22

Hans Moller, *Lobster Traps I*, 27; *Monhegan Harbor*, 38; *View from Our Window*, 70

Peter K. Nelson, *Low Tide, Sunset, Monhegan Harbor*, 93

Paul Niemiec, *Harbor South*, 50

Peter Poskas, *Sea Watchers*, 112

Remak Ramsay, *The Wharf, Monhegan*, 11

Carol Raybin, *Boar's Head*, 106

William Trost Richards, *White Head, Monhegan*, 74–75

Elmer Rising, *Monhegan Hangup*, 20

Marguerite Robichaux, *Midday*, 45

Michael Schweigart, *Monhegan Clearing*, 72

Joanne Scott, *Fire Storm (Inspired by Cathedral Woods)*, 67

Robert Van Vorst Sewell, *At the Dock*, 8

Susan Shatter, *Swirling Water*, 94

Aaron Draper Shattuck, *On the Maine Coast*, 106–107

Henrietta Shore, *A Stroll on Monhegan Avenue*, 52

Morris Shulman, *Monhegan Beach*, 71

Arnold Skolnick, *Lobster Cove*, 102

Carol Sloane, *Day 28, Cathedral Woods, Off Trail 10*, 66

Frederick Dorr Steele, *The Young Kent*, 18

Alice Kent Stoddard, *Andrew Winter Painting Gull Rock*, 16; *A View of Monhegan*, 58

Caleb Stone, *Island Inn, from the Wharf*, 54

Reuben Tam, *Monhegan Headland*, 82

Ted Tihansky, *The Artists' Shirts*, 44

Mary Alice Treworgy, *Monhegan Store*, 49

S.P. Rolt Triscott, *A Gully, Monhegan*, 68 *Blackhead, Monhegan*, frontispiece; *Maine Coast*, 88

Alexandra Tyng, *Aerial View, Monhegan (after a photograph by Charles Feil)*, 40

Unknown, *The May Archer*, 11

David Vickery, *Lobster Cove Spruces*, 73; *Pulpit Rock*, 109

Frederick Judd Waugh, *Pounding Surf*, 104

Stow Wengenroth, *Quiet Pond, Monhegan, Maine*, 20

James Perry Wilson, *Whitehead*, 69

Andrew Winter, *Coast Guard Station, Manana*, 15; *Gull Rock, Blackhead in Winter; Monhegan Island, Maine*, 87

Jamie Wyeth, *Dead Cat Museum, Monhegan Island*, 7; *The Island Schoolteacher*, 63; *The Kent House*, 50; *Obelisk*, 6; *Summer House, Winter House*, 51;

James Wolford, *Monhegan Summer II*, 60

Diana Young, *Artist's Attic*, 56–57

HENRY KALLEM, *CATCHING THE FERRY*, c. 1950, OIL ON BOARD, 22 × 28 IN., FROM THE COLLECTION OF JOHN M. DAY
COURTESY OF ELIZABETH MOSS GALLERY, FALMOUTH, MAINE. PHOTO BY JAY YORK

Selected Bibliography

Aldridge, Richard. *Driving North*. Unity, Maine: North Country Press, 1989.

Bailey, Jan. *Paper Clothes*. Greenville, South Carolina: A Press, 1995.

Beem, Edgar Allen. "The Art of Island Maine." *Island Journal* 10 (1993): 72–79.

Caldwell, Bill. *Islands of Maine: Where America Really Began*. Portland, Maine: Guy Gannett Publishing Co., 1981.

Curtis, Jane, Will Curtis, and Frank Lieberman. *Monhegan: The Artists' Island*. Camden, Maine: Down East Books, 1995.

Day, John M. "Monhegan: The Abstracted Island." *American Art Review* 13, no. 4 (2001): 174–181.

Deci, Edward. "Monhegan Island Artists: A 150-Year Tradition." *American Art Review* 15, no. 4 (2003): 104–113.

Dibner, Martin. *Seacoast Maine: People and Places*. Gardiner, Maine: Harpswell Press, 1987.

Faller, Ruth Grant. *Monhegan: Her Houses and Her People*, 1780–1970. Melrose, Mass.: Mainstay Publications, 1995.

Gussow, Alan. "Reuben Tam: Last Looks at Maine." Exhibition catalogue. Rockland, Maine: Farnsworth Art Museum, 1996.

Island Voices: Poetry of Monhegan. Monhegan Island, Maine: Stone Island Press, 2001.

Jahn, Elena. "50 Years: Growing Up an Artist on Monhegan." *Boothbay Register*, 23 Sept. 1999.

McAvoy, Suzette. "On Island: A Century of Continuity & Change." Exhibition catalogue. Rockland, Maine: Farnsworth Art Museum, 2000.

Mellon, Gertrud A. *Maine and Its Role in American Art, 1740–1963*. New York: Viking Press, 1963.

Mir, Marjorie, ed. *Poet's Cove: An Anthology. Monhegan in Poetry, 2000–2002*. Monhegan Island: New Monhegan Press, 2003.

Newman, Cathy. "Welcome to Monhegan Island, Maine. Now Please, Go Away." *National Geographic* 200, no. 1 (July 2001): 92–109.

Proper, Ida Sedgwick. *Monhegan, the Cradle of New England*. Portland, Maine: Southworth Press, 1930.

Putz, George. "Between a Rock and a Smart Place." *Island Journal* 7 (1990): 77.

Sawin, Martica. "Reuben Tam: Island Paintings." *Arts Magazine*, December 1975, 92–94.

Shain, Charles, and Samuella Shain, eds. *The Maine Reader*. Boston: Houghton Mifflin Company, 1991.

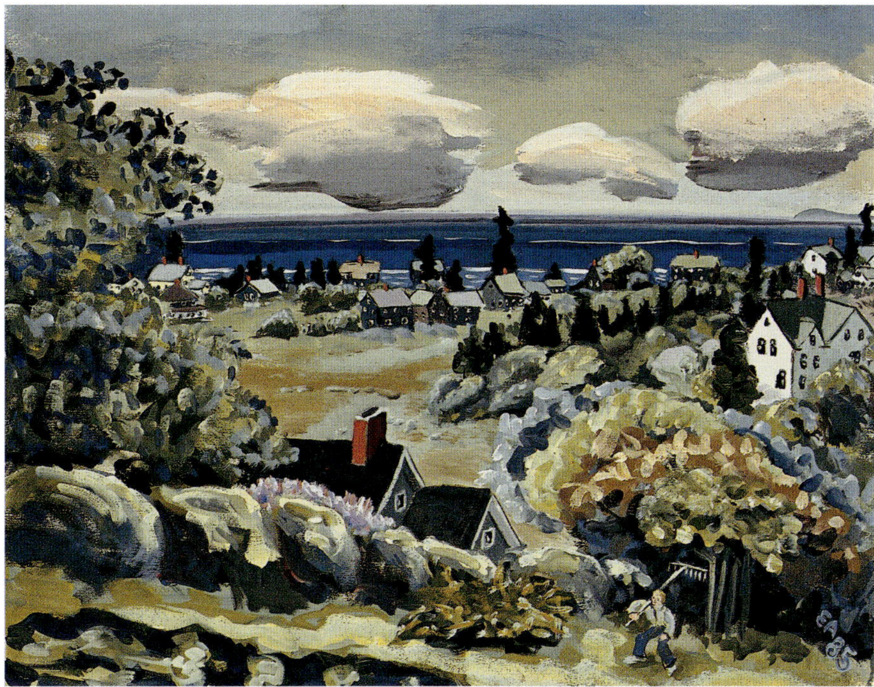

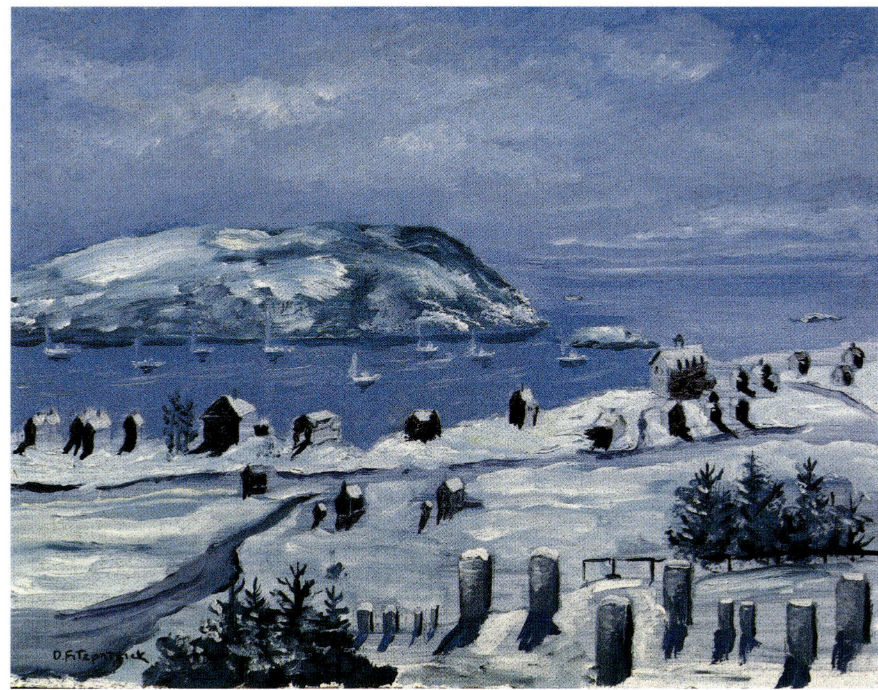

(ABOVE) EVELINA HOLLINS KATS, *MONHEGAN*, 1985, ACRYLICS, 29 x 36 IN., COLLECTION OF IVAN KATS

(BELOW) DYAN FITZPATRICK, *ISLAND WINTER*, 1985, OIL ON PANEL, 8 x 10 IN., COLLECTION OF MR. & MRS. THOMAS DEVLIN

The Chairs

Overturned, freshly painted,
They wait their righting
As summer begins. Soon
Someone will melt into their contours,
Admiring the breaking dawn,
Sounds of the distant surf,
Children playing,

A driving rain,
The setting sun,
The silence of the evening,
Questioning their lives,
Meeting new friends,
They sit.

— KEVIN R. IRVIN

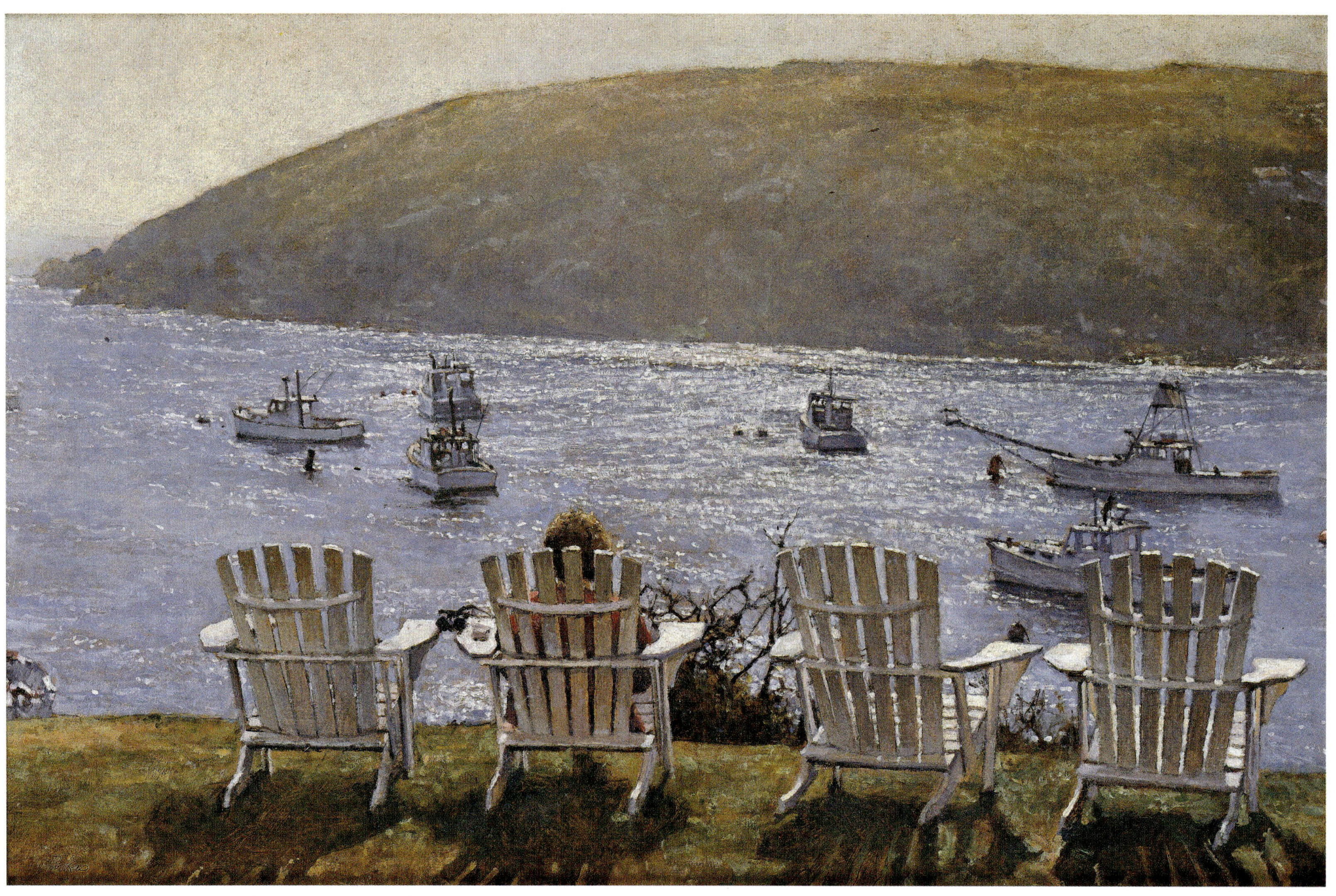

   PETER POSKAS, *SEA WATCHERS*, 1996, OIL ON PANEL, 12 X 18 IN., COLLECTION OF REMAK RAMSAY